Anzia Yezierska

A WRITER'S LIFE

Anzia Yezierska

ANZIA YEZIERSKA

A WRITER'S LIFE

by
LOUISE LEVITAS HENRIKSEN

with assistance from Jo Ann Boydston

RUTGERS UNIVERSITY PRESS
New Brunswick and London

Library of Congress Cataloging-in-Publication Data

Henriksen, Louise Levitas
Anzia Yezierska: a writer's life.

Bibliography: p.
Includes index.
1. Yezierska, Anzia, 1880?–1970 — Biography.
2. Authors, American — 20th century–Biography.
I. Boydston, Jo Ann, 1924– . II. Title.
PS3547.E95Z66 1988 813'.52 [B] 87-9588
ISBN 0-8135-1268-9

British Cataloging-in-Publication
information available

Manufactured in the United States of America

Contents

Reader's Note

ALTHOUGH Anzia Yezierska's seemingly autobiographical work was always fictional, it incorporated small chunks of *verité,* some of which are quoted in this narrative of her life; the sources are clearly indicated in the notes at the back of the book. In a few cases, quotations from more than one page or one book or story of her work are joined, but they are clearly differentiated and identified in the notes. In short, for the sources of all quotations, please turn to the back of the book.

Reprinted with permission of Cosmopolitan *magazine.*

Preface: Who Was She?

"Probably as romantic a figure as contemporary American literature affords is that of Anzia Yezierska, who landed at Ellis Island as a frail, young Polish-Jew immigrant girl, and who now has won her way through dreary hours in sweatshop and scullery to a place among the successful authors of the day."

—*New York Tribune* (November 19, 1922)

She was the heroine of a very American fairy tale. Anzia Yezierska —in 1922 that odd, unpronounceable name was well known in bookstores, newspaper and magazine offices, even movie theaters. For she had been a poor immigrant living in New York's Lower East Side slum, working as a servant, then a button sewer in ghetto factories where twelve-hour workdays were commonplace and even going to the toilet was a luxury. And she had escaped from that terrible dead end by writing stories of protest, in crude, ungrammatical, ghetto idiom, about the desperate lives of immigrants like herself.

Without education, without facility in a new language, and unaware of literary form — according to the accounts she gave interviewers — she "dipped her pen in her heart" and became a famous writer. Her first two books, *Hungry Hearts* and *Salome of the Tenements*, sold to the movies, and she was labeled "the sweatshop Cinderella," a surprising star, an oddity appearing abruptly in the literary world, the girl who had leaped from a Hester Street sewing machine to Hollywood riches.

But how? Anzia was my mother; the stories she told me didn't explain it any better than do the crumbling clippings from that distant past.

It's hard to find Anzia's real face (or her emotion-charged, explosive personality) in the slick pictures and accounts of her life. The smoothing over and sentimentalizing were mostly her fault.

Whenever she talked about herself, to interviewers or even to intimates, she had a way of rearranging or inventing the facts to suit her current feelings. In her erratic life, she proved and also contradicted anyone's rules for getting ahead.

I never knew then how she made that big leap, because at the beginning of her career I was a preschooler, living with my father up in the Bronx; she was "downtown." During the one day of the week when I was with her, I caught occasional reflections of her glory — walking past a window display of her books, meeting an admiring interviewer in her apartment, going to a screening of her film in a movie company limousine — random hints of a life that to me seemed entirely unrelated to my plainly dressed, eating-from-the-pot mother.

Then, after about a dozen years of having all that money and dazzle, of being asked for her opinion on love, marriage, America, and American men each time one of her books or movies came out, she encountered the Depression and new literary fashions. The sales of her sixth book, published in 1932, were dismal. The fad for Anzia Yezierska had apparently passed.

So her life was also a typical American failure; she was the artist forced to bloom too soon, at first embarrassed by too many riches and then startlingly deprived. In spite of that, she managed two more close brushes with success. In 1950, after eighteen years of "silence" (she was writing but not getting published), after a job at $23.86 a week on the WPA Writers Project, she produced an autobiographical novel, *Red Rib-*

A Scrub-Woman Who

By Henry Harrison

"From scrub- woman to novelist" might well be the significant title of a volume depicting the adventures of Anzia Yezlerska. Here is an astonishing story of a Russian Jewish immigrant who came to America some twenty years ago by way of steerage: who became a household servant, a scrub- woman, *bon on a White Horse*, for which she got the best reviews of her career. Her Cinderella history was repolished to a new shine, although in that book she acknowledged failure as the only truth she could believe in and questioned her own integrity when she had been most successful. She was welcomed back to literature with more respect this time. A smashing *succès d'estime*, but the book died at birth.

As a respected but now obscure author in her seventies, she wrote book reviews for the *New York Times Book Review*. She also wrote stories in a straightforward, educated person's language, in protest against old age. Her last story, for which she was paid twenty-five dollars, was published in 1969. She might have been a beginner, struggling for her first notice, although as a reviewer in *Publishers Weekly* recently observed, her last book and later stories "are more skilled . . . the characters more complex, the insights more gripping" than those for which she was acclaimed. With her greater skill and subtler style, she didn't shock and titillate readers as she had when she knew less.

But since her death in 1970, a new interest in Yezierska has grown up, particularly in college classrooms and feminist circles here and abroad. Contemporary scholars, who had to dig through old library stacks to find her out-of-print work, have brought her back. Four of Yezierska's books have now been reprinted, after forty years and more of neglect; scores of doctoral dissertations yearly reexamine her themes. Whether she was ahead of her time, I don't know. In her most successful

Became a Great Novelist

Anzia Yezierska, Who Came to America in the Steerage, Suffered Many Hardships Before She Won Success

A tattered clipping from an unknown source, ca. 1925.

From Literary Digest, *September 8, 1923.*

Digest for September 8, 1923

A GIRL WHO CAME UP FROM DESPAIR

In her early childhood, her people hammered into her "defeat, defeat, because that is the way they accepted the crushing weight of life." The very common lot of the impoverished immigrant was hers, and Anzia Yezierska, now the author of several books that have brought her a measure of fame and fortune, began life in the midst of a bitter philosophy, as well as of a bitter physical environment. Life had crushed her mother, she writes in the current issue of *The Literary Digest International Book Review*, so that "without knowing it, she … fed defeat with the … the blood …

… on the block, will have a birthday tomorrow. And she'll get presents for nothing, a cake with candles on it, and a whole lot of grand things from girls for nothing—and she said I must come. Could I have a birthday, too, like she?"

"Woe is to me!" cried my mother, flaring at me with wet, swollen eyes. "A birthday lays in your head? Enjoyment!" she continued bitterly. "You want to be glad that you were born into the world? A whole lot you got to be glad about. Wouldn't it be better if you was never born already?"

At the harsh sound of my mother's voice, all my dreams took wing. In …

ANZIA YEZIERSKA'S WAY OUT

"By writing out my protests and disillusions," says this immigrant girl, who has become a successful author, "I saved and clarified them. Slowly I began to understand what America had to offer."

… bellion and disappointment, I thrust out my lips with a trembling between retort and tears. It was as if the devil himself urged my mother then to avenge herself upon her helpless children for the aches and wants of her own life. So she went on, like a horse bolting down hill, feeling the pressure of the load behind him.

"What is with you the great joy? That you ain't got a shirt on your back? That you ain't got no shoes on your feet? Why are you with yourself so happy? Is it because the landlord sent the moving …, and you'll be lying in the street tomorrow, already?"

I gazed at my mother with old, solemn …, feeling helplessly sucked into her …ness and gloom.

…'s a poor man but a living dead … she purred, talking more to herself … me. "You ought to light a black … on your birthday. You ought to … your face and cry and curse the day … born!"

… by the maternal tirade, which … been quoted directly from a … of the most gloomy sort, … went silently away. The … of the approaching birthday …led with tears, she says:

…n the edge of the gutter in …ment.

… the pink candles for the …

THE NEW YORK HERALD, SUNDAY, JANUARY 7, 1923.

Fighting Up From the Ghett…

By GERTRUDE ATHERTON.

Anzia Yezierska

From the New York Herald, *January 7, 1923.*

From Good Housekeeping, *June 1920.*

The IMMIGRANT SPEAKS

By Anzia Yezierska

Decoration by W. T. Benda

THE author of this remarkable appeal to America lineage came to this country at the age of nine, of ten children. The next year poverty forced her but the longing for an education was already k less though the prospect seemed to be. It credit of American opportunity that she her education, and finally won an "The Best Short Stories of 1919" are bidding against each other is glad to give this reco

WHEN the editor told me the chance to I ought to out of my her to feel—but loose trained

From Cosmopolitan, *October 1925.*

This is WHAT $10,000 *Did To ME*

By Anzia Yezierska

WAS very poor. And when I was poor, I hated the rich. that I too have some means, I no longer hate them. I have d that the rich are as human as any of us.

When I lived in Hester Street, I could feel life only through the ts and privations of Hester Street. Why were we cramped into crowded darkness of dingy tenements? Because the heartless d such sunny palaces on Fifth Avenue. Why were we ng and wasting with want? Because the rich gorged them with the fat of the land.

nd then it happened. I who thought myself doomed to ter Street had the chance to move myself up to Fifth Avenue. now where are the horns and hoofs that I always seemed to at sight of the well-fed, the well-dressed? Where's the indignation that flared up in my breast when I saw around in limousines? Where's the hot sureness with ndemned as criminals those who dared to have the longed to have but never could hope of having—furs and houses?

gan five years ago, just a few days before Christmas. with cold, I walked up and down the shopping district I caught a glimpse of myself in the mirror of a hat a pinched, starved thing! Worried. Faded, ragged old coat. stepping

Already I saw the throngs mobbing the bookstores for my book. My last letter and my picture in the front page of every newspaper in the country. Everywhere people reading and talking "Hungry Hearts." The whole world shaken with guilty sorrow for my tragic death—but too late!

Yes, on that dark day there seemed no way to take revenge for the cruel neglect of a heartless world but to blow out my brains or plunge under the wheels of the crowded traffic. My last letter was already shaping itself in my head as I hastened back to my room to write it.

How I dreaded to meet the landlady on the stairs! I could not bear to hear her nagging for the rent in my last tragic hour. Trembling with fear I sneaked into my room.

There on the table yellow telegram!

Who would send me a telegram?

I stared at it. hendingly. It was from a

I tore it open and read ng that he could get for well-known moving picture agen the film rights of my book the unheard of sum of ten thousand dollars.

In a flash the whole world changed! And I was changed. It changed still more when, after negotiations for the book had been made, they offered to send me to California to collaborate on the screen version of "Hungry Hearts."

There followed a wonderful trip across the continent, in a private compartment. I had to pinch myself to make sure that I was not dreaming when I entered the diner and ordered roast asparagus, endive salad and strawberries with cream. I with a full hand because a millionaire corpora-

fortune, no matter of luck," earned it for me."

years, the 1920s, I think it was the passion, the nakedness of her words that made her a best-selling writer for over a decade. Her subject was, to most readers, colorful, exotic. Since then, a change of context has made her subject seem contemporary. A rebel against every established order, including the tyranny of men, she quite naturally had been a self-centered feminist even before she'd heard of the marches for women's right to vote. It meant defying her father's and mother's tradition, and she wrote about this as homelessness, being lost between her parents' Old World and the new world in which she could not find a comfortable place. The feeling of not belonging — alienation — was expressed from another pespective at that time, in the literature of "the lost generation," an intellectual minority. Today a majority understand this feeling.

After Anzia died, I found a packet of her letters which I could neither read nor part with at the time; I wrapped up her old manuscripts and other papers and sent them to Boston University Libraries' Special Collections, which had asked for them. When Anzia was alive, I wasn't interested in what had happened to her before I was born or old enough to remember. And I was too familiar with those manuscripts, because she had regularly conscripted me, among others, for arduous editing duty. Her writing had always seemed exaggerated and sentimental to me. I was always correcting her.

But over the next few years I began receiving inquiries from scholars. They surprised me with photocopied documents about Anzia that didn't fit into her life as I knew it. For example, a Columbia University transcript showing that, although she was supposed to have been a primitive who had forfeited her youth in sweatshops and who wrote without knowing how, she had in fact graduated from Columbia's Teachers College in 1904. It should have been obvious that to write as she did in the guise of an untutored immigrant took a certain sophistication.

Taking one of her old books out of a storage cupboard, I reread a story or two. It was amazing: time had somehow contemporized and even improved her writing. I read more stories. Why did they seem to glow now with an artistry that wasn't apparent, to me anyhow, in the 1930s, or for that matter in the forties and fifties, when she was having a hard time trying to sell her manuscripts? I was so provoked by the new sound of Anzia's writing and the new facts I was discovering about her life that I went to see some of my older relatives to check out what she had written or told about herself, as against what had really happened.

Most of the provocation I owed to Jo Ann Boydston, a John Dewey specialist, who by coincidence was investigating Yezierska in another part of the library stacks at the same time (1975) literary researchers had begun resurrecting her books. Dr. Boydston was studying a cache of Dewey poems rescued from the great man's wastebasket and the back of his desk drawer at Columbia University, when she came across Yezierska's trail like a splash of scarlet.

Dewey was known publicly as "a reserved . . . unemotional, almost stereotypical New Englander," Boydston later wrote in *The Poems of John Dewey* (1977). His other books, on philosophy, education, psychology, and politics, certainly gave no hint of passion. Not even his family suspected that he had written these poems. The discarded, crumpled pages, in his handwriting or in his own, error-ridden typewriting, had been secretly collected, unknown to Dewey, during his lifetime. A young colleague who moved into Dewey's office at Columbia University after the older man retired had told a librarian working in an adjacent office about the stuff thrown into the wastebasket.

Turned over to Boydston in 1974, this rescued poetry started her on a scholarly search for clues. The references in the poems to some of his experiences, the inked corrections in Dewey's hand, the typewriter faces, the paper, and other identifying data enabled her to prove that Dewey had actually written them and to fix their approximate dates. The search led her to Yezierska's books because a Mrs. A. Levitas, who later became known as Anzia Yezierska, was listed as the translator on a Dewey research project of that period, a study of a Polish community in Philadelphia.

By reading Yezierska, who was rumored to have written about Dewey, Boydston hoped to find some details of the research project or of Dewey's life that year. She was electrified when she came upon two of his poems (slightly edited by Yezierska and not credited to Dewey) in two of Yezierska's novels. The earlier of the novels, *All I Could Never Be* (1932), is the love story of a young immigrant woman translator and the considerably older professor directing an investigation of a Polish-American community.

I had always known about my mother's relationship with Dewey; she spoke about it often. But I hadn't known about it from his point of view, a perspective revealed in other, very affecting poems Boydston now showed me.

Boydston and other scholars also brought me letters Anzia had written to her publishers and to a film company, and the companies' confidential memos about her. (Who could have imagined that my mother's often hasty, personal scrawls would be preserved today in research libraries at Harvard and Princeton?) Joined to old letters from my father's files, notes in my mother's, some of which I read for the first time, they became, to my further astonishment, a self-portrait of spirited, romantic, egocentric Anzia Yezierska. She reemerges for me in these letters with an extraordinary telescoping of time. It is strangely exciting, a weird shifting of lenses, now that I am so much older, to be entering her life when she was vitally alive. Giddy, capricious, daring, sentimental, and *young*! Exasperatingly self-centered but more reckless, more attractive than I thought my mother was. And, especially, more vulnerable. For all the ghetto shrewdness, which I used to think had made her invincible, the letters show that she was sometimes frightened, uncertain, and easily defeated by the more experienced hucksters she dealt with.

Her letters, though certainly not literary, especially those of her youth, are the essence of Anzia, who runs as she writes, usually excited and ready to explode. The youthful letters, casually self-serving, go skimming over the truth, in contrast to her unflinching self-recognition in the letters of her maturity.

Evidently, from the beginning she wrote letters as frequently and volubly and easily as a lonely woman today would pick up the phone. To me these messages are filled with an aching suspense. From crest to trough, over and over again, they show her rising and falling. For instance, after two failed marriages, "moral bankruptcy," and the end of the Dewey affair, she rises to another crest as a new writer at the moment of her first triumphs, being sought out by editors. Her first book of stories published, her ticket to Hollywood in hand, she is buoyant, exuberant, a conqueror.

Yet even as she travels westward on that Pullman, writing exultantly to her publisher back East, there are small omens of danger, flecks of vanity, naiveté, and simple greed that will grow larger. I kept hoping that she would overcome these omens. It was the incurable hope for a happy ending. Knowing only too well what would happen next made me apprehensive as I went on reading. I had to resist the overwhelming urge to change some words in the letters, smooth out the growing disparities between what she said and what I felt she should have said. As if by editing I could have changed Anzia's destiny — and thereby my own.

I

AMBITION

1

AMERICA

THE YEZIERSKYS CAME TO AMERICA from the Russian-Polish village of Plotsk. Anzia invented a new name for the village each time she wrote about it. She described the family's mud hut in her first book, *Hungry Hearts* — chickens pecking at the earthen floor while her father, an Orthodox rabbi, and the village children, his pupils, chanted Hebrew psalms and prayers and she stood guard at the window.

One day she deserted her post for an instant, just to grab a potato from the table, and the cossacks, catching them all in this illegal religious school, ended the family's livelihood. After that the Yezierskys pawned everything of value for the price of ship tickets to America.

This may be true. They may have lived in a mud hut with an earthen floor. Anzia never corrected those who took her fiction literally, although she frequently changed the details and dates of such events. The only certainty, which I learned from family memories other than hers, is that she arrived here with her parents, three brothers, and three sisters at Castle Garden, New York's gateway for immigrants before Ellis Island replaced it. It was about 1890, when she was from eight to ten years old.

There is no family or public record to pin down the facts, not even a birth certificate. These guesses about her age and arrival date are necessarily approximate. When they landed, the whole family was instantly Americanized. The oldest brother, Meyer Yeziersky, who had reached America a year or two earlier, had been officially renamed Max Mayer at that time by immigration inspectors who could not decipher or pronounce the Polish letters of his true name. He was at the immigration gate to help the family through, and they all received his invented surname and new, easy-to-spell first names. Anzia Yezierska turned into Hattie Mayer.

They came to a dark, airless tenement railroad flat that "looked out at the blank wall of the next house." Her teen-aged sisters went to work sewing shirtwaists in a sweatshop, while Anzia, still too young, learned the English language and American ways in public school. A freckle-faced girl with red braids, enormous and insistent blue eyes, she was doing her share, enthusiastically selling paper bags, pasted up at night in the family kitchen, to the pushcart peddlers on her street.

Anzia's brief schooling, that dangerous bit of learning she acquired before she, too, became a drudge, probably gave her the critical, rebellious eye she now cast on the lot of women in her family:

> My mother . . . dried out her days fighting at the pushcarts for another potato, another onion into the bag. . . . My father [was] a Hebrew scholar and dreamer . . . always too much up in the air to come down to such sordid thoughts as bread and rent.

Anzia Yezierska, about eleven years old.

The first job she could get was as a servant in the home of relatives who had arrived in America much earlier. They were now removed from care and compassion by affluence. Because of their superior environment, they considered room and board sufficient pay for their greenhorn servant. When Hattie Mayer learned at the end of her first, hardworking month that she would get no wages, she moved back to the tenement and to jobs in the ghetto sweatshops.

> I was an unskilled . . . worker, changing my job often and hating each new one [sewing machine operator, laundress, waitress, cook] . . . terrible jobs that stunned me physically. . . . My poverty had a bony hand . . . and I saw no way of escaping.
>
> When all were asleep, I used to creep up on the roof of the tenement and talk out my heart . . . to the stars in the sky.
>
> Who am I? What am I? What do I want with my life? Where is America? . . . What is this wilderness in which I'm lost?

Exploited as a servant or factory worker by fellow countrymen who had reached here a few years earlier and now knew English, she and her family learned from the exploiters that America had opportunities for those who could go to school. Four of Hattie's brothers studied at night and eventually became pharmacists. Of the two born in America, one became a high school mathematics teacher and the other an army colonel. But her sisters, dutiful daughters of a rabbi, married early and had children.

From childhood Hattie warred against such traditions. She fought with her father and brothers, the tradition keepers. Then, perhaps at sixteen she read a poem about the feelings of a factory worker bound like a slave to his machine; it pushed her into open rebellion. That someone had put into words her own anger and misery was overwhelming.

> Like a spark thrown among oily rags, it set my whole being aflame with longing for self-expression. . . . I had nothing but blind, ach-

ing feeling. For days I went about with agonies of feeling . . . birth throes of infinite worlds and yet dumb.

Suddenly there came upon me this inspiration: I can go to college!

To prepare for college, she attended night school after her ten-hour work day, and meanwhile, against her father's wishes, withheld from her wages enough money to pay for a year at the New York City Normal College. During that year she ironed clothes in a laundry before and after classes.

She was seventeen or eighteen, fighting with her family even more because of the differences she now discovered between her own situation and that of the young Americans in her classes. A would-be idealist, memorizing and trying to write poetry, she was also harshly rejecting her parents' ideals. For her dream of the educated life, she finally had to declare her independence from them by moving to a room of her own. This was in 1899, when decent Jewish girls didn't leave their families except to marry.

The room was in the Clara de Hirsch Home for working girls. Hattie enjoyed a brief period of illusion before realizing that the rules and decorum of this shelter were more repressive than those of her parents' home. Like any adolescent, she swung from high emotional happiness to basement despair, suffocating for freedom. Before reaching bottom, however, she had managed an effusive, overblown expression of appreciation to some of the Clara de Hirsch Home's wealthy patrons, and this so deeply impressed the ladies that they voted to pay her tuition to Columbia University. She would become one of the ghetto's first college-educated cooking teachers.

Hattie didn't understand what that meant until she entered Columbia. To her Columbia was a great university in whose halls noted scholars walked like gods on Olympus. She expected to be happy just breathing their air. Then she entered the halls and found that she had to study Food Production and Manufacture, Household Chemistry, Home Sanitation, and the like. During her four years, there, she was able to squeeze four courses of her own choice into her program of study:

Shakespeare, Development of Medieval and Modern Civilization, Political and Social Ethics, and Voice.

To be so close to poetry and philosophy, yet excluded from it, filled her college years with frustration. On the campus she had frequent reminders that she was out of place.

> Every time I had to [go] to the dean's office for a private conference, I prepared for the ordeal of her cold scrutiny. . . . I watched her gimlet eyes searching for a stray pin, for a spot on my dress, for my unpolished shoes, for my uncared-for fingernails.
>
> She never looked into my eyes. . . . She did not see how I longed for beauty and cleanliness. How I strained . . . to lift myself from the dead toil and exhaustion that weighed me down.

College meant "being out for a good time" to the other students. Anzia still worked in a laundry early and late to pay her living expenses.

> I looked at these children of joy with a million eyes . . . with my hands and my feet, with the thinnest nerves of my hair. By all their differences from me, their youth, their shiny freshness, their carefreeness, they pulled me out of my senses to them. And they didn't even know I was there. . . .
>
> One day, the ache for people broke down the feelings of difference from them. I felt I must tear myself out of my aloneness. . . . The freshman class gave a dance that . . . evening. . . . I put a fresh collar over my old serge dress. And with a dollar stolen from my eating money, I bought a ticket to the dance. . . . How the whole big place sang with their lighthearted happiness! Girls like gay-colored butterflies [danced by] in the arms of young men. . . . I took the nearest chair, blinded by the dazzle of the happy couples. . . . A terrible sense of age weighed upon me. Some of my classmates nodded distantly in passing, but most of them were too filled with their own happiness even to see me. . . . The whirling of joy went on and on, still I sat there watching, cold, lifeless, like a lost ghost.

The death blow to her hopes came after graduation, when she had to pass the scrutiny of "other agents of clean society." She felt it was her unkempt appearance they held against her, but in fact the school principals must have recognized also that Hattie Mayer was minimally interested in cooking or teaching, for they doled out to her only the lowest-paid substitute cooking-teacher jobs.

Schoolteaching, to which she had previously aspired, became hateful tedium now. Swerving abruptly with the overwhelming energy she had once applied to her earlier goals, she decided to become an actress. There was no class discrimination in the theater, only the superiority of talent — and more than one friend had told Anzia she had enough emotional excess to be an actress, the way she was always dramatizing the daily encounters in her life: the fat boss at the sweatshop, the cruel dean at the university, the mean, tight-minded school principals who now oppressed her. So she applied for and won a scholarship to the American Academy of Dramatic Arts.

Brothers and cousins now told her bluntly she was a fool, a homely girl with her red hair and wild looks, and already in 1907 about twenty-seven years old. Their ridicule bit into her resolve; nevertheless, she tried to ignore it. She looked more striking but dressed more plainly than most of the other young women they knew. She had thick auburn hair, always slipping out of a large pompadour; the high, rosy-colored, velvet skin and child-blue eyes that go with such hair; a short, strong peasant body; and the self-centered absorption that accompanied an intense, hungry, driving will.

In the first decade of the new twentieth century, even in the black poverty of the East Side there were dreamers who saw their dreams come true: peddlers became merchants, paupers married millionaires. One of Hattie's older sisters married a cousin in New York who became a prosperous cloak and suit salesman in Los Angeles; they lived in comparative luxury. Another East Side girl, Hattie's friend Rose Pastor, captured James Graham Phelps Stokes, a young philanthropist and social worker who was also a millionaire.

Such golden examples stirred a constant ferment in the East Side: the movement of do-gooders and uplift crusaders into the exotic neighborhood of ghetto immigrants, and the fierce drive of Hatties and Roses and Sammys forcing their way out. Young East Side thinkers talked about better working conditions in the sweatshops, socialism, Emma Goldman, women's suffrage, Havelock Ellis, even birth control. Hattie recited the poetry of Walt Whitman and Rudyard Kipling in her acting exercises and read to herself the urgings of Ralph Waldo Emerson on self-reliance. She knew that all great things were attainable if one persisted.

And yet, the simplest, the most desired goal continually eluded her. At sixteen she had fallen in love with her beautiful older sister Annie's suitor because he was a poet. Although her sister rejected him, Hattie followed him around for weeks in silent adoration. At last she declared herself — and he laughed at her! In college, for which she had abandoned her family, she had been an outsider, hungrily looking in. Now at the Academy of Dramatic Arts, she was making women friends, aspiring actresses with whom she shared the same ambivalence: the need to be an independent, free woman; the ache for love.

She reached in both directions when she moved to a room in a Socialist dormitory, the Rand School. The school, near Gramercy Park, offered educational and cultural activities that made it a meeting place for young intellectuals with similar ideals. But for Hattie it had so far proved lonely. Her sister Annie, the warmth of humanity, and especially the comfort of recognition were still in the crowdedness and dirt of the tenements. She kept returning, although she was not altogether welcome; she couldn't get along with the men of her family. An outsider now in her parents' flat, she fought with her two younger brothers who remained there and, at Annie's, with her brother-in-law, whom she despised for keeping her sister pregnant and in poverty.

The sisters had always been very close, chafing under stern patriarchal dicta, which the older girls, unlike Hattie, accepted as the laws of God. Despite Hattie's urging to the contrary, they obeyed their husbands' demands in the same way. But they treated Hattie as a daring, willful, and lovable child; they mothered her.

Bessie died suddenly from pneumonia; Fannie and her husband moved to California. So Hattie, still in need of family warmth, spent her free time in Annie's flat while Annie's husband was out. She was teaching nearby at P.S. 168 on East 105th Street, a working-class neighborhood of first- and second-generation immigrant families, Italian, Irish, and Jewish.

At Annie's, Hattie practiced her drama school lessons, laughing in a range of scales and styles, sobbing, screaming, fainting — just dropping to the floor — while Annie's young children watched in amazement, her first audience.

After the scholarship ended, Hattie became discouraged over her chances of getting into the theater and decided to become a writer instead. Annie was an inspiration. Only two or three years older than Hattie, before her marriage Annie had been a ravishing blond beauty whom men followed in the streets. Married at eighteen, she had five babies in the next ten years. She was to have five more. Childbearing and poverty had not discouraged her; she was creating an oasis in the slums. She had organized the women of her neighborhood into a mothers' society, which worked to gain social benefits for all of them. She won for Oscar, her fifth child, a scholarship to a private school. Through these activities, she came to know leading activists and philanthropists of the East Side, who sometimes visited her in the tenements.

Annie had a vivid way of talking about her life, for instance giving details of her children's conversation and gestures that captured the whole experience. Hattie urged her to write them down, and she tried — but it was too difficult for her. Annie had been a sweatshop worker from the age of fourteen, while Hattie was still going to school. Now she was studying English grammar from her children's schoolbooks.

Annie's mimicking of her children and neighbors gave Hattie an idea and she started writing "The Free Vacation House." The story of one of Annie's vacations, it boiled with the bitter humor of a ghetto mother who took her children to a country home where the poor could spend a free week, provided that they kept to the backyard, didn't wrinkle the bedspreads, didn't raise their voices, didn't walk on the grass, and didn't step into the beautifully furnished front parlor and porch reserved for the patronesses of this charity.

With Annie's help, Hattie was writing the story in the words of such a mother — the idiom of the Jewish immigrant. It didn't sound natural

Annie, née, Helena Yezierska, and four of her children.

when she tried to translate it. Hattie carried her handwritten manuscript back to Annie's repeatedly. They worked on the phrasing while Annie was ironing, cleaning, or cooking. Hattie would coax Annie to remember how her neighbors spoke, the Yiddish expressions they used, and then they would rework it into a strange but picturesque English.

The story was an oddity when Hattie first submitted it to a magazine. It was rejected. She sent it out again and again, and rewrote it each time, injecting stronger feelings, inventing harsher incidents to make it more dramatic, so that it no longer resembled Annie's experience or Hattie's original story. It had a compelling life of its own. Meanwhile, she started on another story.

Along with the stories, Hattie brought her fashion finds to show

Charity Trust Opposed by Women

Humiliation of Poor Is Deplored

Children to Be Sent to Country

Mothers' Aid Society, Which Furnished Food to Needy in Winter, to Send Hardworking Mothers and Tots to Shore and Mountain.

To obtain funds to send poor mothers to the country during the Summer, the Mothers' Aid Society, of which Mrs. Helena Katz is the president, will hold a series of entertainments and dances to realize the amount needed. The second of this series will take place within the next few weeks at one of the leading halls of Harlem.

The organization, which is composed of mothers of large families, was organized a few years ago. These women visit the families in need in Harlem, giving whatever relief is necessary. Rents are paid by the organization, and coal, wood, food and clothing are purchased for the unfortunates.

The society is self-supporting and is trying to do away with charity organizations. The motto of the society is, "Help the poor mothers in Harlem who have met with misfortunes in life." The Mothers' Aid Society meets in the Young Men's Hebrew Association every week. The society has a membership of eighty women.

In an interview with a representative of the New York American yesterday, Mrs. Katz said:

"We want to help the unfortunate mothers in Harlem, who, although longer vacation than any child. First, because she works hard from morning until night. A mother works until nine or ten o'clock. She has always something to do. If it isn't getting the meals for her husband and children, it is washing, sewing, darning or making the house look neat and clean.

"To send these poor women away it is necessary to have money. Without money we are unable to do anything. We have at present about $500 in the treasury, but it is not a sufficient sum to send all the women we wish away to Summer resorts.

"I take this opportunity through the columns of the New York American to make an earnest appeal to the young men and women of Harlem to co-operate with us in raising the necessary funds.

TO GIVE ENTERTAINMENT.

Mrs. Katz is the founder of the organization. At first there were only a handful of members, but to-day the membership has increased greatly. It is expected that within the next year hundreds of mothers, in comfortable circumstances, will join the ranks.

Mrs. Katz is the mother of eight children, and finds plenty of time to

Anzia's sister Annie with her fifth child, born in 1907. She had been Helena Yezierska in Poland, but was renamed Annie Mayer by immigration officials. Resuming her own name, Helena, she became Helena Katz after marriage.

Annie. She had a mania for clothes. She was a "girl starving for beautiful clothes. . . . The hunger for bread is not . . . as maddening." Especially she liked to buy the big hats of that period; but as soon as she opened the hatbox to show off her new purchase, she started stripping off the flowers and ribbons to make it more like the hat she had in mind. Perfection remained always out of reach.

Once she gave Annie a hat she had just bought and instantly discarded. But when Annie put it on, the hat suddenly looked beautiful again. That was Annie's magic with hats. Hattie asked for it back. Her hunger for clothes and love was underlined by her awareness (despite fierce assertions of independence) that years were passing. She was twenty-seven or twenty-eight. "I can't bear to be left out of life, an old maid," she wrote later in the character of someone like herself. "Outside in the street, it was sunshine. It was Spring in the air. Other girls were enjoying themselves with their young men. The whole world was alive." At night, "couples . . . embraced in hallways, lay together on roofs. I passed them all with eyes averted."

She had always felt like an outsider until, one early spring night, she went to a party at a friend's house, and the letters began.

Parts of a letter from Arnold Levitas to Anzia's friend Miss Kalisher, dated March 10, 1910.

2

L O V E

"NEW YORK, MARCH 10, '10 — My dear Miss Kalisher," wrote my yet-to-be father to Hattie's friend, the party giver, in the flowing loops and swooping curves of a self-conscious penman:

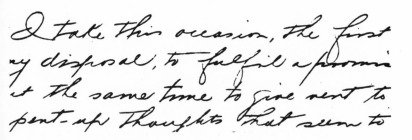

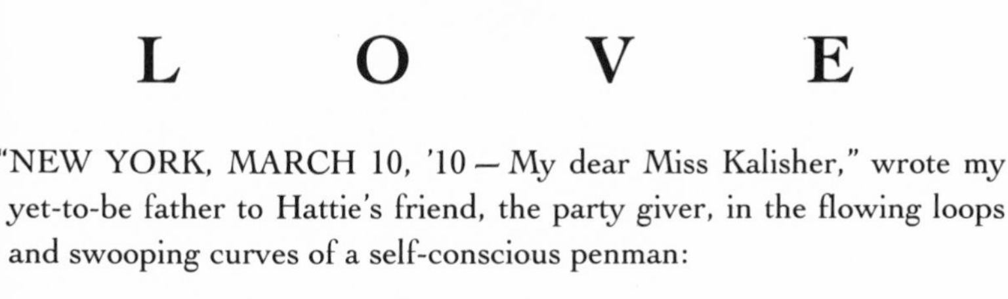
I take this occasion, the first
my disposal, to fulfil a promis
t the same time to give vent to
pent-up thoughts that seem to

But since the first occasion does not always happen to fall on a moment of inspiration — especially when one is surrounded by cold facts, documents, dictionary and copy prosaic, historic and scientific, as is the case with me [he was a printer and proofreader] — I beg for indulgence if I do not altogether conform to the time-honored eloquence that is to grace an epistle to a member of the fair sex.

I would like to express my gratefulness for the opportunity you afforded me to meet so many nice peopie under such favorable circumstances. The solar plexus blows and uppercuts delivered by Mrs. Murray to my poor, unfortunate brethren, and which consequently had the effect of filling me with sorrow and sadness, were more than overcome by your kindness and that of some of the other charming young ladies. . . .

I would ask you to kindly remember me to Miss Mayer, of whom I carried away a very favorable impression. Some girls there are soothing as a tonic, others like to scratch their names on our nerves. You and Miss Mayer belong to the former class.

I enclose the article on Unionism about which I spoke to you and which, I hope, will be of some interest.

I would deem it a privilege to have your comment on it, and trust that you will not consider it impolite if I were to request its return — this copy being the only one in my possession.

Hoping that this finds you in the happiest of moods and best of health, I beg to remain,

Very sincerely yours,
Arnold Levitas

He wasn't in a hurry. In 1910 he was thirty-one, courtly, correct, admired by women, a collector of epigrams, jokes, and other ornaments of conversation. He had two married sisters and a widowed mother. Many years before the four of them had emigrated from Libau, on the island of Kurland, a German-speaking part of Latvia.

In the packet of letters I found after his death in 1934, only two were written by him: this one of 1910 and the carbon of another he wrote

Arnold Levitas, ca. 1920.

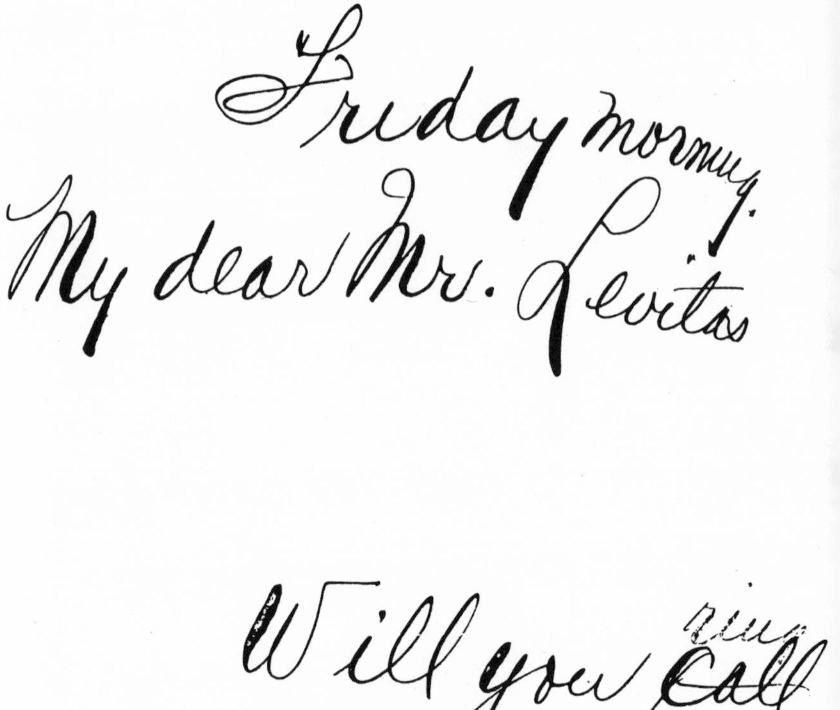

Friday morning.

My dear Mr. Levitas

Will you ~~call~~ ring me up on Sunday morning at about ten at the Rand School 778 Gramercy.

Parts of a 1910 letter from Anzia to Arnold.

Here's a little verse for you that I know you will appreciate.

With cordial greetings,

Hattie Mayer

to Anzia after the marriage had ended. She never saved his letters. But despite the end of their love, a second marriage, and moves to other apartments, he saved all of hers plus the two he wrote beginning and ending their time together.

Three weeks after Miss Kalisher's party, Anzia wrote to Arnold Levitas. It is easy to imagine, in the interval, her happy receipt from Miss Kalisher of the compliment in his letter, the beckoning word she must have sent him through the same friend, and his stately response — because she now simply invited him to visit her.

She was always in a hurry; she crossed out the inelegant word, but left it there in her oversized, egocentric handwriting. Perhaps he hesitated after answering, because on April 19 she had to nudge him:

My dear Mr. Levitas

Do you still possess that little verse I once sent you as I have no other copy and need it just now. Will you kindly return it to me?

Please give my warmest greetings to your sister. I hope I may have the pleasure of meeting her again soon.

Hattie Mayer

On May 23 (she never dated her letters; these dates come from the postmarks on the envelopes) she asked him to come and see her — she needed his help with "something" — and after that she offered free professional advice:

[June 5]

My dear Mr. Levitas,

This is just to remind you not to forget 1/2 cup of orange juice *before breakfast every single morning without fail*

Any of the following vegetables for lunch or dinner (with your meat or eggs) celery, lettuce, spinach, cauliflower or any other greens.

The food we eat is almost as important as the thoughts we think and if you will follow my suggestions for a week, you will see how your complexion will clear and all indigestion will disappear.

H.M.

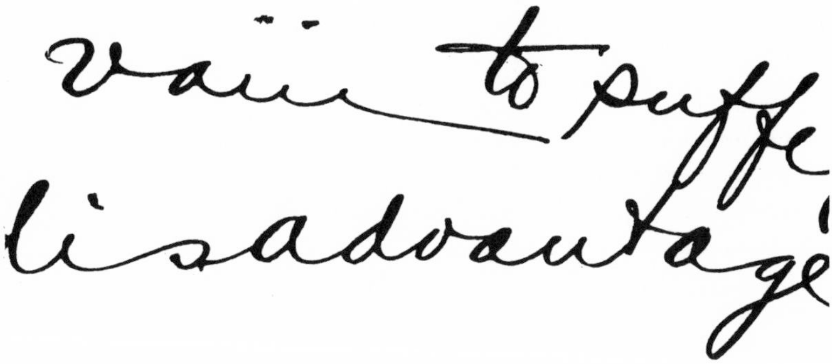

Part of a letter from Anzia to Arnold, June 1910.

> I almost forgot — Please return my postal as soon as you receive this for I want to tear it up. This snapshot hurts my vanity. I know I will never win the first prize at a beauty show; still I would not look quite so bad if I were not overshadowed by such a handsome man.

How incongruous these fluttering effusions, in that large, imperious hand!

"My dear friend," she called him in her next letter, about a week later; she was desperately in earnest:

> I'm just back from the commencement, and am so sorry, so very sorry to have missed you.
>
> Can you come to see me Friday after work. I feel so terribly lonesome.
>
> Anzia [the first time she took back her own name]

In July, as she returned from a country excursion, Arnold Levitas was first in her thoughts. She wrote:

> Did you get the thousand messages of love . . . I sent you . . . ? This kind of wireless telegraphy saves . . . superfluous writing.

She said she wanted to begin the lessons in German he had agreed to at her request:

> One of the most beautiful things about friendship is the free boundless way in which we give and take from one another. I do not hesitate asking you to help me with my German, because I know what a pleasure it would be to me to be of the smallest service to you.
>
> Anzia

During her long loneliness, from adolescence through her twenties, men had approached her who she thought were completely unattractive — coarse, insensitive, or just homely and graceless. Men she found attractive did not approach her, apparently deterred by her intensity. Her standards of honesty, she said when she explained her solitude, were too high. But in this exciting new adventure, her first experience of continuing courtship, she found it impossible — especially when Arnold delayed or hesitated — not to use the female guile she scorned. It was so obvious that he required it.

She was meeting him on weekends in Northport, Long Island, where he now worked for the Edward Thompson Printing Company. On a Monday evening in October she sent him a poem she had copied to speak for her — two stanzas of fervid emotion whose theme was:

> We love, and love is the Eternal Breath
> We draw together with a single will
> The highest end of being to fulfill . . .

The next day she wrote for herself:

> [October 10]
>
> Dearest,
>
> If I could only tell you how I love you! How my spirit follows you all over wherever you go — how my one prayer night and day is, — how can I best help you — how can I become your *real friend*,

your true comrade! Up till now, I haven't begun to love you, I was simply drawn to you irresistibly and blindly, but the more intimately I know you, the more deeply I love you. Now I really love you. I feel it by the light and beauty and the hope and the joy that has suddenly opened up all around me. — How I wish I had words for the thoughts of my heart, but you have the power to look into my inmost depths and read the inexpressible.

Your own forever,
Anzia

Had she assumed too much?

[October 24]

Dear Arnold,

I hope that all is well with you as I have not heard from you for so long.

Anzia

[October 26]

Dear Arnold,

Our notes must have crossed. I did not write till now, because I was waiting to hear from you. . . .

I was surprised at your silence, but there was nothing left for me to do, but wait quietly till you thought of me.

I need not tell you how glad your friends will be to see you next Saturday. If you can, stop in to [see me at] the Rand School first as that is so near . . . your way home. . . .

Always your friend,
Anzia

[October 27, restored as friend and nutritionist]
Thursday

Dear Arnold,

. . . I shall expect you . . . between two and two-thirty. . . . You mustn't travel for two hours on an empty stomach. At any rate . . . I shall have some crackers and milk for you.

Will tell the boys to be at your house. . . . They are all coming to see me this evening. How I love them all more and more! Gordon with his idiosyncracies and Jaffy with his. How I wish I could do something for them. God bless them a thousand times!

Anzia

The "boys" were good friends of Arnold's including Jacob Gordon, a successful lawyer and man-about-the-East Side, and Max Jaffy, who was in the printing business. She had met them through Arnold, perhaps at Miss Kalisher's party or, later, when Arnold took her to an evening at his sister's home.

Acquaintance with Arnold had brought her at once into a circle of gemütlichkeit (his family and friends were all German Jews) she hadn't experienced before. These people had time for nonpurposeful sociability, the slow, decorous exchange of graceful compliments and anecdotes during an evening at someone's home that permitted young men and women to look each other over. For a time Anzia bloomed and softened in this company. The sudden wealth of male attention and the elation she expressed in her letter to Arnold must have provoked the desired effect on Saturday night; she and Arnold must have reached a romantic understanding, because afterward she wrote to him happily, freely:

Sunday evening

Dear Love,

I greet you again at Northport. I put my arms around you and press you close to my heart, and kiss your dear lips and eyes and hair. God bless you and keep you my dear one! May God help you *to be* — just *to be* the best the highest that is in you.

Anzia

Between letters, the courtship now flourished at the Rand School, his mother's or his sister's apartment or Annie's. At weekend parties with friends, they listened to phonograph records of Caruso's arias or Kreisler playing Massenet's *Elegie*; they may have danced to Strauss waltzes and to fox trots, rewinding the phonograph each time a record was played.

They also had tea and cake and uplifting conversation about Ibsen's plays, about Socialist theories, whatever could be politely discussed. Perhaps this was too stately for Anzia's temperament. The goals she was at last reaching at twenty-nine weren't all that she had expected. She became moody. After so many years of wanting to escape from her loneliness, was it possible she didn't really want this?

[November 2]
Wednesday

Dear Arnold,

I have been ill and absent from work since Monday. I am still very weak and unable to write, but I just want to tell you how happy your dear letter made me. . . . Will send you Shaw's plays as soon as I can get around.

Good night my dear one, if I'll read your letter over a few more times I shall be well.

Lovingly yours,
Anzia

Her next letters, their envelopes addressed to "Arnold Levitas, Esquire," are an early revelation of Anzia's demon. While he was in Northport, she had been seeing one of "the boys," and was now faced with the luxury of two choices. She couldn't make up her mind. She appealed to Arnold for his "understanding" when he came in to see her and wrote to him gratefully after each visit. For example:

[November 4]

. . . May heaven bless you. You have been so good, so kind, so beautiful to me! Just like an angel in my hour of need. . . .

[November 8]

My darling angel friend,

My little room does not feel so very lonely though you have just left it, for you have left behind you the light and benediction of your dear presence. . . . No matter what I may do, I feel I can always come to you and rest my head on your dear heart and be soothed and consoled.

I kiss your feet in prayerful gratitude for all you are to me in this hour of need.

Your most grateful
Anzia

Arnold, persuaded of his own nobility and bewitched by Anzia's whirling turns, had no choice. But she couldn't help being grateful that he was permitting her to hold him in abeyance while she tried out several attitudes and, finally, dismissed him as she went off with his friend instead:

[November 10]

Dear Arnold,

Hard as it was for me to tear myself away from my parents, it was a thousand times harder to finally resolve to separate from you. You know how I have struggled to be true to myself and to both you and Gordon — but I have come at last into the light! Yesterday Nov. 9th Gordon and I were married by Mayor Gaynor at City Hall.

Because I have found the strength to fight and win my battle I feel in my heart that you will have the strength to win yours. I know that we will both be stronger and better and deeper because we have known and been close to each other even for such a short while. I hope that after a while when time has calmed us all that we will always have you as our very best friend.

Sincerely
Anzia Mayer Gordon

Jacob Gordon was a prominent lawyer and, compared to Arnold, well-to-do. Although Arnold was certainly handsomer, Gordon was "my kind," Anzia once said, explaining her brief first marriage to her daughter. Unlike the romantic role she fell into with Arnold, she was more at ease and more honest with Gordon. He understood that she was a non-comformist, an ardent rebel; in fact, he appreciated it. Arnold, had he realized it, would have been shocked and disenchanted. Nevertheless, although Anzia and Gordon had mutual sympathies and interests and were comfortable with each other, immediately after they were married they discovered they had taken too much for granted.

"'SPIRITUAL BRIDE' HAS RULED OUT CUPID," reported the Hearst wire service, headlining a story about the eventual dissolution of their marriage. "LET OTHERS PROPAGATE RACE, N.Y. TEACHER SAYS." The *New York American*'s headline ran: "'MENTAL' BRIDE'S VIEWS ON WEDLOCK. MARRIAGE 'IDEAL FRIENDSHIP' ONLY. HUSBAND A 'FEARLESS COMPANION.'"

She couldn't explain (probably even to herself) why she abruptly married and then left Jacob Gordon, a man she admired more than Arnold, but whom she couldn't sexually embrace. Speaking to the reporter, Anzia said the marriage failure was due to "a misunderstanding." But in fact she had never tried to tell him how she felt. She had expected Gordon to understand it without words. So, in the blur of cloudy but lofty sentiment, she went on "explaining":

> "To me marriage has always been an ideal state of perfected friendship, of flawless mental companionship.
>
> "Of course, I knew of what I might term the standard viewpoint of matrimony, but only vaguely. Its real significance did not dawn upon me until after I had married the man whom I thought of as the perfect friend. . . .
>
> "I have come to think now that I knew not the difference between friendship and love. Some day, perhaps, mad, overwhelming love will come to me. Until then I shall remain in the sphere of lonely singleness. I have come to the conclusion that the work of propagating the race can be carried on by those whose convictions are in accord with natural lines upon this subject."

Although the marriage and annulment shocked Anzia's friends and relatives, she received admiring letters from newspaper readers in other parts of the country. From Dutchess County, New York, a man wrote:

'Mental' Bride's Views on Wedlock

Marriage 'Ideal Friendship' Only

Husband a 'Fearless Companion'

Mrs. Gordon Tells of Strange Theories on Matrimony; Separation Suit Brought.

"I have the deepest respect and admiration for Mr. Gordon. No one could have inspired loftier sentiments in a woman.

"I did not realize that my views on marriage were unusual until after we were married.

"I have always looked only upon the mental side of marriage. My thoughts on matrimony have always been confined to the platonic relations of man and woman. I wanted a chum, a friend, a mental companion. Mr. Gordon wanted a mate.

"To this day my husband and I are the best of friends. We shall always remain perfect friends."—*Mrs. Harriet M. Gordon.*

Mrs. Harriet M. Gordon, bride of a [h]alf year, whose theory is that marriage [sh]ould be a "strong, spiritual friendship, [no]thing more," yesterday granted an in[te]rview to a reporter for The American [in] which she explained her views on [ma]rriage.

Mrs. Gordon's husband, Jacob D. Gor[do]n, a young lawyer, with offices in this [cit]y, recently instituted proceedings for [a] separation at Patchogue, L. I.

[R]esumed Her Maiden Name.

Since parting from her husband on [th]e evening following their marriage, [No]vember 9, 1910, Mrs. Gordon has been [livi]ng under her maiden name in apart[me]nts in the neighborhood of Gramercy [Sq]uare. She continued teaching also [un]der her maiden name in one of the [lar]gest public schools in Manhattan.

Mrs. Gordon was found by an Ameri[can reporter] in her classroom yesterday

Hattie Mayer Gordon,

[...]est intellectual attainments, a man of whom any woman would be proud.

From the New York American, *May 23, 1911.*

Dear Lady:

I am a Presbyterian preacher . . . nearly seventy years of age . . . married about 42 years. But for the last 15 years with the consent of my wife have been living in innocence with her. For you to live as you do is very commendable. It shows that the kingdom of heaven is coming upon the earth as a thief in the night, as Christ said it would.

And from Omaha, Nebraska:

Pemit me to congratulate you on your stand. Too long has passion been mistaken for love! And the worst form of ignorance of the Edenic state of the marital relations has so long borne sway in all the homes of Christendom, that the real beauty and sanctity has been dwarfed if not completely shattered. . . .

Do not grow discouraged. Press onward, look upward, and take hold of God's hand by faith and he will lead you and save you out of this evil world.

That was not Anzia's goal, however. The news stories were published when Gordon sued for separation, which was six months after she had left him. Leaving Gordon's home in Patchogue, Long Island, the evening after they were married, Anzia had written and telephoned for help, and Arnold had instantly responded. Years later, talking to her daughter, she recalled that he came out to her temporary quarters in Patchogue and "went on his knees to me," begging her to return to him — a gesture for which her acting lessons had well prepared her. She discovered how much she had missed him. For the next ten days, she worked at her cooking-teaching job in New York and came back each night to mull over her situation alone in Patchogue. Arnold persisted. Twelve days after her wedding to Gordon, Anzia wrote Arnold breathlessly that she was yielding to his persuasion:

[November 21, 10:30 A.M.]

Dearest,

I am writing this in the train and this paper is the only thing I could find in my bag. I haven't much to say as I just left you and all my thoughts seem merged and

~~confused~~ consumed into one all-absorbing you! You! — nothing but you!

I can't see, I can't hear, I can't feel, I can't think of anything but you and only you.

Anzia

I may be able to write a sensible note in the evening, but I know you will understand this. . . .

Lovingly,
Anzia

Later that day, she asked for more evidence of his devotion:

[8:00 P.M., by Special Delivery]

I am at present at Mrs. Ollesheimer's hotel waiting for her to come. [Mrs. Ollesheimer was the philanthropist-patron-adviser who had paid a part of Anzia's tuition at Columbia University and who took a continuing interest in her.]

My heart is aching terribly. My whole family is against me, because I have left Gordon for you. My brother from Cornell University came over specially from Ithaca to condemn and ostracize me with the rest of them. Even my sister whom you seemed to have converted to . . . our side is not very encouraging. . . .

Mrs. Ollesheimer has just returned. I have told her all about it. She is sorry for me she says, but can have nothing to do with me . . . [for] leaving the man I married. See what I give up for you. Father, mother, sisters, brothers, . . . Mrs. Ollesheimer, the whole world, all society, all for you. Can you love me enough to make up for the bleeding heart-ache that I must suffer in tearing myself away from all those dear to me? . . .

It is frightfully lonely in my room tonight. All are deserting me. Will you always stand by me? Will you ease the heart-ache and the loneliness. . . .

Heartbroken
Anzia

And at 9:30 that same night:

My darling,

I just received your sweet love note and in one breath all my gloom and heartache vanished. As long as you stand by me, I can stand ostracism and slander and calumny. — No trial is too difficult. . . .

Also received the two checks which I need just now. . . .

Your loving
Anzia

Without pausing to brood over the marriage she had just quit, she drew a circle of letters around Arnold and herself, ardent even in apology:

[December 1]

Dear Arnold,

I feel like a monster for the way I behaved last night. Instead of cheering you up, I only added to your depression. . . .

I'm looking forward most anxiously to next Saturday. In the meantime write to me. . . . If you are tired, just write . . . Anzia I'm tired, I will understand. Let me feel that you feel me with you at all times, not only in your moments of inspiration and vision, but in moments of failure — depression. What is the good of my being with you, unless it is [that] I'm your rock of refuge in your hour of need.

Most lovingly yours,
Anzia

[December 2]

Arnold dear,

I'm enclosing a copy of the note I am sending to Gordon. I hope it meets with your approval. . . .

A terrible sadness has seized me. . . . I'm looking forward most anxiously to meeting you tomorrow. . . . I feel that you are perhaps the only one in the world that understands me.

Your lonely and desolate
Anzia

The enclosure:

My dear Gordon

Do you remember your oft repeated saying "the way of the transgressor is hard?" I have experienced its full meaning. I have learned that it is the mercy and justice of the higher law that the transgressor will ever have it hard, that his hardship can never be less than the depth of his wrong.

I suppose you thought that I have not written till now from sheer irresponsibility. It was not so. In rushing over to Arnold, it took me some time to realize that I deserted you and then I was too exhausted to put my thoughts together and write. My life will ever be blighted with the memory of the suffering I have caused you.

I have a favor to ask of you. I may not deserve the favor, but if you treat people according to their deserts, how many would escape hanging? I want you to meet Arnold in my room next Saturday at six.

Arnold feels nothing for you but the old friendship which has bound you from the first. All ill-feeling has burned away in suffering.

Let me know if you can come.

Hattie

Through the next few months she was needed after school hours at her parents' flat. Unable to meet Arnold, she wrote him frequently.

[December 7]

. . . My mother is dangerously ill. . . .

Since Sunday she does not let me . . . near her bedside. I can only come . . . in the kitchen when she doesn't see me. You can imagine how I feel.

Her mother's anger had been provoked by Anzia's repeated rejection of her parents' pleas after she left home. This daughter had shown such contempt for their beliefs, she had deeply offended them.

[December 15]

. . . you know *dearest* how my heart clings to you *now* more than ever before. Your changeless devotion, your undying faith in me when everything was against me, was but "bread cast upon the waters," which will return to you in your hour of need.

From now on, I shall no longer waver. I am yours forever and always. Our home shall be a home of *perfect love* and Faith.

Your own loving
Anzia

P. S. Darling, — I just received your sp. del. I thank God for your awakening. You are going to be one of the greatest men I know. From now on I shall focus all my energies, all my thoughts just to serve you. The two of us together will do some great things for the world. . . . You have kindled in me the deepest, the most consummate love that one soul can feel for another.

Arnold moved back to New York and a new job. During their reunion her demon must have burst out once more, for she conceded:

[January 9]

Dear Arnold,

I was so stupid and inconsiderate. — I'm awfully sorry.

Most regretfully
Anzia

But most of her letters during this period, when they were meeting infrequently, expressed only her loneliness.

[February 9]
Thursday

Dear Arnold,

I just came to the Rand 7 P.M., and they told me you phoned. I thought you were to *meet* me at the restaurant and I purposely came down (from my mother's flat uptown) for I felt so heartsick and depressed. . . . I had to see you if only for a few moments. I'm on my way back to my mother's and am writing this in the train. I want to see you so much. . . . I feel so bad. If I saw you for a moment tonight I'm sure the heartache would have eased. . . . I don't know how I'll pull through the terribly long night and my mother so ill.

After the crisis passed, after her mother improved, she and Arnold met more often. Now, when nothing stood in their way and all that she had evoked in her letters could be realized, she seems to have become uneasy. Probably she was afraid that in an uncontrolled moment she might push him away again, too far this time, and find herself alone. Yet the bland texture of their everydayness together seems to have disturbed her also. The last letter she wrote to him before they married was an omen.

[March 11]

Dear Arnold,

I came to school, but I broke down, I couldn't teach. I don't know what's the matter with me, but I crave to be alone — just to be alone. My nerves are unstrung and I want to be all alone to pull myself together. . . .

I'm sorry I must try your patience so much, but I can't help it, I can't pull myself together unless I'm all by myself. . . . But step in for a little while on Friday.

Yours,
Anzia

Shortly after she wrote this letter came the public disclosure of Gordon's suit for separation. In the newspaper interviews, Anzia betrayed her underlying sadness. Despite all her protestations, she was still lonely, uncertain, troubled by a growing suspicion that she was running from one extreme to another. After all her promises, reversals, and new promises to Arnold, she no longer had the confidence to change her mind. They were married, probably soon after school vacation started, in July 1911. Although she changed her name in the school records to

Anzia Levitas that September, the wedding was a religious ceremony, without legal validity. A delay in the court's annulment of her marriage to Gordon must have made that necessary. Arnold was a stickler for correct form; his relations with Anzia's sisters and brothers, as well as his mother and sisters, were important to him. But the nonlegal marriage suited Anzia's purposes (her secret reluctance to commit herself "forever"). She evidently persuaded him that it was nobler not to bind each other.

THE LUSTER OF ILLEGALITY, however, could not enliven the dullness of marriage for Anzia after the honeymoon. Her teaching job was over for the summer, she had their new apartment to arrange, but she had never confessed to Arnold that she was not a domestic science enthusiast, that she was not at all interested in the decoration of platters, the creation of desserts, and good housekeeping. In fact, Anzia liked the simplest arts-and-crafts decor — fishnet curtains to let the sunshine in and skip the sewing, plainness of food, freedom from chores and obligations.

She was about thirty by that time and had spent most of her life fighting to free herself from other people's orthodoxies. The strain of silently opposing Arnold's expectations, the effort to avoid the truth, must have weighed heavily. When school started again in September, she was pregnant. In those days, pregnant women stayed home. Preparing the nest, she also had time to pursue her interest in women's rights, socialism, and other contemporary progressive causes. To enlighten her friend Marcet Heldeman, a former classmate from the American Academy of Dramatic Arts, Anzia gave her a copy of a book translated from the Swedish on the new woman, with an introduction by Havelock Ellis. The book, *Love and Marriage*, propounded a radical (for 1911) philosophy about sexual morality, free love, marriage, and divorce.

Delighting in the unexpected friendship of Haldeman, a petite, very pretty, warmhearted girl from a small town in Kansas, Anzia had enjoyed sharing these ideas with her. Haldeman, who seemed the ideal young native American, had been open to such new and daring points of view even though her father was a banker, in fact one of the wealthiest men in Kansas. But when Anzia brought this friend to meet lively, sociable Annie, Haldeman turned more of her attention to Anzia's sister and her children, which made Anzia jealous of Annie once again. Compared to Annie's tenement flat, and Anzia's furnished room, Haldeman lived in splendor at the Four Arts Club. There she arranged a party for Annie and her children. She also enchanted the little girls with unusual treats — a trip to the theater, a new dress, or some other magnificent luxury.

Haldeman dutifully returned to Girard, Kansas, after her New York years and became a bank officer, but she evidently did not lose the cosmopolitan tastes she had acquired in New York, and she maintained her friendship with Annie and Anzia. She married a young Jewish newspaperman, Emanuel Julius, who came out to Girard from New York to work on the Socialist weekly *Appeal to Reason*. He added his wife's family name to his own and, as Haldeman-Julius, he became the publisher of the Little Blue Books, which he started with a loan from his wife. These were the first paperbacks, only three and a half by five inches in size, a tremendous success, selling all over the country for 5¢ and 10¢. Some were reprints of great classics; some were recent books by controversial authors — for example, Upton Sinclair, Bertrand Russell, Morris Hillquit, Clarence Darrow, Havelock Ellis; and one was the book Anzia introduced to Haldeman: *Love and Marriage*.

Nevertheless, despite *her* self-designed name, Marcet Haldeman-Julius felt free, in a letter to her daughter, sometime after Anzia became famous, to ridicule "Anzia Mayer" for "calling herself" Anzia Yezierska. "Anzia, I suppose, thought a Russian name sounded more interesting. . . . I think it is all very silly. You take my advice, Alice, and keep *your* name just as it is as long as you live."

AS THE DREARINESS OF WINTER, 1911, overtook Anzia, she was inspired by a dream of escape. Some artist friends had moved to San

Francisco; her sister Fannie was now in Southern California. Thoughts of the golden air they were enjoying spurred her to action. As soon as the snows came, she convinced Arnold that their future might lie in the West.

Anzia went ahead of Arnold to scout for it and in the meantime to enjoy Fannie's care during the pregnancy. Arnold remained at his job in New York, waiting for the right moment to join her. On February 17, 1912, emotionally warmed up again, she wrote him an apology from Long Beach:

> My dear Arnold,
>
> I just received your letter. I feel thoroughly and painfully ashamed of myself . . . as if someone had *deservedly* slapped me in the face . . . [for] the guilt was all on my side. . . . It is poignantly humiliating to get a sudden focused glimpse of all the pettinesses and selfishnesses of one's nature. You remember that excruciating moment of . . . the "scarecrow" who thought himself a lord and suddenly saw himself face to face in the magic mirror that revealed him to be nothing more than a . . . broomstick and a bag of hot air. . . . In the despairing moment of self disillusion . . . he felt his real soul being born. As I read your letter, I underwent the agony of the scarecrow. . . . There's much that I want to say to you now. . . . It is at such moments of mere word misunderstandings that one feels most keenly the pain of separation. One glance into one another's eyes, the mere touch of the hand . . . and in a lightning flash misunderstandings would vanish and we'd feel all the more deeply the irresistible current that has drawn us together from the first and draws us ever closer through all clouds and storms. Dearest, do you not feel even now as I'm writing to you these shortcomings and failures that have risen up for the moment high as mountains to obscure us from one another, melting away in the love hidden deep in our hearts and which lights up most vividly in an hour like this. It is because of the purity and sincerity of our love, that an act of selfishness or pettiness in either of us causes so much pain. . . . Dearest, how I wish we could sleep together tonight! How much

we could give to one another at this moment. How our hearts and souls would open up and rush together and soothe one another, — and in that irresistible melting moment, in the white flame of the flowing together of our naked beings, . . . we'd realize even more deeply than we have ever before, how indissolubly one we are.

Anzia was apologizing for having confided one of their secrets to Marcet, who evidently couldn't be trusted.

In reference to Marcet's gossipings to my sister. You know one of my besetting sins which I'm trying to overcome is lack of tact. In an unconscious and unguarded moment . . . I may have told her something which if she had more sense, she would not have carried to my sister. . . . If I have been foolish and indiscreet enough once to afford a gossip food for his gossip, I shall not add to my folly by trying to stop [her] mouth. . . . But my friendship with Marcet comes to an end.

In fact, it didn't. The friendship with Marcet continued far longer than did Anzia's marriage.

Arnold dear, now that I've had a good cry over your letter, I feel a little relieved. . . . I cannot bear to have anything but love between us.

Your erring and most repentant wife Anzia.

From Fannie to Arnold:

Feb. 25, 1912

My dear brother Arnold

I read your last letter over carefully. Under the circumstances as favorable opportunities for the development of your career seem to be opening up in N.Y., it would certainly be rash for you to think of coming to a place where you are not sure of things.

We all try to make it as comfortable as possible for Hattie. But I don't know what it is with Hattie that she is not as happy as she might be. I think actually the main cause is that she misses you. Although she will *not* admit that. She is looking splendid! The climate out here agrees with her. But I do believe that Hattie is a little too active considering her condition.

For instance Hattie took a notion to go to S.F. and Berkeley the other day, where she was invited by some of our friends. I tried my very best [to insist that she should] *not undertake the trip,* as it is about 500 miles from L.A. Any other time, I would not mind so much, but not in her condition. But she was persistent. . . . She wanted a little change and nothing could keep her . . . from going. You know by this time that Hattie has a mind of her own. One thing I am certain, is that Hattie will *not* stay away long. For she cannot have it any wheres more pleasant and convenient [than] she has it in my house. . . .

With kind regards,
Your sister Fannie

Although undated, the letter below followed a ten- or twelve-day interval and proved that Fannie was right:

Arnold dear,

I have not been well the last week. I took a boat trip on the ocean and it suddenly grew stormy and windy and it upset me so that I nearly had a miscarriage. But I'm much better now for my sister is taking such good care of me. . . .

The baby and myself . . . came very nearly being on the other side of heaven. Hereafter I will have to be more careful. Your inspiring letter with the verses was like wine to me in my illness.

Your loving Anzia

The next day:

Dearest,

. . . I'll tell you how it all happened. You know how anxious I was to see Miss Pollak [one of Anzia's art-circle friends who had moved from New York] when I went to Cal. But she lives in Oakland near San Francisco, a 24 hr boat-trip from Los Angeles. My sister dissuaded me from making the journey all along, on the ground that sea-sickness might seriously affect me at this period. Even Miss Pollak who was anxious to see me dissuaded me from the trip. (She could not come to see me as she owns a little art store to which she is bound every day.) At first I listened to the advice given to me. But . . . I was in such splendid physical health that I thought nothing on earth could harm me. There seemed something even alluring in the possibility of danger, — to be all alone at night on a stormy ocean seemed poetically irresistible. Besides the plain truth is this: I was itching for a change — to talk to a live human being like Miss Pollak. At my sister's I have all the love and tenderness, all the luxurious comforts a person can wish for — sunshine, flowers, automobiling, the finest food, and the most loving service of my sister who treats me like a mother her one child. I appreciate it — but — there isn't one *live* person here to talk to. No possibility of any mental or intellectual intercourse with anyone. My brother-in-law while he has a good heart and means well is unfortunately a coarse, vulgar boor whose mentality has been reduced to money-making and lustful physical enjoyment. The people he surrounds himself with are those of his own calibre, whose idea of sociability is time-wasting . . . meaningless, purposeless conversation [about] women or card-playing. My sister who has always been preoccupied with the children and the care of the house and who never had a chance of coming in touch with people of ideals, gradually adapted herself to the path of least resistance and is unconsciously stagnating in the quagmire of her husband. . . . I do not thrust my views on them. I merely stand back and look on . . . you can imagine how lonely . . . I feel at times and why I look forward so hungrily from one week to the other for the letters from you. . . . You can imagine how I could not help longing for Miss Pollak. Well, to make the story short, on the way to Miss Pollak . . . a fierce wind and storm arose, the ship nearly turned over and instead of being on the water 24 hours we barely made it in 56 hours. I was terrifically sea-sick and was in danger of a miscarriage but heaven, with the help of a very good doctor, saved me. When I got to Miss Pollak she put me in bed at once and made me stay there for two days.

As soon as I was well enough she treated me to an intellectual feast of the Gods. She invited some of the most interesting people of Oakland and San Francisco and a few days in the society of people of my own kind rejuvenated my whole being. . . . I went back to Los Angeles yesterday. With the refreshing and invigorating memory of [the] visit, I will be content with Long Beach till baby comes. . . . But I hope in the future to be able to be in Oakland near Miss Pollak. When you decide to come to California, I am sure you will prefer Oakland, or San Francisco or Berkeley to Long Beach.

Miss Pollak seems charmed and delighted with our picture together, the first postal picture that you sent, in which you stand so tall and straight. Can you possibly send another one as she is very anxious to have one. She is in love with you before she [has] even met you.

Acknowledging in this letter the packages Arnold was regularly sending her — literary and political magazines and other gifts, which she felt she needed for intellectual nourishment — Anzia vetoed his idea of also sending gifts to her hosts as "really unnecessary"; but, she conceded, "perhaps for my brother-in-law . . . one or two ties." Arnold's attentiveness to her wishes made her purr:

Your sweet beautiful letters are on my lap as I write to you. The mere feel of the paper which you touched and handled soothes and refreshes me like the touch of your hand or the sound of your voice or the kiss of your lips. I'm living in the dreamy anticipation of the future when you, the baby and I will be together working and struggling for something higher and higher and higher. In the meantime I feel like you, that distance does not divide us, that though 3000 miles apart, we are more closely bound together than some of our married friends who hold on to one another's coattails. The bond that holds us transcends time and space. . . . In millions of years we'd rush back to one another just as irresistibly as now. And the reason for this is — that both of us are parts of one ideal — the ideal which you can only realize when I give my best to you and when you give your best to me.

Lovingly your wife
Anzia

[March 11, 1912]

My own dear husband and sweetheart,

. . . Have read your letter to Fannie in which you appoint her my guardian and advisor in your absence. . . . There's only one person in all the world whom it is a joy to obey and that is my own dear husband because there's no one in all the world whom I love as much as my own dearest Arnold Levitas.

. . . Fortunately I have come in touch with a few very interesting people, with whom I started a class in the study of socialism. Have also joined the Polytechnic High School where I . . . study German.

She was expelled from this high school when the principal decided that Anzia's expanding figure, which she made no effort to disguise, was an improper, too graphic demonstration of real life for the other students.

Before leaving for New York, Anzia had told Arnold she planned to do some writing, perhaps poetry, while she waited for the baby. Now, she confessed, her circumstances were so "very trying . . . I could not do . . . my writing in such an atmosphere. . . . All I could do [is] watch my brother-in-law play pinochle. . . .

My sister is ill and worn out most of the time from the harmful preventives of conception which she is so often forced to use as she does not want more children and her husband is most inconsiderate in his desire. Have given her Dr. Robinson's equipment with all the medicines. One box has run out. Will you send another. . . .

. . . If the doctor's predictions prove true, we will have a wonderful baby. I never was in better health and I feel as light as a feather. . . . I feel sure the baby will be the image of you, your eyes, your hair, and your graceful slender body! . . . It is as if something light and angelic were beating in me and opening up the wonders of the heavens. . . .

Your Anzia

From across the country and after months of separation, the thought of her marriage completely enchanted Anzia again. Her letters grew cozier and more loving with each week. Writing to Arnold on March 14, she called him "Dear Hubby," and declared that she now understood his inner nature more deeply than any of his relatives or friends:

Your real self . . . I am in touch with and feel and understand 3000 miles away as well as if I were with you day and night. In fact I feel myself getting closer and closer to your real self since I'm away. It will not be possible for me to tear myself away from you again, you can be sure. The thought of being together again and the thought of the baby between us seems like a far off beautiful dream too perfect to be realized.

My sister just brought her baby in my room; that means I must stop writing. It's a velvet skin, blue-eyed golden-haired, pot-cake little man of 8 months that magnetizes your body and soul on the spot. And you forget all that you want to do at the touch of his velvet little hand.

This little gentleman wants me to take him now and so the letter must be put away at once. . . .

Lovingly yours,
Anzia

Free from any responsibilities and pressures, lovingly ministered to by her sister and Arnold's gifts and letters. Anzia perceived how much finer was her marriage than that of her sister. The fact that Arnold's letters regularly enclosed small checks, like an allowance, also explains the childlike sweetness, even meekness, she expresses in all the 1912 letters from California. Always a believer in the power of words to transcend deeds, she was writing propaganda as much to convince herself as to persuade and hold Arnold.

Thursday

My dearest,

. . . Ingersoll's selection on Love was something I have admired for a long time, and to think that you of all people should guess the very thought of my thoughts!

Your Anzia

Thursday

My dearest Arnold

It seemed to me, when I thought of the many great moments spent together, that I had already tasted life's deepest and sweetest joys, but as I read your last letter, and felt between the lines, the unfolding of your heart and brain into . . . rich, strong, independent manhood, I . . . [knew] an unutterable . . . joy — deeper and sweeter than any I have yet experienced. If you had scaled the heights of fame, if the whole world applauded your greatness, I could not have felt prouder of you than I do now. It seems hard at times to believe that you are really my husband, for you tower so mightily above me — . This picture you sent me is the first photograph that brings out all that I see in you. I cannot part with it, I like it so much. Please send me another for Miss Pollak.

My sister tells me that most women feel a great weight dragging them down during the latter months of their pregnancy. I feel as light as a feather and the baby within seems like a live electric leaven lifting me in space. I think it must be the soul of a poet growing inside me rather than a little body of mere clay, for all its movements seem so thrillingly light and sinuous as a poet's. . . .

With loving embraces,
Anzia

Anzia, a month after the birth of her child. The smiling pride in her achievement remains on her face, although the baby has just been lifted from her lap.

Anzia gave birth to a girl on May 29. Her sister Fannie had a photographer take pictures of the new mother (see illustration) when Anzia returned to Fannie's home from the hospital. About two months later, Anzia and her daughter took the train back to Arnold, ending a rare period of peace and tenderness in her life.

3

HATE

"AT FIRST IT SEEMS IMPOSSIBLE TO GO [through] your husband's pockets for money, or to ask your grocer to add a few dollars to your bill. The first time you do it, you hate yourself and are unable to meet your eyes in the mirror. . . . Then . . . you become hardened. Self preservation makes it as natural for you to keep on deceiving your husband as . . . for couples to keep on living together when they have ceased to love one another."

Anzia filled a large pad with these ideas for a true-confession-style story, "Rebellion of a Supported Wife," one of her early attempts at popular magazine writing, which she began soon after her return from California. She never finished it, no doubt interrupted by the emotional turmoil she was describing. She found the time, the anger, and the inspiration to write it when she came back to real life with Arnold after leaving the haven of Fannie's care.

> How little people can tell from the outside of a man's life the sort of husband he is at home. Many a man who is considered the blessing of the community . . . a free and generous gentleman in all social circles, may be stingy as a miser at home. . . . Usually [those] . . . who are so . . . liberal with their own needs that they never know the amount . . . they have in their pockets, demand that their wives render them . . . [an] account of expenditures to the minutest fraction of a cent.

They lived in one of the Vanderbilt Apartments, looking out on the East River, a new development of "model" dwellings exemplifying the latest and best in architectural design for living. Their apartment was furnished by Anzia with the deliberate simplicity of Mission chairs and tables, fishnet curtains, and a monk's-cloth sofa covering. But the aura of perfect comradeship and understanding she had created for them by mail, the sensitive poet she had discerned in Arnold, the loving, kitchen-minded idealist she had persuaded him (and herself) she would be — all these illusions seemed to evaporate after her return. In the same notepad she reported other painful facts of "a supported wife's" condition:

> Women who have known the independence of earning their own livings before marriage . . . feel most poignantly the humiliations they have to live through while being "supported." If there was some way out, they would all rush back to the offices, shops or factories. But they cannot go back. . . . By the time they realize the full meaning of being "supported," they have a baby or two to care for. A baby is like the ball and chain of the prisoner that keeps him bound to his cell.

Arnold at first had no suspicion that Anzia felt oppressed and that he was the oppressor. Although he was easily roused to anger — by her "extravagances," for instance — he got over it quickly. Throughout his life his mother had demonstrated that the natural delight of women was to be the servers, and of men to be the consumers, of cooking and other housewifery. A scrupulously honest respecter of the right way to behave, a sociable man who especially enjoyed family gatherings in his own home, he could not have imagined any other kind of marriage.

When he got angry — a sudden, terrifying, explosive outburst — Anzia was startled and then frightened. He had been so patiently understanding before they were married!

> I tell my husband, "When I have to come to you for money, where wouldn't I run to be able to get away from . . . the anger you heap on me. . . . These are times when every feeling within me turns into poison and hatred."
>
> "Witch! Fury! You never showed your real venom till now."
>
> "I never had any venom in me till now. If I have turned into a witch and a fury, who is to blame?"

For a while Anzia kept her feelings confined to this essay because she was also furious at herself for having deliberately walked into the trap.

> Levitas. Why did she kill herself so to get him — ? . . . She broke away from her own only to get into another den of relatives. Small talk about cooking, theater, etc., bores her to madness.

Most of these smoldering notes about a woman's enslavement as "a poor man's wife" were actually based on observations of Annie's marriage, which predated Anzia's by sixteen years. After Anzia became a wife and mother like Annie, she continued to run back to her sister, complaining now about their common lot and also discussing or working over stories they had worked over before — dreams that had the glorious fairy-tale possibility of someday freeing her from her "prison cell." To get away from the cell temporarily, she often hired Annie's older girls, aged ten and fourteen, as cheap labor to clean the East Seventy-ninth Street apartment or watch the baby, Louise, nicknamed Tinker Bell.

By that time Annie had borne seven children; one had died; her youngest was fifteen months old. Compared to this older sister, Anzia was living a luxuriously comfortable life. Every room of Annie's slum tenement flat was crowded with beds. Annie's husband, Abram, according to Anzia, who despised him, dined in good restaurants and gave Annie only pennies to feed his family. Enraged by what she perceived as his brutishness and Annie's meek acceptance of it, Anzia flung accusations at him as if it was her own battle. In a sense, it was.

> "All I want," said John, aggrieved, "is a hot cup of coffee and a decently set table. I can get it at any restaurant for ten cents. And that little I cannot get in my own home. Either the coffee is lukewarm, or the table isn't decently set, or you haven't the time to wait on me."
>
> "Why don't you wait on yourself?" I broke out. "Why don't you help me a little in the morning with the baby — ? You see your . . . wife in need of help, buried alive in the kitchen, and instead of giving her a hand, you expect her to wait on you.
>
> ". . . Will you stop your nagging?" he shouted, "Hereafter I'll have my breakfast outside. I can't stand it any longer." With this he slammed the door.
>
> A man can always put on his hat and go, I said bitterly to myself. But a woman with a baby — The massed social pressure of the entire world is against the mother who wants to get away from her place of bondage. . . . They do not have to use dogs . . . to hound the slave back to [her] master, they simply make it impossible for her to leave her baby anywhere."

When Anzia finally expressed this despair out loud to Arnold, he was outraged. His own mother, he pointed out, had three children and earned their living while baking, cooking, cleaning, scrubbing, and washing laundry — without complaint. Sometimes after these quarrels Anzia fled with the baby to Annie and stayed overnight, crowding Annie's flat still more, aggravating Abram, who ran out of the house whenever Anzia appeared, and also tantalizing Annie's children, who, after doubling up to make room for her, had to watch hungrily as she prepared special custards and other delicacies for her baby.

Arnold and Anzia patched up their quarrels, but the disagreements would always erupt again, and they grew worse. When Tinker Bell was two years old, Anzia found a solution: she hired a nursemaid and went back to being a cooking teacher. It gave her more money, freedom, and even, with the release from home and baby, the joy to start writing:

> May 29, 1915
>
> Baby mine! You perfect one of my imperfect self.
> You melting tenderness born of my hardness
> You precious sunbeam fused out of my tears.
>
> You are just three years old today
> But ages before you were born, I dreamed you and
> loved you into being.
> Your little radiant body, how it lights up the very
> air
> Your eyes, your hair, your little lips, your little
> limbs, how I worship . . . every atom
> of you!
> What music so heart-stirring as the sound of your
> happy voice?
> What saint or divinity could so lift me . . . as the
> touch of your little hand?
> Oh sweet spirit of dancing sunshine, (She left the poem
> unfinished.)

But the joy and the feeling of freedom were brief. More than ever, after she recovered a degree of independence, she and Arnold found out how far apart they were. For instance, they totally disagreed about the extra money, Anzia's salary. (How much should be kept for herself?) They bickered also about the decline of social entertainment in their home, now that she was holding a job. These disagreements brought up a much thornier issue: her housekeeping, or the lack of it.

Suddenly Anzia's desperation was pushed aside by an extraordinary event, a fantasy come true. Her first story, "The Free Vacation House," written and rewritten for years, and sent out repeatedly, was accepted for publication! The *Forum* didn't pay much money, but it was a highly respected, in fact a highbrow, magazine.

She knew now that she was meant for more than keeping house and baking cookies for Arnold and relatives. She wrote to Fannie about it, and in writing back Fannie mentioned that she was going to a hospital soon for surgery. Anzia yearned to be with that warm, motherly sister, just to escape the fights, perhaps even to help Fannie. Her yearning sparked a sudden impulse:

[June 3, 1915]

Dearest Arnold,

I did not mean to leave in that hurried manner. But it was such a terrible heartache to tear myself away that I did not know what I was doing.

In a month I shall be back, and I know we will both gain a closer sympathy and understanding for one another because of the separation. If you can forgive and understand my going, then you will write me daily about the little darling — our one beautiful dream in common.

Lovingly yours
Hattie

Sitting up in a coach train for four and a half days, she was returning to the freedom she had known without Arnold. Twice before she had escaped to Fannie's home in California: first, when she was lonely, unmarried, depressed with her old-maid, cooking-teacher job, and then again when she was pregnant and seeking relief from the boredom of marriage. She had written to Fannie, and each time Fannie had answered with urgent invitation: "Come! I'm waiting for you. I need you! We need each other." And when Anzia came, she recalled years later, "Gewalt! what a holiday it was for us both! We had so much in common!"

Before taking the train this third time, Anzia sent the first hurried explanation to Arnold on a scrap of paper from Grand Central Station. The return address she wrote on the envelope was Fannie's home in Hollywood; instead of reaching Arnold, this letter was returned to her at Fannie's home because she had misaddressed it. She had forgotten the number of the home she had recently moved to with Arnold, a new apartment house in the countrylike Bronx at 863 East 176th Street. She had written 563 instead. She repeated the mistake with her next letter, which she wrote while sitting up in the train. This, too was Returned to Sender:

Dear Arnold,

Please send a special delivery or night letter telling me how you and the baby are.

It is a million times harder than you can imagine to be away from the little darling. . . . I would give up heaven and all its glory to be near her. Will return just as soon as my sister is over the operation.

Awaiting most anxiously to hear from you,

Anzia —

Send the night letter. I shall appreciate it.

About a week after she reached her sister's she at last addressed a letter correctly:

Dear Arnold,

I'm enclosing a few of the letters that were returned to me because of wrong address.

Why did you not write a line since your night-letter? How are you and the baby? . . . How is your mother? Has Anna remarried?

Sit down and write me a long letter. My sister is surprised that you have not written till now.

Am on my way to San Francisco for a few days to see Mrs. Levy. When I return I shall let my sister go for a few days vacation, for she needs to get away. In about ten days, I shall return to N.Y.

Remember me to all our friends.

With love to you and the baby,
Anzia

Kiss and hug the darling for me.

In San Francisco, she renewed her comradeship with Miss Pollak and her circle of artist friends, whom Anzia considered "some of the most interesting people in Oakland and San Francisco." With her story about to be published "by Anzia Yezierska," she felt like one of them.

But in July she had to return to the Bronx. Whatever her resolves, which seemed so easy to aim for while she was writing letters to Arnold, when she faced him in person she rediscovered the same impasse they had reached before. To Anzia the Bronx was "the uptown ghetto," a place where "all the women sat around together with their baby carriages, darning and mending, discussing what was cooking in their neighbors' pots," and where a woman like Anzia who was interested in writing was suspect.

> "She's such a lady, when she goes to the market, she don't even bargain herself to get things cheaper like the rest of us. She takes it wrapped up, don't even look at the change. Just like a Gentile."

She wrote these comments years later from memory, in a story called "Wild Winter Love," about a woman whose urge to write and to live differently from her tailor-husband's wishes was destroying their marriage. In this story, a quarrel starts as the husband calls to his wife:

> "Come to bed already, I waited up for you long enough. It's time to sleep."
>
> "Oh, Dave! Stop bothering me. I only just got started. Why can't you go to sleep without me!"
>
> No sound for a while.
>
> "*Nu*? Not yet finished?"
>
> "Let me alone, can't you? I've scrubbed and cooked and washed all day long. Only when the baby is asleep [is the time] I take to myself."

"Gewalt!" Dave's voice, raw with hurt, rose into a shriek. "There's an end to a man's patience. My gall is bursting. You're not a woman. I married myself to a *meshugeneh* with a book for her heart."

"God! What does that man want of me?"

"You know what I want. I want a home. I want a wife."

Anzia stayed on in the Bronx with Arnold nine months more. There were increasing arguments over money, and one night, in the face of Arnold's thunder-and-lightning rage, she dressed and packed her suitcase. Still in his robe and pajamas, Arnold stood in the hallway barring the door. His shouting and Anzia's weeping woke their three-year-old daughter, who came running into the hallway in terror. They were so engulfed in their bitter fight that they didn't see her.

Anzia left that night; a couple of days later, while Arnold was at work, she returned and took the child from the nursemaid. Writing to the friend of her East Side days, Rose Pastor Stokes, Anzia said the quarrels had grown "unbearable"; she had found a furnished room nearby for herself and the baby. She was still teaching night school, but now would have to earn more to support the two of them.

Stokes, then a frequently published journalist with many magazine connections, sent a check, which Anzia returned. What she wanted was her friend's help with her stories and in finding "literary work" — in fact, her access to editors. Stokes had probably been the one who helped her reach the *Forum* when she had been making the rounds with "The Free Vacation House."

On April 6, Arnold's thirty-seventh birthday, he received a letter from a friend of Anzia's:

Dear Mr. Levitas:

I just learned from my sister that Hattie left New York taking the child with her. Of course I can understand how you feel about it. Yet — do not take this very much to heart. In spite of her eccentricities, Hattie is an excellent woman, and I am sure the child will get excellent care. Besides, knowing Hattie as I do, I believe she will not absent herself for long. The same impulse that made her leave will bring her back. Let us hope her return will be soon. In the meanwhile — be of good cheer.

With kindest greetings,
Sincerely yours,
Rose Shomer

Giving up her New York efforts to be self-sustaining, Anzia had taken Tinker Bell with her to California, to the safety of Fannie's home, until she could find the means to reach her goal in San Francisco. During the next two and a half months, receiving no word from her, Arnold must have written frantic, angry, accusing letters both to Anzia's sister in Hollywood and to her brother Henry in Berkeley. Finally, Fannie answered:

June 19

My dear Arnold,

Just received your letter of June 15th. Although you made me feel terrible . . . in your previous letter [saying] that I am the cause of Hattie and the angel Tynkabel being out in California, I often wanted to write to you and explain to you in detail from A to Z how very wrong you are.

She was too poor a writer and too burdened with urgent business, Fannie wrote, to clarify the situation in a letter. "I often wish that I could have a heart-to-heart talk with you [so] that you would not feel so very bitter against Hattie." The death of her older son in an auto accident and the grave financial reverses of her husband — sorrows she didn't mention to Arnold — had prevented Fannie from answering sooner. "You don't know, dear Arnold, what I went through the last 8 or 10 months. Hattie and your mixed-up affair has only added [grief] to make a nervous wreck of me. Life is so very short altogether. Why shouldn't there be more harmony?" She took time to add that the "angel Tynkabel is feeling and looking fine. . . . There are very few mothers who are more devoted to their children than Hattie to her Tynkabel. She is taking the best care of the child. . . . Your friend Fannie."

When was Arnold's wife "Hattie," and when did she turn into

Anzia? Some of her old friends and relatives could not forget the old name. But to her newer friends and younger relatives, especially after her first story was published, Hattie, taking on the persona of the artist-writer, had become indisputably Anzia. Even her little girl, after giving up the word "Mama," had learned to say Anzia instead. To Fannie's husband, whether she was Hattie or Anzia (he stumbled over both), she was constantly annoying. He was growing exasperated at the new disorder in his home. His children were older and therefore less obtrusive than Tinker Bell, his wife more attentive to his needs when her sister wasn't there. Prodded by his irritability and by her own distaste for his presence, Anzia packed up precipitously, without funds or a job, to seek her fortune in San Francisco.

This time the lure was not only Miss Pollak and the pleasure of Miss Pollak's circle. Anzia expected to see a New York poet named Hugo Seelig who was then in San Francisco. She had met Seelig in New York when her marriage had started disintegrating; and although he was too poor to provide any financial aid, his heart seemed to be available.

Since her adolescence (she was now about thirty-four) Anzia had enshrined poets in her personal Valhalla. She tried poetry herself, a paean to freedom and the future, now that she was free from Arnold's terrible outbursts over money, free also from his Bronx relatives:

> I am a spendthrift in love
> I am thrifty and wise and prudent in everything but love,
> I cannot help it.
> My heart rushes out of me in a surge of reckless longing and
> desire at the passing shimmer of beauty.
> Eyes, lips, a smile whisper to me a thousand secrets.
>
> I never count the cost,
> I never stop to think whither,
> I can only follow the beckoning shine of love —
> I can only sing out my heart's hunger for beauty.
>
> All my life I've spent myself on love —
> All my life I've let go all for the fleeting rainbow gleam

of beauty.
My hands are empty,
My house is bare.
I stand alone in the dimming memories of vanished loves,
But in me I feel [them] beating still —
. . . I have spent love — and bought beauty.

With Tinker Bell somewhat slowing her pursuit of this poetic creed, Anzia arrived at Miss Pollak's, where she undoubtedly spoke freely of her great plans. She must have expressed her anger and boredom with Arnold, his card-playing relatives and their gemütlichkeit, and she probably contrasted all that with Seelig's aestheticism and literary nobility. But Miss Pollak, who had been wholly convinced by Anzia's previous accounts of her "ideal" marriage, as well as by Arnold's photo and his idealistic, love-filled letters, could not adjust to Anzia's sudden change of love. Anzia was so wrapped up in the new romance that Miss Pollak became concerned about Tinker Bell.

The next messages Arnold received from California confirmed his worst fears: two telegrams from the secretary of the Women's Protective Bureau of Oakland, Beatrice A. McCall, stated that his little daughter was suffering from neglect and volunteered the bureau's services to rescue her. No longer Anzia's friend, Miss Pollak had called the bureau into action. The secrets Anzia had confided were now being used against her. After leaving Miss Pollak's home, she had found a job with a San Francisco settlement house — to demonstrate and live in a model flat; but the job required that she board her daughter elsewhere.

Regarding this substitute care, Beatrice McCall followed up her telegrams with a more alarming letter:

City of Oakland, California
City Hall
Women's Protective Bureau
August 19, 1916

My dear Mr. Levitas:

The conditions surrounding the baby are at present about . . .

what you would suppose they are. Hattie has changed her address numerous times, dragging her from one place to the other. I heard indirectly that she was going to place the child with some people who are at present mixed up indirectly with the bomb throwing episode in San Francisco.* Of course the baby gets no care, and both Miss Pollak and myself are extremely distressed about it.

When I telegraphed you I didn't know that you were not married. . . . This . . . deprives us of the legal right to the child. You see, I thought that, [considering] the way the child is . . . being taken care of, a father who could offer a good home . . . and decent surroundings would of course have the preference, but under the law you have no right to her. . . . I think that the matter will have to rest now, and if you will be in readiness to come [when] I wire you to come, I will not send you that wire unless I believe that there is some good reasons why we might get the child. . . .

Thanking you for your quick co-operation, I remain,

Cordially yours,
Beatrice McCall
Secretary
Women's Protective League

Arnold's by-now frantic telegraphed inquiries to Fannie were answered by Anzia's brother:

Berkeley, Y.M.C.A.
Berkeley, Cal.
August 21, 1916

My dear Arnold:

There is nothing very serious in those telegrams you received. They are the result of a "scrap" that Hattie had with Miss Pollak who was in part responsible for her coming out here. As for Fannie, she is 500 miles from here and just at present is financially

*The bombing had occurred a month before at a "preparedness" parade in San Francisco. Nine spectators were killed, many others injured. News reports ascribed the act to "anarchists" who were opposing U.S. entry into World War I. Tom Mooney, a leader of the International Workers of the World (IWW) and his assistant, Warren K. Billings, had just been arrested.

worried and that is why she doesn't write. She is just as much interested in Tinkabel as ever.

There is a possibility of some plan being evolved soon for giving you charge of Tinkabel. I am in touch with Miss McCall who sent you those telegrams. I didn't know she sent them until after she had done so or I would have suggested writing instead.

For the present I can't write you anything more definite. Tinkabel is well and happy and attending school. With regards, I am

Sincerely yours,
Henry Mayer

Henry, younger than Anzia, was then studying for a doctoral degree in physics at the University of California. He had apparently failed to impress Miss McCall as trustworthy.

City of Oakland, California
Women's Protective Bureau
City Hall

My dear Mr. Levitas:

. . . I did as you suggested and sent for Mayer in Berkeley. He hastened to get the news to Hattie that you were contemplating coming and that I was going to assist you. All the time he was here he pretended to be much in disgust at her actions. He then informed the sister in L.A., who hastened to inform Hattie, so that the aforesaid lady is spending her time cursing us all. She thinks that she has hidden the child but we know where she is.

You have in this state absolutely no legal ground to stand on unless Hattie does something else. We cannot arrest any parent of a child for failure to provide if they even contribute ten dollars a month to the support of the child. She is doing this now. Also the court will permit an immoral woman the custody of a child providing the child is boarded elsewhere and out of sight of her indiscretions. The religious ceremony [by which Anzia and Arnold were married] does not amount to anything except as it means your good will. Of course Hattie is keeping the child, mostly because she thinks she can win back this individual Seelig. We are hoping she will get tired or do something unusual and the thing for you to do is to come. I will wire you whenever I think there is a possibility of your getting the child. She is at present with a pretty good woman in a suburb and is quite well. . . .

Cordially yours,
Beatrice A. McCall
Secretary

Although the efforts of McCall and Pollak had thus subsided, Anzia was now overwhelmed by another unexpected blow. In a letter to Rose Pastor Stokes on September 28, 1916, she wailed:

I could not write to you — and cannot yet — because I am so dead. The man I loved died and with him went all the life out of me.

Besides this death came poverty — at present I'm working as investigator for the Hebrew Charities — the dirtiest, most dehumanizing work that a human being can do.

I see how the people are crushed and bled and spat upon in the process of getting charity and I must keep my mouth shut or lose my job. . . .

Your encouraging words about the stories I sent you make me work harder than ever. My one release, my one prayer is my writing. If it were possible for you to get Everybody's or the Metropol interested in publishing some of the stories I sent you, you would save me from the "Charities."

Seelig had not, in fact, died, but he was dead to her. Although he had flirted with her in New York, it appears he was not ready to solve the problems of a runaway married woman with a child. "Love Cheat," a story Anzia published years later about "an empty sensualist" who pursued casual sex, not love, may have been inspired by this harsh, wounding experience.

She had recovered enough three weeks later to write Stokes that now she planned to stay at the detested job until she had collected "enough material for the plot" of a play about charity and enough money to live on for a year. "Do you know I envy Billings his life sentence in prison. In one blow he is freed from the dragging down wear & tear of making a living — and in the solitude of the prison, he can think out his thoughts . . . as he never could while chained to his stomach needs." A poor person had to commit a crime "to get away from the worries of the world," she added. "If I did not have Tynkabel to care for, I would be in prison writing."

Stokes understood Anzia's theatrics: besides being a published writer and playwright, she was herself the East Side heroine of two highly publicized, highly dramatic romances. One was with the millionaire Graham Stokes who, in 1904, because of his Socialist convictions, had ventured into the Lower East Side to work at the University Settlement. Passionate, red-haired Rose Pastor came to interview him for the *Jewish Daily News*. They were married a year later.

The second romance was with radical politics. Rose Pastor Stokes was a former cigar-factory worker, educated by self-study. After her front-page wedding, at which, according to the *New York Times,* the Lower East Side mingled with Park Avenue, she and her husband devoted themselves to Socialist causes. Her poems, articles, and plays were on working-class themes. She also continued to lead strikes and walk picket lines. By 1916 temperamental and political differences had cooled her marriage, but her radicalism and writing nourished each other.

Both were valuable to Anzia in her desperation that autumn of 1916. As she schemed to escape from poverty and helplessness by selling her unorthodox, anti-establishment stories, Rose Pastor Stokes was the rescuer she clung to by mail. Anzia's frantic letters, always asking for "news about the stories I sent you," disclosed her ever-present anguish. Now it was about Tinker Bell, the need to find foster care for her daughter when Anzia changed jobs, her constant anxiety over money to pay for it.

Memories of her tasteful home and her real friends in New York must have haunted Anzia by this time; and Arnold, in retrospect, must have seemed truer and far more dependable than those she had formerly dreamed of in San Francisco. The old wounds of her marriage were almost forgotten. At least by Anzia. She made one more try:

From 644 Grove Street, San Frañcisco
to Arnold Levitas, 863 E. 176th Street,
New York City October 23

Tynkabel — Early in the morning, just waking up —
Mama, dear, I want to go to my papa.
Mother — Do you want to go away and leave me?
Tynk. — No — I don't want to leave you. But I want to go to my papa. He is so lonesome.
And I love my papa. And I want to sing him . . .
Ah-h-h papa! like he was a baby —
And I'll tell my papa I go to kindergarten
and I can sing and dance — and I can dress myself — and draw pictures of a house and a boat. — and I never put my fingers in my mouth no more.

This peace offering met silence. Humbled by misery, Anzia perceived at last that she would never be forgiven — there were no more ways out — and collapsed. Her brother Henry came at once from Berkeley to revive her, offering his and Fannie's wisdom, which this time she accepted. Henry's wire to Arnold in late October said everything in ten words: YOU MAY HAVE TINKABEL. MOTHER ILL. TELEPHONE INSTRUCTIONS AT ONCE.

"I have decided to tear my heart out of my body," Anzia wrote to Rose Pastor Stokes the same week. "I have decided to send Tynkabel back to her father for a few years until I get back on my feet. At present I have to knock about from pillar to post. . . . Her father can give her the permanence of a home & good food which is so important." She would let Fannie bring Tinker Bell to New York and would ask her sister also "to go to see you before bringing the child to Mr. Levitas so you could be a witness later that I have not abandoned her."

Resolutely, Anzia stayed at her job and her nights of writing. Feeling desolate in January 1917, six weeks after Tinker Bell had left, she wrote to ask Rose "the biggest thing in the world" — to see Tinker Bell "whenever you can" and "take her on your lap and sing to her" the wordless Yiddish lullaby Anzia used to sing to her daughter, "Ah-ah-ah babele," and tell her "I asked you to do it while I'm away from her."

"Mr. L.," she added, "hates me with black hatred because he took . . . as a *personal* insult my refusal to 'legitimize' the child by marriage." Instead she allowed Mr. L. to "legitimize" her daughter by adopting her.

But when she wrote to him a month later, on February 13, 1917, Anzia called him, gratefully, "Dear Arnold":

> I thank you *so much* for the few lines you sent me. I was ill with anxiety for the baby, and I can breathe different knowing that she is well and happy.
>
> My heart aches so for you and the baby! I'm struggling to hold on to my present position as a means to be able to do things for the child later on.
>
> Arnold — do not forgive me — but try to be *kind* to me and let me know about my darling baby.

And on April 16:

> Arnold,
>
> Although you have the power to revenge yourself on me for all the wrongs you have suffered, and cut off the child from all memories of me, I feel you love [her] too deeply to wreak such vengeance on me. I want to ask you again to let me know how she is, at regular intervals. . . .
>
> I have not written to her recently because my heart broke and died in parting from her. . . . In case I cannot save up enough money to see her this summer, I shall try to see her in the early fall. . . .
>
> That which is truly ours, no power on earth can take from us. You can no more keep her from me than I could have kept her from you. The mere fact that I could have surrendered her to you when all my ideals left me bankrupt proves to me that she was the one true ideal saved in my bankruptcy.

On June 12:

Dearest darling

Selma's mother wrote how much you and Selma [a child who lived next door in the Bronx] enjoyed the play Hansel & Gretel. I was so happy to read . . . it. And I have asked Selma's mother to come to see you often and tell me how you and Selma play together. . . .

Mother has to work very hard for a few months to finish some work. . . . But remember darling mother will come to you as soon as she possibly can. In the meantime you and mother are together in heart and in mind because we are always thinking of one another.

Your loving mother

Louise, at five, could not write back how she really felt, the truth of her endless sorrow, because she was, in effect, a prisoner in the enemy camp. She had come abruptly from California to dark New York in November, from Anzia's bohemian, extravagantly voluble, hectic arrangements and love to the cold rigidity of Louise's paternal grandmother. Louise's father was away at work daytimes and some nights; she was left with an austere old woman who hit her when she got angry and kept voicing her disgust with Louise's mother.

The separation lasted a year. For Louise it was a term in a sunless wasteland. Meanwhile, Anzia, keeping to her stern routine in San Francisco, could not sell another story, despite her first success more than a year earlier. She couldn't give up either. Getting her stories back from Stokes, she worked over them again. One story in particular gripped her in her despair and kept her working late. It was written as if told by an East Side woman, in the same ghetto idiom as "The Free Vacation House." This woman, now married and worn out with children, reencounters the lover she had known when she was young:

For years I was saying to myself — Just so you will act when you meet him. Just so you will stand. . . . These words you will say to him. . . . But he came upon me so sudden, all my plannings . . .

smashed to the wall. The sight of him was like an earthquake shaking me to pieces.

It was the story of Annie's youth, her first great love, but imbued with Anzia's more vivid, stronger emotions — "Where Lovers Dream." Anzia was, in a sense, now writing about herself:

It ain't that I still love him, but nothing don't seem real to me no more. For the little while when we was lovers I breathed the air from the high places where love comes from, and I can't no more come down.

Meanwhile, in New York Louise had celebrated her fifth birthday.

[June 16, 1917]

Dearest Tynkabel

I was . . . delighted to receive your beautiful letter and the precious flower of your birthday. I read the letter over and over again and I'm still reading it. Whoever wrote it for you is full of heart and please thank that person for me.

. . . I just feel like packing my trunk and leaving everything and running to you. But I must finish certain work. . . . Although it is very, very hard to wait . . . [it] is made lots easier knowing how wonderfully kind your papa is to you. . . .

Your loving mama

[August 13]

Dear Arnold,

I was so deeply touched by your brief note, that I have not words left to write even to Tynkabel. So please read to her an imaginary letter that I might have written —

As for Mrs. Kobbe and the dressmaker — Arnold *please* believe me — I owe them *nothing*. I paid Mrs. Kobbe a month in advance and I only stayed 3 weeks. She told me that I could let Tynkabel play with her little girl. And I cannot conceive of any claim for money she may have on me unless it be for letting Tynkabel play with her girl.

And this is the case of the dressmaker. I bought a suit and the skirt was too long. She herself offered to help me shorten the skirt. This work took less than 3 minutes. I offered to pay her 50 cents for it then and there. But she refused to take the money and insisted that she did this out of friendship and because I introduced her to Mr. Lasky. If I owed either of these "babbling tongues" any money, you may be sure I would have sent it to them. Arnold please believe me. I do want to "wash the slate clean" but I owe neither of these women one single cent.

I feel so sorry to have had to drag out this dead and buried skeleton of the past. I beg you to forgive me for the mere reference to the past. It is a sore and hardened wound that must not be touched again.

I thank you from the depth of my heart for the miracle of your *large understanding*. . . .

Please look into Tynkabel's eyes for the utterance of the words that fail me.

Anzia

[August 31]

Dear Arnold,

. . . I have not received a letter for over three weeks. If in my ignorance I have said anything or done anything to have roused old wounds, I beg of you to forgive me. Do not punish me by withholding my letter from Tynkabel.

Anzia

That fall, Louise started public kindergarten, but she lacked the required birth and vaccination certificates.

[September 10]

Dear Arnold,

Have written to Fannie [in Santa Monica] to go at once to the hospital where Louise was born and get the certificate. If the hospital is out of existence, she will go to the doctor or the bd. of health. . . . Louise was vaccinated in May when we lived in the apt. on E. 79 St. I cannot recollect the name of the doctor. But I remember we used this doctor several times when baby had a cold, and once I recommended him to your sister Marie for her baby.

Thank you for the letter and the pictures. I need not tell you how much I appreciate both.

I was all in from ceaseless longing for the baby. . . . The gratitude I feel that she is well and that you no longer judge and condemn me, gives me renewed energy to go on with the work set before me.

Anzia

Fannie, as she reported to Arnold later that month, immediately drove to Long Beach to ask the Board of Health for Louise's birth certificate, but learned that the birth was not registered there. It had not been compulsory in earlier years for doctors to register births. Fannie called on the doctor who had delivered the baby; he couldn't find any record of it, but promised to look further. She phoned him several times thereafter, fruitlessly.

[October 6]

Dear Arnold,

Getting the birth certificate is delayed somewhat for the following reason: You remember I did not like the treatment in the hospital and I left after staying a week instead of two weeks. I paid for that one week and I paid the doctor a separate fee of $25. But he sent me an additional bill for extras and for the week which I did not and could not stay. . . . I naturally refused to pay that extra bill, and now when I come to ask him for the birth certificate, he threatens to withhold it unless the bill is paid. And he happens to be friends with the doctor at the head of the bd of health at Long Beach — But of course I shall get this matter straightened out, without paying a cent to the doctor. I shall go to the public defender of Los Angeles and ask his advice about this. This accounts for the delay.

Anzia

Anzia's familiar maneuvering over pennies must have greatly annoyed Arnold by then. He was meticulous in observing rules and paying debts. He took such obedience for granted. It was necessary for the smooth functioning of society. But Anzia, a born rule breaker, forever fighting her way out of tight corners — out of her family, the ghetto, the university, the schools she worked in, her marriage — couldn't help bending and twisting the customary order to make room for her greater, more urgent needs. Writing Arnold on October 19 from Fannie's home in Santa Monica, she promised again, "Will get the certificate shortly." A month later Anzia had reached New York without it. She had saved the money for the fare by just such penny hoarding as had angered dressmaker, baby-sitter, and doctor. She felt she had truly won her way back when she received a modest check from *Metropolitan*, a leading popular magazine, for "Where Lovers Dream."

Y.W.C.A.
122nd St. & Lenox Ave.
New York, N.Y.

Dear Arnold,

When the baby rushed over to meet me and put her arms around me, it was not like a child embracing a mother, but like a *true mother* embracing a lost child. . . .

All that I in my highest moments aspired to be & was not that child naturally is. . . . I said to her "Come somewhere for a walk," & she tactfully disengaged herself & said, "I must first call up to my grandma and ask her if I may go." My eyes overran with tears . . . & she hastened to assure me with "Oh mama . . . I must mind her." That child's faithfulness [to you and your mother] may be a divine compensation for all the pain and sorrow that I have caused.

. . . This is what I would like to say to you. . . . I do not wish to be trailing a shadow in your future happiness.

If you find someone you love, you can marry & have a new family & . . . Louise as well. I love the child so that I do not need to possess her bodily. I am content with what naturally flows to me from the child's own heart. . . . The separation has only proven to Louise and me that we are inseparable. . . .

Anzia

Anzia spent Thanksgiving Day, 1917, in Rose Pastor Stokes's Greenwich Village brownstone, a handsome town house that Stokes still shared with her husband although they now led separate lives. The confidences she and Anzia exchanged over Thanksgiving dinner must have put Anzia in a mood of renewed hope. Compared to what she learned about Graham Stokes, Arnold must have seemed a warm-hearted, sensitive man. She sat down and wrote him a letter overflowing with gratitude "for the splendid care you and your mother have taken of Louise," and enclosed a $5 check as a gift for his mother. "As soon as my work begins," she wrote, "I hope to send your mother something each month — in appreciation of the love and the patience with which she cares for the child, which is beyond price."

Arnold answered these effusions, as he had her earlier effort toward reconciliation, with cold matter-of-factness. She was stung. In an attempt at formality to match his, she typed her next letter to him. The return address was her father's apartment on East 114th Street. Anzia had moved out of the Y and was still staying a day or two at a time with friends and relatives. The job she had just found had not yet started.

[December 25]

Dear Arnold:

As long as the statement is given out that we are legally divorced, it seems to me Louise would suffer no embarrassment if I resume my own name. I do not wish to hold on to a shred of anything that is no longer mine.

You have been *superhumanly tolerant* [despite] all the mountains of evil slander that have been brought to you by kind friends such as Mrs. Reynolds. . . . My only wish is to free your path from me as much as I can; that is why I shall resume my own name, and that is why I forego my one longing and my one consolation, and see Louise as seldom as I do.

If I would have known what splendid care you and your mother are taking of Louise, I might have risen to the strength of not coming back to N.Y. until you were married and happy. . . . Great happiness or great sorrow lifts us to the heights where we can look down upon wrongs and betrayals we have suffered, and forget and forgive.

But in this case . . . the wrongs and malicious slander have heaped up so high that it is humanly impossible to forgive. You have been wonderfully tolerant. . . .

I have paid, and am paying and still must pay for my mistakes before an inescapable divine court. . . . But it is great to lose, to suffer, and not go under, to feel all the sorrows of life sweep over you, and not be annihilated. Life is never so deeply beautiful as when we seemingly have lost it. It is then we come face to face with the mystery of our own unconquerable soul. . . .

Sincerely yours,
Hattie Mayer

Arnold had just enjoyed Christmas with his daughter. Unlike Anzia, to whom Christmas recalled Polish terror (a pogrom), he relished the Santa Claus tradition. He was a Jew who ignored Jewish rituals while embracing America's, and for that matter Germany's, charming Christmas customs. Watching his five-year-old girl unwrap her stocking gifts and those around the tree, he was in an expansive, gemütlich mood until Anzia's letter arrived. Her readiness to blame another more than herself was so galling that it provoked him to an immediate reply:

December 26, 1917

Mrs. Hattie Mayer
New York City
Dear Madame:

I feel that it is necessary to disabuse your mind of some of the mistaken views which you seem to hold.

Let me assure you that I received absolutely no information of any kind from Miss Reynolds. I saw her only once after you left, and then I merely related to her the fact of your leaving with the child. She merely expressed regret and nothing else.

Secondly, I wish to assure you that the information which I received from other sources could not possibly have influenced my mind in any way.

My attitude at present, and for several years past, is entirely the result of your actions and your behavior during the several years in which we have lived together . . . particularly the latter part of your sojourn in New York and your abrupt departure.

I do not wish to bring these matters up again; but they have been of a nature to root out my entire respect for you. I am not holding any grudge; but I cannot go against nature.

If my forgiveness will do you any good, I assure you you have that. More than that — you have my sympathy. I certainly hope that as you are realizing the true significance of life you will some day find that which you are seeking and which we are all seeking.

There is no use traveling on a false trail. . . . I hope you realize, as I do, that our paths lie widely apart. Let us . . . begin over again in some other direction. Our past mistakes and faults will help us choose better in the future.

With best wishes,
Sincerely yours,
Arnold Levitas

4

REAL LOVE

IT TOOK ANZIA A WHILE LONGER to give up her still-flickering belief that Arnold might even yet relent. Sometime in December 1917:

Emanuel Sisterhood of Personal Service
318-320 East 82nd Street
New York, N. Y.

Dear Arnold,

I would like to speak to you about some *urgently important* matter [affecting] the welfare of the baby. Would it be possible for you to come down here any time next Saturday. If that is not convenient I can meet you . . . anywhere. I would appreciate it as a great favor if you could [do this] . . . as I [would] feel terribly embarrassed to come up to your house.

I have commenced work here to-day, as managing housekeeper. For a while, I shall have very little time to myself. Instead of coming for the baby, I shall send a girl for her, if that is agreeable to you. If you could bring Louise here next Saturday, you could leave her with me for the day and I shall get someone to bring her home. . . .

Anzia

In fact, it was to avoid facing Arnold's mother and the gossips who had been Anzia's Bronx neighbors that she hired Annie's daughters to take Louise by subway to and from the weekly visits.

The elation of finding a job — "managing housekeeper" — soon evaporated. Even as the Emanuel Sisterhood was discovering that Anzia's impressive credentials — her Columbia University diploma, her teaching and settlement house experience — were hollow when it came to overseeing the daily care of the institutional iceboxes, windowsills and doorknobs, the new job was becoming painfully tedious to Anzia. But when she tried once more to qualify as a schoolteacher, even though she was better groomed than in the old days and professed a new willingness to conform, she encountered the same cold appraisal of her appearance and personality. Who knows what deeds were marked against her on her record? Perhaps the many times she had claimed sickness or "nerves" as a pretext for not meeting her classes, or even the times she handed over a cooking lesson to a more experienced student; certainly the fact that she had abruptly quit her last teaching job three years before, with no warning. She, who now considered schoolteaching a dull and sterile way station en route to something better, was turned down with no hesitation by the school authorities and offered only the randomness of low-paid substitute teaching.

Simmering with anger that December week, unwilling to accept their final no, she picked up a newspaper and read that Professor John

Dewey, Columbia University's distinguished, internationally known philosopher, psychologist, and educational theorist, had just made a stirring speech to a mass meeting of schoolteachers. The meeting was called to protest the firing of three New York City high school teachers of liberal political beliefs for "holding views subversive of good discipline." Dewey told his cheering audience that "it is not the teachers who are under indictment; it is the method of administering the public school system of New York City in relation to the teachers."

Exactly Anzia's feeling. She had seen Dewey's name frequently in the newspapers of that wartime period, writing or speaking out against autocratic school or university administrators, on behalf of the teachers' right to be different, to hold unpopular, even extreme, views. He had also written sympathetically about immigrants as contributors to American culture, an unusual position in that time of overheated nationalism.

His assistance to minority and sometimes radical political causes, including women's suffrage, during his years at Columbia had made Dewey "a kind of father figure for a succession of movements . . . that needed . . . linkage with the American tradition," notes Lewis S. Feuer, a Dewey scholar. The year before, 1916, Dewey had been applauded enthusiastically in liberal circles on the publication of his clarion *Democracy and Education*, a book whose very title appealed to Anzia; certainly it was what she was seeking — democracy, fairness, the right, no matter what her heritage and personality, following her graduation from Professor Dewey's own institution, to be a teacher in the public schools.

It seemed only logical to try to enlist this eminent crusader in her own fight for democracy. Fired with the aptness of her case, she walked into Dewey's office the next morning to make an appeal. The fact that she had no appointment made her visit more dramatic from her point of view. She brushed past the secretary and, once she started speaking, not giving him time to learn who she was, she found it easy to capture Dewey's attention. She had chanced upon the ideal man at just the right moment for her needs.

A New Englander who had inwardly rebelled against his Puritan inheritance, according to Feuer, "All his life Dewey sought sustenance from flamboyant, . . . emotionally expressive personalities." They had included such originals as Albert C. Barnes, inventor of Argyrol (then widely used as an antiseptic) and renowned art collector; Carlo Tresca, the Italian anarchist; sociopolitical journalist and bon vivant Max Eastman; Russian author and revolutionary Maxim Gorki; and the "brilliant young Jews at Columbia University who became his favorite pupils." These people provided the warmth and excitement that had been ironed out of him in a rigid Vermont upbringing. "Somehow they helped him . . . to mitigate the thinness, the schematic, abstract character of his own responses."

"He was a big man in his middle fifties," wrote Anzia, describing in fiction her first meeting with Dewey. "A great head strongly modeled; the forehead jutted out, throwing his eyes into deep shadow. . . . Those eyes . . . had a penetrating intelligence that could see through people. "The . . . noble head, the white hair like warm sunlight about his face . . . contrasted strangely with a slipshod appearance — clothes worn anyhow, pockets bulging with papers. . . . She noticed the loose shoelace dangling from his old-fashioned high shoes, and his tie knotted awkwardly to one side. He was a man too absorbed in his work to look at a mirror. . . . His simplicity made his greatness less formidable.

"As she followed him into the room, she caught the quick inquiring glance and the droll twist of his eyebrows."

Anzia said boldly she had come to give Dewey the chance to practice what he had been preaching. She declared that she had been excluded from her rightful place as a schoolteacher because she was a non-Anglo-Saxon, an immigrant with not-so-neat ways. Not mentioning her current disdain for schoolteaching, she told him she had dreamed and worked and starved to be a schoolteacher through years of hardship in sweatshops and laundries, attending preparatory school at night and at last college. She had believed in the immigrant's dream of America: opportunity. But as soon as she arrived at college, Columbia University itself, she had discovered "big fences put up against me, with the brutal signs: 'No trespassing. Get off the grass.'" She was not even allowed into the classrooms of literature and philosophy for which she hungered. Instead she had to swallow "barren . . . dry, inanimate stuff . . . hammered out in lectures."

John Dewey, about 1917.

Slaving in a laundry from five to eight in the morning before going to classes every day, and from six to eleven each night, she had won her university diploma. And now, she said, its benefits were denied her. Columbia University Teachers College was *against* democracy in education.

> "After graduation the opportunities for the best positions are passed out to the best-dressed.
>
> I have been tricked . . . considered unfit to get decent pay for my work because of my appearance, and [it's] to the advantage of those who [use] me that my appearance should damn me so as to get me to work for low [substitute] wages."

To prove that she was worth far more, she had brought along her two stories — "The Free Vacation House," published two-years earlier, and the about-to-be-published "Where Lovers Dream." And to prove the class prejudice of the school authorities, she asked Dewey, as one of the leading authorities on education, to judge her teaching for himself.

Her intensity, the aggressive and impassioned speech, even her blouse pulled partly free of her skirt, her red hair slipping out of its pompadour in wisps around her flushed face — all these unconventional traits, which had so offended school principals and deans, were persuasive to Dewey. As if he had nothing more important to do, he traveled to the elementary school where she was substitute teaching and sat, a quiet, gray-haired observer, at the side of the room, while she led a class of schoolgirls through a hastily improvised cooking lesson. But when it was over, the class dismissed, and she turned to him to support her claim, he said candidly that she ought not to waste time trying to be a teacher. He had read her two stories, and it was obvious she had more talent for writing.

Emboldened by his interest, and by his wrinkled jacket, Anzia asked him why he was so different from other educators, the frigid Anglo-Saxon "bosses of education" who had humiliated her. "You've got none of that what-can-I-do-for-you-my-poor-child look."

Since for quite different reasons Dewey had often felt as outraged by academic orthodoxy as Anzia, he was charmed. He told her that she should write the story of her experiences with American education; it would be valuable. He invited her meanwhile, as another educational experience for both of them, to audit his graduate seminar in social and political philosophy beginning the following month, January 1918. She might contribute to the seminar by telling about the immigrant's encounter with the institutions of American democracy.

Dewey was fifty-eight. Yezierska was about thirty-five, but her unconventional behavior and her challenging, dramatic way of speaking made her seem even younger. He was ready just then for another protégé or friend — to fill the space left by his children, who were now all adults, and by his wife, who since the tragic death of their youngest child, Gordon, at the age of eight, had grown increasingly detached and critical. He had recently also endured public criticism from former students and disciples when he abandoned the pacifist philosophy to support the Wilson government and the country's entry into World War I.

For Anzia, this great man's immediate acceptance of her, at a time when she was rejected and discouraged elsewhere, had a powerful, tonic effect. She rushed through the next day's work in a "transforming holiday spirit"; her job seemed effortless. She was filled with an unnameable excitement, which she tried to describe later in fiction:

> On her way back from work . . . jostled and pushed by the [subway] mob, she thought of [all] she wanted to write to him, but in her room, when she put pencil to paper, she could only wrest out of herself one line . . .
>
> Generations of stifled words — reaching out to you — aching for utterance — dying on my lips unuttered —

In that exalted state she put the unfinished sentence, with no signature, into an envelope and mailed it to him. It reached his desk with a pile of other letters, but Dewey recognized whose message it was in the giant handwriting. In fact, the line inspired him (their relationship was already developing its own tacit understanding) to write a poem in answer:

Generations of stifled worlds reaching out
Through you,
Aching for utt'rance, dying on lips
That have died of hunger,
Hunger not to have, but to be.

Generations as yet unuttered, dumb, smothered,
Inchoate, unutterable by me and mine,
In you I see them coming to be,
Luminous, slow revolving, ordered in rhythm.
You shall not utter them; you shall be them,
And from out the pain
A great song shall fill the world.

And I from afar shall see,
As one watching sees the star
Rise in the waiting heavens,
And from the distance my hand shall clasp yours,
And an old world be content to go,
Beholding the horizons
Tremulous with the generations
Of the dawn.

He had been thinking, as he wrote, of his own stifled world, generations of Vermont farmers and tradesmen, as well as of Anzia's ghetto ancestors. Part of her attractiveness to him was that she spoke vividly and without inhibitions of feelings most people kept hidden. She had the emotionalism — he called it eloquence — which he felt he lacked, the reason his poem predicted that hers would be a song to fill the world while he watched in mute admiration "from afar."

But in his seminar, which she attended with a remarkable group of graduate students, she usually sat in awed silence. Around the table with Dewey were Irwin Edman, later to become noted as a critic-philosopher and chairman of Columbia's philosophy department; Paul Blanshard, an ordained minister, who later reached prominence as an editor, social critic, and author; Brand Blanshard, Paul's brother, who was to be the head of Yale University's philosophy department; Margaret Frances Bradshaw, who afterward married Brand and wrote an important book on aesthetics; and Dr. Albert C. Barnes, even then successful, famous, and rich. Among these brilliant students, she felt painfully uneducated, an outsider. They shared her opinion. Accustomed to Dewey's generosity toward such "waifs," they assumed he had admitted her to their seminar out of compassion.

Outside the seminar room, however, the passionate, unpolished, demanding Russian Jew and the seemingly austere Puritan, already past middle age, were reaching an extraordinary level of exchange. Sometimes he was like a father explaining the world to a child. He tried to answer her questions about the students in the seminar who considered her, she felt, not even human.

"Why do I need them so terribly, when they don't need me?" she demanded. "I'm so drawn to you cold Anglo-Saxons, but you always thrust me out, at arm's length!"

He said she was in too much of a hurry. "If you want to understand people, you must stop blaming them for being what they are. . . . Your attitude should be that of an explorer [in] a strange country. . . . No one's ways are better than anyone else's, but if you happen to migrate into a foreign country, you must learn the ways of its people. Learn to give what you want to give them in their terms."

Dewey also tried to teach her to laugh at herself, especially in her writing to laugh at her "damned Slavic seriousness," as he called it. She was affronted. Only many years later, recalling in her novels her conversations with him, did she come to appreciate what he had meant to teach her.

But paramount in all their encounters were his reading and encouragement of her writing, the fact that he valued the originality others had condemned and that he kept assuring her of her great talent.

"You are translucent," he wrote to her once when he was out of the city on a speaking engagement, "and the world's own understanding and love shine through you. . . . You *are* but you don't yet fully know that you are. You feel as if you wanted to be. You suffer from striving, but it is unnecessary. *You are already*."

There were other times when she became the guide, taking him at his request on tours of the Lower East Side. "At first I [was] embarrassed about showing him the dirty streets, the haggling . . . and the smells from the alleys of the ghetto where I lived. But what I had thought coarse and commonplace was to him exotic." He was enchanted by the richness of feeling, the passion for joy and for fighting to be discovered around the pushcarts and tenement stoops — the extreme opposite of the hidden emotions and reserved manners of his own society.

Now no longer a supplicant, Anzia also volunteered criticism of his writing, offering sharp advice. "Why can't you write the way you are talking to me?" she demanded, remarking on his "clear head and cold heart." She said he wrote in such abstract, undemocratic language, only a handful of scholars could understand it. "Your book [*Democracy and Education*, some pages of which she had now read with dismay] . . . was meant to be the Bible of America. . . . You could light up the lives of millions." But because of what she considered his ponderous verbiage, he had failed, she thought. "In your books you are an intellect talking to scholars" — both terms of disparagement in her vocabulary. "In your letters [to me], . . . you are St. Francis, loving the poor."

When Anzia later made uncredited use in her books of poems and letters Dewey wrote to her, and even excerpts from his published writing, she edited them freely. She even slipped some of his phrases and sentences into her stories. He wrote this poem for her understanding:

> I wake from the long, long night
> Of thoughtless dreams, fancies
> Nor pleased nor vexed. And despite
> The sleep of untroubled trances
> Joyless, griefless, begins the round
> Of day's unillumined duties,
> A silken web in which I'm bound.
> Earthward my eyes, lest the beauties
> Of a life not yet trammeled distract
> My ordered paces from the path
> And I no longer keep the pact
> With my possessions, and the wrath

Of stern-eyed freedom break the chains
Which keep me from the wilderness of tears
And turn me loose to suffer in the lanes
Of thorn trees unpossessed as yet by man.
From which no harvest shall I reap
Save stabs and flames of pain, and wan
Exhaustions among th' unshepherded sheep
Of thoughts which travel th' untracked wild
Of untamed desire. Either this, or else I creep
To a cooped-in grave smothered by the treasure piled.
My friend your hand I ask along the lonely steep.

It is one of the poems that was found, forgotten in his desk, and published years after his death in *The Poems of John Dewey*. But Anzia, who had seen it when it was written and had kept it, shaped it for her own use in *Red Ribbon on a White Horse*:

I arise from a long, long night of thoughtless dreams
Joyless, griefless begins the web of unillumined duties,
A silken web in which I'm bound.
Earthward my eyes,
Lest your spirit keep me from the pact with my possessions
And lure me to your wilderness of tears,
Where no harvest shall I reap, save stabs and flames of pain
And wan exhaustion among the unshepherded sheep of thought
Who travel through trackless wilds of untamed desire.

Through the seminar Anzia attended, Dewey had also developed a warm friendship with his businessman-student Albert Barnes. The two men enjoyed long talks at dinners after the seminar sessions. Partly to continue their association, Barnes hit on a plan for a summer research project to which Dewey readily agreed. It would employ the seminar students to test in a real-life situation the theories discussed around the seminar table. Barnes was an ardent disciple who had distributed Dewey's

Democracy and Education to all his factory workers in Pennsylvania; now he offered to finance the project and suggested the site and subject: an investigation of a Polish immigrant community in the Philadelphia neighborhood that had been Barnes's birthplace.

The purpose would be to find out why, as a group, these former Poles resisted assimilation, retaining their own language and customs, and why in the next generation they continued their separateness, politically and culturally, from the rest of the city, even during the war. Perhaps the study would show how to overcome such ethnic isolation.

To be able to test his theories and at the same time provide summer jobs for his prize students delighted Dewey. In particular, he hoped the project would employ Anzia so that she could escape from the poorly paid substitute teaching job and use the comparative freedom to write. Her story "Where Lovers Dream" had just been published, but the check she received for it would probably support her frugally for a few weeks at most. Barnes was offering a salary of a hundred dollars a month — in 1918, generous pay for novice investigators, and for Anzia, munificent. But when Dewey proposed her as translator for the study, Barnes was skeptical. He had never spoken to her, although he was friendly with the other students. Anzia had uttered scarcely a word during the seminar. Shy with the younger members of the class, she was far more intimidated by this brusquely forthright, middle-aged scientist-businessman.

To persuade Barnes of her ability, Dewey sent him a typescript of "Soap and Water and the Immigrant," the story she had just written, at Dewey's suggestion and with his editorial help, about her grievances against American educators. In it she told how she had faced the cruel scrutiny of the dean of students "as one strapped on the operating table [faces] the surgeon approaching with his tray of sterilized knives." The dean always criticized Anzia's grooming: "Soap and water are cheap. Anyone can be clean."

The student had found them costly. "I, soaking in the foul vapors of the steaming laundry . . . with my dirty, tired hands . . . [was] ironing [the dean's] clean immaculate shirtwaists," reinforcing the pedestal from which the dean looked down at Anzia.

> But this last time when she threatened to withhold my diploma, because of my appearance . . . something burst within me.
>
> I felt the suppressed wrath of all the unwashed of the earth. . . . My eyes blazed fire. I didn't care for myself . . . nor the whole laundered world. I had suffered the cruelty of their cleanliness and the tyranny of their culture to the breaking point. I was too frenzied to know what I said or did. . . . I saw clean, immaculate, spotless Miss Whiteside shrivel and tremble . . . before me.

The story failed to convince Barnes. In an answering letter to Dewey, he wondered whether "the abnormalities . . . she manifests" would not make her unfit for working on the project. More arguments from Dewey by letter and a meeting with Anzia finally convinced Barnes that she could contribute to the study. Or perhaps he simply yielded to Dewey's urging. She was to be employed as translator and researcher, and in advance of the other investigators she would go to Philadelphia to find housing for them.

Sometime before Anzia began this job, Dewey, in a gesture typical of his generosity to the protégés he aided throughout his career, brought her a typewriter, supposedly for her Philadelphia assignment, then reached into his pocket and pulled out all the money he had with him. He had just been paid for an article, he explained, and until she earned her first paycheck from Barnes, he wanted to make it possible for her to do her "real work."

The gift — his belief in her — was overwhelming. "I have learned to abase myself. Now I must learn to abound," she wrote to him soon afterward, a letter she also recalled in *All I Could Never Be*. Dewey had gone to San Francisco as soon as the semester ended to deliver a month-long series of lectures at Stanford University. "But want, want, want has so eaten itself into my bones," she confessed in the letter, "I do not know how to abound.

> And so you must forgive me if, when I try to tell you how I rejoice, I can only weep and thrust on you the shadow of my unreasonable sorrow.

Tell me, how can I learn to work calmly? I have that aching sense of being in debt for this free time. How shall I ever make good to you my freedom? And yet — I can think of no deeper happiness on earth than to be indebted to you.

He answered her like a loving father:

Dear Love of God,

I have your note, beautiful as your soul. . . .

While in my twilight, a beautiful garden with the brightness and perfume distilled from all the ages, is suddenly opened to me. . . . The advantages are . . . on my side. It is foolish to say do or don't to anybody, but when you say you weep, I must say don't. . . . You need to be buoyed up and my arm should be sustaining you. . . . You have not been cared for in the past. . . . You should be taken somewhere in the country and be fed beefsteak and eggs and whatever is nourishing. . . . I have the feeling that you do not think sufficiently of your body, that you are inclined to think of such things as mundane and to be a considered last. . . .

You ask how you can learn to work calmly. . . . Since you have begun to ask you will soon find the answer yourself. In time your body will discover what your soul already knows, that it is free, that you are not just having a reprieve from prison, but are out, once and forever.

What you have to say will be said. . . . Live in peace and confidence. Anxiety to produce is not for you.

Anzia's first letter from Philadelphia to Arnold and Louise gave only a slight hint of her activity: her return address was in care of A. C. Barnes, 24 West Fortieth Street, in Philadelphia.

May 17, 1918

Dear Louisa's father,

I would like to ask you . . . to let me know once a week if possible how the child is faring and . . . at any time of sickness [to] please call for me immediately.

> I was knocked out for several days because of the doubt that made you question me about the matter. And though underneath the wound still hurts, I'm so rushed with work out here that I cannot indulge in the luxury of sorrow except at rare moments when I'm too tired to fall asleep.
>
> Anzia

> Dearest love,
>
> How are you? Does your papa hug you a little more and does he play with you more than he used to of late? Tell me all about everything.
>
> Your loving mother

The reason she used Barnes's address was that she had met immediate obstacles on her preliminary assignment — to rent a house for the investigators in the Polish neighborhood they were going to investigate. The people she talked to were suspicious. The local politicians were opposed to such an investigation. The advertised houses she inquired about suddenly became unavailable.

Her next letter, on May 27, was from a furnished room at 3127 Richmond Street. She told Louise:

> I'm coming to your birthday on Wednesday evening. I'm so anxious to see you my precious darling. I saw pictures and I love them all. . . .
>
> Your loving mama

Meanwhile Barnes, who relished a fight in what he considered a good cause, jumped in to solve her difficulties by buying a house for the student investigators right on the riverfront bounding the Polish district. The house was also near the shipyards, which employed many Polish workers. Barnes wrote Dewey, gloating equally about his purchase and about Anzia's ability to ferret out the hidden facts regarding the Philadelphia Poles. Believing from his brusque manner that Barnes disliked her, Anzia would have been astonished at the admiring comments in his letters to Dewey. She had given him enough information, Barnes wrote, to confront and probably eliminate certain local politicians — "the three bastards who are opposing us."

While looking for the house, Anzia's daily encounters with the local Poles were uncovering (and she was reporting to Barnes) a tangle of political intrigue that extended far beyond Philadelphia. The war had started a contest among Polish groups in the United States, led by exiles from abroad, for American funds and political support. The eventual prize would be control of the future government of Poland — the new republic to be carved out of Imperial Germany, Austria, and czarist Russia by the Allies after the war.

Two factions were dominating this competition even in Philadelphia: the KON, the Polish acronym for the Congress of National Defense, led by Socialist worker-intellectuals; and the Polish National Committee, which was based in Paris but was represented in the United States by the pianist Ignace Paderewski and his wife. After examining its goals and past connections, Dewey characterized the Polish National Committee as "a small party of conservative reactionaries . . . tied to the Czar before the war."

Although the contest in the United States was focused on Washington, smaller versions of it were taking place in each Polish community. In Philadelphia, the Polish-American religious and political leaders were evidently afraid of any investigation because it might upset their tight control of votes and funds for Polish war relief. They were doing their best to stifle the Columbia University study; they told their followers not to talk to the outsiders.

Another conflict was brewing among the novice investigators. In Dewey's absence (he was still at Stanford University), Paul Blanshard had designed a questionnaire to be filled out by the subjects of the study and convinced his brother and friends that this was the way to begin collecting information. Anzia told them heatedly it was not. She was outraged by their so-called "scientific" approach to human problems; it reminded her of the cold condescension of the social workers who in her youth had humiliated her family and her neighbors. The other four said she was too emotional and unschooled for the research. Injured and angry, she abruptly withdrew from their discussions.

At this impasse, the students wrote to Dewey about Anzia's obstructive incompetence and put a copy of their complaint on her desk. For whatever reason, the study was not progressing. Barnes, who visited the house frequently, wrote Dewey, criticizing the students for being so full of textbook wisdom they could not apply it to real-life matters. But of Anzia, he wrote that it was inappropriate to criticize an artist, and that as a true artist she was keeping aloof from the "science" the others were trying to impose. She was staying in her room, writing stories and awaiting Dewey's coming.

Smiling at the childlike artist, Barnes was as unaware of the intensity of Anzia's vigil as of Dewey's letters to her, which inspired it. She was lonely, bruised by the rebuffs she had once more encountered. But she consoled herself with her writing, knowing that Dewey would read and approve it. He alone believed in her. Even in the beginning, and despite her rudeness, "when she came to him . . . he [accepted] her instantly."

At night she took walks along the river, "recreating my every experience with him, the way he looked at me, the words he said, trying to hold close the golden moments of being understood." Sometimes, thinking of him in California with his family, she had doubts. "I was aware how far from me he was, how unpossessable, . . . withdrawn into a world of culture and beautiful living where I could never enter." But a letter from him would immediately restore her. "I know him as neither his wife nor children could know him. . . . He could never share with [them] the thoughts he shares with me. We . . . understand one another . . . profoundly."

In his letters (which Anzia later memorized or copied into her novels), Dewey expressed thoughts he could not have spoken. He confessed his habitual fear of emotion, his "evasion of life," the aridity of which she had made him stunningly aware. Perhaps he might learn from her, he wrote, to let feeling speak. "I must begin humbly like a child to learn the meaning of life from you." For he thought she was both natural and "eloquent with the beauty of the world."

He was also writing poetry. As an indication of his feelings, he enclosed in one of his letters the poem "I wake from the long, long night /

Of thoughtless dreams, fancies . . ." (which appears in full earlier in this chapter). "The beauties / of a life not yet trammeled" expressed his view of Anzia's life:

Earthward my eyes, lest the beauties
Of a life not yet trammeled distract
My ordered paces from the path
And I no longer keep the pact
With my possessions . . .

For *his* life, Dewey saw two stark choices — either to stray from that ordered path into a dangerous wilderness, "th'untracked wild / Of untamed desire . . . or else I creep / To a cooped-in grave smothered by the treasure piled." It was an apology and a plea: "My friend your hand I ask along the lonely steep."

Struggling with unfamiliar emotion, always mindful that he was twenty odd years older than she, he wrote poems that he never sent her. This was one of them:

Across the white of my mind's map
The livid equator shines like a welt
As if the sun had drawn its belt
Around the bulging girth
Of my hot swollen earth
Where desert sand waves vainly lap
To quench a heat they but swallow
As fire after fire doth ceaseless follow.

He could not forget nor escape the incongruity of his situation:

So let it be till judgment day shall roll
The spread out heavens as a scroll,
And fervent heat dissolve away
The loins of fire and head of grey.

Writing this poetry must have been for Dewey a confessional, a private refuge from his extraordinarily consuming yet not fully satisfying professional and family activities.

His Stanford lectures completed, Dewey left his wife in San Francisco about June 21, 1918, and took a long route back, going northward first to Portland, then staying a couple of nights at Glacier House in British Columbia. He needed a respite before he faced the problems awaiting him in Philadelphia. It was July 6 when he reached New York; a day or two later, he arrived at last in Philadelphia.

Calmly, swiftly, he resolved the quarrel dividing the research group. He met first with his young students. Anzia waited outside the room as they discussed her. Inside, Dewey not only rejected their complaints about this over-excitable Pole; he told them they had much to learn from her. Paul Blanshard, of whom Barnes had been the most critical, was dropped from the project, along with the questionnaire he had designed and to which Dewey, too, objected.

When Anzia and Dewey were briefly alone together, after weeks of increasing intimacy by mail, the air was electric. She said she was sorry for causing him so much trouble, but her dispute with the students didn't seem to bother him. She talked about her writing. He listened, but seemed distracted.

Finally, in embarrassment, he broached the real issue between them. He asked her to try to understand what he was about to say: that he was not free. He wanted to preserve their rare understanding and friendship, not destroy it. He was trying to return to a safer distance, but Anzia, shocked, would not allow him to.

> He drew from his pocket a worn bundle of letters. Her letters.

This is her account in *All I Could Never Be*.

> "Keep these for me. Will you?
>
> A puzzled frown gathered between her brows. . . . Her eyes swept the deep drawers of his desk, the tall files. . . .

"Why can't you keep them?"

"Because I don't belong to myself."

"It's fear," she burst out. "You fear to feel. You fear to suffer — "

"No. I was only trying to save you from finding me out." . . .

She put the letters in her purse, talking to herself. "This is murder. Murder for the sake of safety."

He was, she believed, retreating to the security of his possessions, his lofty position in the world. Like all Anglo-Saxons, coldhearted and clearheaded, he was concerned with propriety. He denied it.

"I know you better than you know me. I am older. . . . Remember what I tell you now in a comparative moment of sanity. You suffer infinitely more than I do. . . . I was only trying to protect you — "

"I do not want to be protected," she burst out fiercely. "I want to live. . . . I want life . . . in all its terribleness — in all its suffering. But not safety. Not death."

At the door she said simply, "You don't want to see me any more?"

"How can I help wanting to see you? You are fire and sunshine. . . . You make life full of daily wonder."

And then: "Maybe you know best," he said humbly. . . . Your instinct may be surer than all my reasoning."

But her accusation stirred him to a stronger reply after he left Philadelphia — a poem Anzia probably never saw:

Riches, possessions hold me? Nay,
Not rightly have you guessed
The things that block the way,
Nor into what ties I've slowly grown
By which I am possest.

In this poem, titled "Two Weeks" (the interval before he returned to Philadelphia), he wrote of "the tie, the iron band" of home and family, and added:

What I am to any one is but a loan
From those who made, and own . . .

Yet would I have you know
How utterly my thoughts go
With you . . .
In a ceaseless quest . . .
What happens at this minute . . .
Has she written or shall I wait
In sweet trouble of expectancy
For some fresh wonder yet to be?
Whate'er, howe'er you move or rest
I see your body's breathing
The curving of your breast . . .
I watch the lovely eyes that visions hold
Even in the tortured tangles of the tenement
Of a life that's free and bold . . .

While I am within this wonder
I am overcome as by thunder
Of my blood that surges
From my cold heart to my clear head —
So at least she said . . .

In every stanza he continues to argue with or answer another of her remembered comments:

Then there's that matter of youth and age.
Youth's felicitous, undaunted rage
For living against long years age has spent

In bare existence. . . . You say you have lived longer and most.
Truly, if you measure by what is deep and tense –
The only scale of quick youth. But if by the host
And unnumbered diversity by which age counts
Rather than passions few and deep, then not so. For each
Of the many says to every other, Renounce, renounce;
The horizon is too far to reach.
All things must be given up.
Driest the lips when most full the cup . . .

I told you my diet should be prose.
I didn't know there would always float
Before my sight the waving lily and the beckoning rose,
Or that even on the city's hard paved streets
My thoughts should ever shape themselves into a boat
To bear you on every wind that blows . . .

Although he intended only to supervise and advise the researchers in Philadelphia, Dewey was almost immediately drawn into a more active role by their first reports. As a longtime champion of liberal political causes, he was galvanized by the evidence that the most reactionary faction among the contending Poles in Philadelphia and elsewhere was winning the American government's support. "In view . . . of a war waged in behalf of democracy and the freedom of oppressed nationalities," he wrote later in his *Confidential Report: Conditions among the Poles in the United States*, it was natural to ask "why a group which is monarchical, representative of conservative economic interests and largely anti-Semitic should occupy such an important semi-official political status."

He therefore assigned himself to interview leaders and spokesmen of the several factions, including Paderewski and members of the KON. Then, with Barnes's concurrence, he set about using whatever influence he could exert, including that of friends in government, to bring his perception of the Polish situation to the attention of the Wilson administration and the U.S. Military Intelligence.

These activities took Dewey to New York, Chicago, and Washington. He was in Philadelphia for short periods that summer, staying at Barnes's home, and in touch with the original researchers only intermittently. There was little chance for private conversation with Anzia. He was probably glad of that for a while.

Meanwhile, Anzia, reinstated to the research group, was interviewing women of the Polish community in Philadelphia for her share of the project and also carrying out assignments Dewey had given her, along with others in the group, to help his larger investigation. Both troubled and exhilarated by her recent encounter with him, she waited for what would happen next.

In this mixture of elation and suspense, she wrote to Arnold in mid-July, asking "Dear Louisa's father" to bring their daughter to stay with her for a summer month because the Philadelphia house had a spacious yard where Louise could play: "I know nothing can make the child happier . . . and loving [her] as you do, I know you will not deny her the little joy of being with her mother whether the mother deserves this or not." Perhaps she also wanted to show her daughter to the most important person in her life. But Arnold, who probably had other summer plans for Louise and himself, did not take her to Philadelphia.

DURING THE SUMMER OF 1918, Dewey found the opportunity to present his version of Polish political affairs to the Commission of Inquiry, which Colonel Edward M. House, President Wilson's political adviser, had set up to prepare for the future peace conference. But although Dewey sent the commission several memoranda of explanation in the following weeks, he was unable to change its fixed position. Convinced of the urgent need for another viewpoint in U.S. government circles, he then arranged to meet with Colonel House on August 5 at House's summer home in Massachusetts. Barnes accompanied him. House was polite, but this effort also seemed to have no effect.

That same month Dewey, through separate channels, reached the U.S. Military Intelligence Bureau, which appeared to be more receptive to his ideas. The MIB asked him to write an "extensive" report on his findings about the Poles. To supplement the information he had already gathered, he assigned Irwin Edman, whom he considered the ablest of his students, to attend a convention of Polish Americans in Detroit. He asked Anzia to see one of the Philadelphia Polish fund raisers, show him an "anonymous" letter Dewey had obtained from another, opposing Polish politician, and report to Dewey the first man's reaction. "Mystery business," Dewey wrote to Barnes in explanation.

Anzia relished the conspiratorial nature of the assignment. Having known the ghetto in Poland, where Jews were brutally terrorized by the czar's cossack soldiers, she had a natural hostility toward the old aristocratic regime represented by the Paderewskis. She also had an aptitude for intrigue. Her report on the "interview with Mr. Alexander," with its implications of fraud and misused funds, reads like melodrama.

> Mr. Alexander's face was a study as he read the letter. Every word . . . worked like an electric shock. . . .
>
> "Read it," he exclaimed, throwing the letter into my lap. Then he began pacing up and down the room, muttering incoherent interjections.
>
> "I'll send a copy of this to Mr. von M. [Judge von Moschzisker, a Polish-American leader in Philadelphia] at once," he panted. . . . "The grafters! I saw to it that they shouldn't get a red cent from Pennsylvania. And they know it. That's why they put me on the blacklist." . . .
>
> He . . . reread the letter, and then fingered it nervously with an inward look, . . . as if he were stirred to the depths.
>
> . . . After a while he asked me about my interview with Mme. Paderewski.

Referring to Helen Paderewski's successful fund-raising efforts in other U.S. cities, Anzia told Alexander the lady said she had not received any money from Philadelphia and that Pennsylvania was the only state that had not invited her to assist in its money drives. (Perhaps Alexander's Polish Citizens Committee had collected money that wasn't going to Poland, was Mme. Paderewski's implication.)

> He flared up at this and called Madame "a damned liar." He maintained that [when] Madame wrote to Mrs. von M. asking for Christmas presents for the soldiers. . . . Mrs. von M. appropriated $300 from the Emergency Aid treasury and the Polish Citizens Committee also sent $300.
>
> "As for her not being called to Philadelphia, she never will be called. We believe in home rules. . . . We do not need her."

Then Alexander suggested, in turn, that Mme. Paderewski was using the money she received in this country to establish "her segregated White Cross" and that "she was putting over in America what the French Government did not permit her to start in France. . . . I left him rereading the letter feverishly and muttering that he must see von M."

5

AMBITION

BY LATE AUGUST 1918, the Philadelphia study was ending fruit-essly, blocked by the effective opposition of the local Polish authorities while Dewey gave his attention to the larger possibilities in Washington. As the researchers in Philadelphia packed their files, getting ready to eave, he worked on his report at the modest Dewey farm in Huntington, Long Island. He also wrote dutifully about his difficulties with the Poles and the U.S. bureaucrats to Mrs. Dewey, still in San Francisco.

Anzia finished her investigative duties with an official letter to "My dear Prof. Dewey," enclosing a message from Alexander, and adding in the conspiratorial vein she had lately adopted, "Jan Kohnet shot a bombshell in Polish politics!! . . . Shall tell you of this later on. A.Y." They were to meet again, with more privacy, in New York.

On September 1, the Columbia group gave up their Philadelphia house and dispersed. Anzia returned to "restaurant work" in New York, according to a letter Dewey wrote to Barnes. She may have taken a job as a waitress, but she had saved much of her summer's salary and, as Dewey informed Barnes, she had plans for starting "a small community centre in New York." He also wrote Barnes about another job possibility for her of which she was unaware. One of the leaders of the KON, whom Anzia had encountered on an assignment, planned to set up a Polish Bureau in Washington and wanted to employ "someone who knows Polish and English to write his English articles for him and also to become throughly familiar with Polish politics. . . . He was impressed with Yezierska-Levitas."

A few weeks later, Dewey sent his completed *Confidential Report: Conditions among the Poles in the United States* to the Military Intelligence Bureau and to President Wilson. He wrote another analysis of the Polish study for the *New Republic.* And sometime during the interim he also wrote a poem about Anzia, which he could not have shown her:

> There stirred within me
> The ghosts of many a love . . .

which he had stifled in the past. The ghosts rebuked him: "You shall not let our sister in / To perish in this sepulcher . . .

> By every touch of hands that did enhance
> Desire till distance lost its stern avail,
> By the drops of blood that trait'rous started
> In warm wonder whene'er we met
> By every ling'ring kiss with which we parted,
> By every sacred tear that wet
> Th'innocence of our unopened scroll of love . . .
> You shall not let our sister in . . .

But as he persisted in the new love, the old relented:

For all we might have been
Eternally is she:
The surprise of the flushed welcome of the day
After th'encompassing mystery of night,
The tender twilight creeping to the sky's last ray,
The certain faith the new born day doth plight
To each unsullied hour . . .
In her we yet shall live,
To her our unlived lives we give.

Although he wrote the poem for himself, he sent her a letter shortly before they were to meet again, echoing its sentiment:

Dear love of God!
All whom I ever loved I love in you . . .
Your father, your brother, your son, your lover. . . .

Anzia's feelings for Dewey were by now a strange mixture of reverence and recognition. He was both godlike and familiar. In *All I Could Never Be* she described his resemblance to her father.

The feeling of familiarity shocked and amazed her. Absurd! Her father had lived . . . in the ghetto of Poland. This man a Gentile, an American. And yet for all their difference, there was that unworldly look about [his] eyes that made her feel her father . . . as he might have been in [the] new world.

Trying to encompass nevertheless the strong and growing sexual attraction between them, she found aesthetic, illogical explanations that disguised it.

We're drawn to each other by something even more compelling than the love of man for woman, and woman for man. It's that irre-

> sistible force as terrible as birth and death that sometimes flares up between Jew and Gentile. . . . It's because he and I are of . . . different races that we can understand one another so profoundly, touch the innermost reaches of the soul, beyond the [understanding] of those who think they know us. . . .
>
> My writing is but a rushing fountain of song to him. . . . He excites . . . and releases my imagination.

She also discovered, to her delight, that she was able to affect him.

> In some way I do not understand I've been the means of bringing some release to him too. I've awakened in him a new worship of life and beauty that none of the women of his class can ever dream is in him.

By late September, Dewey had gone as far as he could in his efforts to present his information about Polish political intrigue to President Wilson's advisers. He was temporarily free from obligations, even from "the iron band" of family, when he came to see Anzia at last in her New York tenement.

They left her furnished room and stepped out into a lingering Indian summer sunset, when all New York's windows were open. They passed neighbors sitting on the front stoops, children at play in the streets, enjoying the open-air freedom of the city on a warm evening.

They walked to a restaurant for dinner and afterward to a park. In *All I Could Never Be* (1932) and again in *Red Ribbon* (1950), Anzia recreated the scene, which obsessed her and which she could never again make right:

> The light and shadows fell from the silent elms above them. . . . They did not speak — the faint rustle of the . . . leaves . . . might have been their voices.
>
> Far behind them was the city with its noise and crowds. They seemed all alone, at the edge of the earth. . . . They leaned toward each other, his hand groping for her hand. He kissed her fingers, one by one.

> With her fingers drawn through his, they looked at each other, frankly, understandingly. . . . In the slowly silvering sky, the last pale tints of the sun's reflection drifted and died. . . . With a small sound of tenderness, he drew her to him. . . . He bent his head to hers and kissed her.
>
> "Do you love me?" he whispered, drawing her closer to him, kissing her neck, her mouth. . . . "Dearest!" Suddenly his lips pressed her lips with fierce insistence. . . . A wild alarm stiffened [her] with fear. The shattering impact of his lips, . . . his hand fumbling her breast! "My dearest one! . . . Do you love me?"

Anzia, the "spiritual" bride of her first marriage, clenched her lips against a stranger. "Instead of a god, here was a man — too close, too earthly." Terror, disillusion, then distrust welled up. The ghetto's atavistic suspicion of outsiders momentarily possessed her. "[She] had not dreamed that God could become flesh."

Equally shocked, Dewey immediately released her. Where was the volatile, adoring worshiper, ready to burst into flame at a touch? In all their meetings before, he had been cautious, restrained, reluctant to yield to impulse. She had continually beckoned, even insisted on this moment, coaxing him against his good sense into self-betrayal. From a passionate, alluring woman of thirty-five, she had changed without warning to a prim, incongruous adolescent. The picture of himself as an aging fool, which he saw in her frightened face, repelled him.

> They stood awkwardly, looking away from each other. After a while, he turned to her . . . back in his habitual low monotone. "Perhaps we had better go home." She nodded.
>
> They walked [back] slowly. . . . Silence grew thick between them — a separating silence, like a wall of ice. . . . At the door she was torn between asking him up to her room and the fear that if she did, . . . she'd hate him. . . . He settled it by bidding her good night in an absent voice and walking away.
>
> The moment he turned the corner she wanted to run after him and beg him to come . . . with her.

She spent the night reliving the scene.

> He had left the track of generations of puritan training to burst into that blaze of life. And she, who had longed for the warm intimacy [with him, the Anglo-Saxon] . . . that had always been locked to her, had resisted . . . not only him but herself. . . . Now she was awakened . . . with all the abandon of first love.

She went to see him at his office the next day, ready to throw herself at his feet. But he had turned overnight into a polite stranger, his eyes averted, looking down at the work on his desk; he could not pause to speak with her for more than an instant. He was too busy.

In spite of the rebuff, she came back again the next day, more fiercely determined. This time, he frowned and said, "Not now."

> "Now! Now!" She pounded his desk. "Now I must talk to you — "
>
> "There's nothing more to talk about," he said. . . .
>
> She flung herself against the stone wall. . . . "Why are you so different?" . . . Her look was so intent that he turned. . . . In that instant a curtain seemed suddenly to have been drawn aside and she saw how tired he was. His face had grown thinner, paler, lines . . . creeping stealthily across the forehead. Shadows dulled his eyes. Even his hair had lost its luster. . . . For the first time she saw that he was old.
>
> Dimly . . . she glimpsed the disappointment, the disillusion drowned in his busy-ness. . . . She was appalled at the sadness in his face.
>
> "You have a great capacity for unhappiness," he said.
>
> "My unhappiness in only loving you."
>
> Harsh lines rose between his brows. "You want love, but you do not want me. You do not love me. You only dramatize your want of love — "
>
> "You're all that I want in life. You've given me myself."
>
> His eyes softened and he bent toward [her]. "Some day when

you're older, you'll see I have nothing more to give you. I've given you everything I had."

Then he asked her to return his letters. "You must realize this is a delicate matter." Frantically she refused.

In *Red Ribbon* she wrote that she burned the letters years later, when she realized that she was holding on to a now-lifeless memory. By that time she had memorized and had borrowed sentences from them for her stories. But in *All I Could Never Be*, the earlier, more passionate book, she wrote that she returned the letters after a taste of success had calmed her, with a note explaining why she had kept them: "I was like a person with only one light in the room, afraid of the dark."

Still kind, but distant, Dewey had tried to help her get another job. It was a busy kindness; he was departing within days on a sabbatical leave. He was rejoining his wife in San Francisco to lecture for three months at the University of California. But one sees by the poems he did not show Anzia that he had been deeply affected, too.

Now he also recognized her volatility. He must have been shocked into awareness of the risk he had taken and was ready and glad to get away, for in California he accepted the subsequent invitation of a Japanese university to visit, and in Japan a similar invitation from China, which together were to keep him out of the country for three years.

Before his departure, Anzia had refused his offers of help, too proud to accept his impersonal kindness now. But when he left, she discovered a greater despair. She was thrust back into a terrifying isolation. She could not return to her family or friends for refuge. Her mother was dead, her father remarried; she had fought with her brothers and her sisters' husbands. She had arrogantly, confidently spurned them all when she was living "the higher life" under Dewey's sponsorship. Now she was totally alone.

Wherever I went [in] the street, the subway, in every crowd, I looked for him. . . .

I felt I was falling, falling into a dark, soundless canyon, plunging into lower depths of loneliness than I had ever known. My life cracked. Everything was tearing open and splitting apart.

. . . I clung to the memory of his voice, his eyes when he loved me. I read and reread his letters. The more I read them, the more I believed he still loved me. I had only to read the first words of his letters: "Dear love of God!" and doubt vanished, the bleak years of loneliness dissolved, life lay open in all directions, all that I lacked was mine.

I had to write what love meant to me.

To the piece of paper she unburdened herself as if talking to a close friend, to John himself. Sometimes she found momentary relief as she wrote feverishly, chaotically, trying to understand why he had left:

He had given me something divinely made of the golden haze of faith & dreams — & I wanted to have & to hold [it]. That's why I lost the creative gift he imparted. His leaving me has taught me 2 things: this light . . . is there — like sun & stars are there — not to be owned. A lamp to guide us in our darkness. . . . I don't belong to those who have a place in this world. I belong to the outcast, the beggar, the mad, the lost. . . . We lost ones have this covenant of sun & stars to go by.

She filled pages with such fragments. The pages piled up on her table, she was sucked into a wilderness of words. She pulled herself away from the table one night to escape from the chaos and went outside.

These were the streets she had walked through with Dewey. She remembered the delight he had found in scenes she despised. For him the noisy crowds were a pageant. He had marveled at the vitality of the people as they argued, shouted, cried, or exulted, carrying their private lives from too-small tenement rooms out into the streets for any passerby to witness. And suddenly it was as if he were there, to open her eyes:

I saw my own hump of inferiority. Here was life, right here on my own block, in the house where I lived. . . . Hanneh Breineh, the janitress, cursing and shrieking at the children she loved till they fled from her in hate. The old Jew, sitting on the sidewalk, discussing the *cabala* with his cronies. . . . In all of them I saw a part of myself.

Returning to her room, she pushed aside the jumble of pages and started to write whatever she knew about these people, the ideas coming faster than she could get them onto the page. She wrote about the pushcart peddler she had known since childhood. She saw him sending his first letter home to his family, still in Poland, the kind of letter the peddler had paid someone else to write and which her father, as the only literate person in the village, was often given to read:

To my worthy wife, Masheh Mindel, and to my loving son, Susha Feifel, and to my precious darling daughter, the apple of my eye, the pride of my life, Tzipkeleh! . . .

First, I come to tell you that I am well and in good health. May I hear the same from you.

Secondly, I am telling you that my sun is beginning to shine in America. I am becoming a person — a business man.

I have for myself a stand in the most crowded part of America, where people are as thick as flies and every day is like market-day by a fair. My business is from bananas and apples. The day begins with my pushcart full of fruit, and the day never ends before I count up at least $2.00 profit — that means four rubles. Stand before your eyes . . . I . . . Gedalyeh Mindel, four rubles a day, twenty-four rubles a week!

She wrote more notes during the next days about the other immigrant Jews she knew, especially about her mother and father.

The writing became an absorbing, growing thing. It fed and devoured me. It blotted out nights and days until I plucked out of the contradictions of a human being the living seed of a story.

This story became "The Fat of the Land," about Hanneh Breineh, an anachronism from the Old World, an overwrought, gesticulating, yelling, loving shrew like Anzia's mother; and about her children, who, like Anzia, grew up to become so successfully American that they were embarrassed by the ghetto habits of their ignorant mother.

In the stories she had written before, Anzia had tried to capture the Yiddish-into-English idiom and feelings of uneducated immigrants yearning for understanding, but she remained separate from them, an onlooker. With "The Fat of the Land," she embraced her own family. Although she was still fighting inside herself against her father's harsh judgment of her, she wrote with rare compassion and love about her dead mother in this new story. She seized hold of its powerful emotion in pages of notes, but it was still shapeless, too big for her. She caught a childhood memory in the flash of an early scene:

> Hanneh Breineh . . . heard the noise of her famished brood [returned from school] and topped their cries with curses and invectives.
>
> "They are here already, the savages! They are here already to shorten my life!" . . .
>
> The children, disregarding her words, pounced on her market basket. . . . They tore the bread and herring out of [the] basket and devoured it . . . clamoring for more.
>
> "Murderers!" screamed Hanneh Breineh, goaded beyond endurance. . . . "From where should I steal to give you more? Here I had already a pot of potatoes and a whole loaf of bread and two herrings, and you swallowed it down in the wink of an eye."

She scribbled another fragment — Hannah Breineh confronting a flunky of the impressive apartment house to which her children, now grown and well-to-do, had moved her to live on "the fat of the land." It was a place where she felt "cut off from air, from life, from everything warm and human":

> Hannah Breineh returned triumphantly with her purchases. The basket under her arm gave forth the old, homelike odors of herring and garlic, while the scaly tail of a four-pound carp protruded from its newspaper wrapping. . . . [She] strode proudly through the marble-paneled hall and rang . . . for the elevator.
>
> The uniformed hall-man, erect, expressionless, frigid with dignity, stepped forward.
>
> "Just a minute, madam. I'll call a boy to take up your basket for you."
>
> Hannah Breineh, glaring at him, jerked the basket savagely from his hands. "Mind your own business! I'll take it up myself."
>
> Angry lines appeared on the man's face.
>
> "It is against the rules, madam," he said stiffly.

Struggling with a theme bigger than any she had ever attempted before, Anzia was also contending with her own self-doubts. Despite the two stories she had published, despite the strong assurances Dewey had repeatedly given her, she was not convinced that she was yet a "real writer." And that winter the story she first wrote from these notes was repeatedly rejected; she sometimes faltered.

She was working as a waitress, living frugally in a furnished room in the ghetto, trying to be the artist John Dewey had discerned in her. "Show him what's in you," she admonished herself. "If it takes a year or a million years, you've got to show him. From now on . . . you've got to work . . . by day and by night, you've got to push yourself up till you get to him and can look him in his face eye to eye." But she knew that she didn't have the technique, the glossy skill an editor would instantly accept as professional. In a hurry to pick up the missing gloss, like a coat of varnish, she took money out of her hoarded savings to enroll that fall in a creative writing class at Columbia University's Extension Division.

To the class she brought "The Fat of the Land," her still unpublished story, hoping for a quick lesson. The class pounced on it. This so-called story spanned twenty years and had too many characters, violating cardinal short-story rules that had been repeatedly expounded by the teacher. Moreover, its heroine was *disagreeable*:

> "Oi! Mrs. Pelz; if you could only look into my heart! I'm so choked up! You know they say a cow has a long tongue, but can't talk." Hannah Breineh shook her head wistfully, and her eyes filmed with inward brooding. "My children give me everything from the best. . . . but — but — I can't talk myself out in their language. They want to make me over for an American lady and I'm different." Tears cut their way under her eyelids with a pricking pain as she went on: "When I was poor, I was free, and could holler and do what I like in my own house. Here I got to lie still like a mouse under a broom." . . . The doorbell rang, and Hannah Breineh jumped up with a start.
>
> "Oi weh? It must be the servant back already!" she exclaimed, as she tore off her apron. "Oi weh!"

"It's not a story," the teacher and students agreed. "It has no plot." "Over-emotional." "Feeling without form."

But their criticism, instead of discouraging her, fed Anzia's rage. Having lived through months of desolation alone, she was indignant — to have paid so much money for the class and not receive any help! When the teacher returned "The Fat of the Land" to her at the end of the class, she clutched with protective, maternal love "this living thing of hers that they were killing." Rejecting their advice, she sent it out again, unvarnished. She gave up her job.

> I was a hermit [enduring] . . . a self-imposed imprisonment. . . . My body starved; for much of the time I lived on graham crackers, stale bread, mush and milk. My brain adapted itself, slowly, to the art I had set out to master.

"If the method I evolved is unconventional, lacking in form, so much the better," she later told an interviewer in the flush of early success. "I care nothing for the ready-made mental garments of the writer who has been fitted by colleges and short story classes."

For a long time the hermit collected rejection slips. They made her so stubborn that she went to the magazine offices and sometimes succeeded in waylaying an editor: "You want something good? I got it! I can wake up your readers." The editors she confronted found these merchandising efforts as bizarre as her stories.

The stories had become her whole existence, freighted as they were with everything she had lived through, even the glory she had known with Dewey and her expulsion from his Eden. In the end, although she strongly believed otherwise, Dewey had recognized the truth of her — that Anzia could not love him. But she had desperately needed him as a father, a lover, a brother, to care for her and make her whole. Without his love and acceptance, she had nothing, she *was* nothing. That was why she fought now to sell her stories. She *had* to be something.

Just as the creative writing class was ending, "Soap and Water and the Immigrant," which she had written under Dewey's direction, was accepted by the *New Republic*, for which he served as roving editor and contributor. He was probably responsible, before leaving the country, for its acceptance. This small success inspired her to return to her notes about Dewey with a now-coherent idea for another story, the romance of an immigrant sweatshop worker and her American night school teacher. "The Miracle" turned out to be a lyrical remembrance of Dewey. It mistily transformed the unhappy ending. The girl was almost true to Anzia's life; the teacher, although he spoke mostly with Dewey's remembered words, was the prince of a fairy tale.

> My teacher was so much above me that he wasn't a man to me at all. He was a God. His face lighted up the shop for me, and his voice sang itself in me everywhere I went.

The sweatshop worker told the teacher, when she first came to his classroom, that she wanted above all to become an educated person.

> "I'll help you," he said. "But you must first learn to get hold of yourself."

> "Friend," I said to him. . . . "If you could teach me how to get cold in the heart and clear in the head like you are!"
>
> . . . Then he said: "I am not so cold in the heart and clear in the head as I make-believe. . . . I am bound by formal education and . . . traditions. . . . I am repressed by the fear and shame of feeling. You could teach me . . . how to be natural."
>
> "I'm not so natural like you think," I said. "I'm afraid."
>
> He smiled at me out of his eyes. "What are you afraid of?"
>
> "I'm afraid of my heart," I said, trying to hold back the blood rushing to my face. . . . "How can I learn to keep myself down on earth like the born Americans?"
>
> "But I don't want you to get down on earth. . . . That is just the beauty and the wonder of you. We Americans . . . need more of your power to fly. . . . You are the promise of the centuries to come. You are the heart, the creative pulse of America to be."
>
> Classes ended, night school closed for the summer.
>
> As I faced the emptiness of my long vacation, all the light went out of my eyes. . . . "A lot my teacher cares for me once the class is over."

So she "shot out a letter to him," as Anzia had once written to Dewey when he was away, and as she was trying to do even then, although he had gone beyond reach.

> "You call yourself a teacher! A friend! How can you go off in the country and drop me out of your . . . head like a read-over book you left on the shelf of your shut-down classroom. What good are all the books you ever gave me? . . . I can't live inside my head as you do."

As soon as the girl in the story posted the letter, she realized that it was unforgivable and she yearned to retrieve it. Returning forlornly to her room, "I saw my door open. . . . Am I dreaming? There was my teacher sitting on my trunk! My teacher come to see me . . . in my dingy room."

In the same words Dewey had used in a letter to Anzia, the teacher told the immigrant girl, "Without you I am the dry dust of hopes unrealized. You are fire and sunshine and desire. You make life changeable and beautiful and full of daily wonder." His arms enfolded her in this fairy tale, and he said gently, "'Tell me, do you love me?' kissing me on my hair and on my eyes and on my lips. . . . I could only weep and tremble with joy at his touch."

Writing that story — from which she was able to gain such emotional comfort — was a turning point for her. She sold it, probably on the first submission, to *Metropolitan*, a popular magazine for "women's fiction." Sonya Levien, the sympathetic editor of that magazine, a year and a half earlier, had virtually started Anzia's career by buying "Where Lovers Dream," about her sister Annie's faded romance. Success breeds success: on her next try, after countless rejections, Anzia sold "The Fat of the Land" to the important literary magazine *Century*, whose editor had undoubtedly been impressed by reading "Soap and Water" in the *New Republic*.

Within the next few months, editors started opening their doors to her. One after the other, she sold stories that had gone begging for years.

What had happened between the winter of 1918, when she was repeatedly rejected, and the spring of 1919, when her stories were suddenly found acceptable? Not much was changed in the manuscripts. Perhaps they had been burnished by her persistence as she sent them out again without pause and, unwilling to tolerate their rejection, even took them in person to the magazines.

But when one story after another appeared in print at last, they looked and read quite differently than they had in manuscript, even to editors who had rejected her. From being a strange and freakish writer, she had become an acquired taste. Novelty was desirable, once someone had tested it.

Early in 1920, Edward J. O'Brien, the distinguished editor of *The Best Short Stories* series, chose "The Fat of the Land" as the best short story of 1919 and dedicated his year's collection to her. She was, though still struggling to pay her rent, a "wanted" writer. Editors sent her letters asking for her stories.

"In the intoxication of this sudden recognition," she wrote of her experience at that time, "all my hunger and longing for love turned to ambition. I saw a place for myself. I saw work. I, the unwanted one, was wanted. If I could not have love, I would have fame, success."

Yet, with each story, which she sent to Dewey as soon as it was published, she still hoped for love. She expected to hear from him. Against the rush of mail she was now receiving—invitations from strangers, remembrances from former friends, requests from editors—his silence was incredible to her. "There was in her now a power that he had dug up out of the confusion that wasted her. . . . How could he help being interested in the way she used the gift he had discovered?"

How could he remain aloof from her now?

"You make too much out of nothing," said a version of Dewey in her story "To the Stars." In that story, he was a college president who helped an immigrant writer, but found her gratitude excessive (as had Dewey).

> "Nothing?" Her eyes were misty with emotion. "I was something wild up in the air. . . . I couldn't get hold of myself all alone, and you—you made me for a person."

II

SUCCESS

6

F A M E

BECOMING A SUCCESS, in the early months of 1920, was not as simple or as profitable as Anzia's envious friends and relatives imagined. True, she was getting gratifying letters from magazine editors and other newly acquired readers; and thanks to Edward J. O'Brien, magazine checks were arriving often enough to pay the modest rent, so that at last she could live by her writing.

But just barely. Although she now could sell almost any story she wrote, the checks usually came on publication, four to six months after acceptance. Because she was a new writer, the amounts were small. The

O'Brien award, thrilling as it was, had so far brought only survival money.

She still lived in a bare furnished room, eating minimal meals cooked on a hot plate. Now, working even harder than before, a pulse of recurring excitement, the thrill of being recognized, kept her company as she worked, went to sleep, or woke to work again. After days of writing through the hours into the night, grabbing any food at hand, she would run out in a hurry, usually to Annie, to test what she had written, hear how it sounded. But no one could replace Dewey as that necessary listener, could give her as much assurance.

The work itself stimulated and solaced her and helped her to withstand the loneliness. It was always "a torture of chaos . . . and doubt . . . so much dirt through which I have to dig before I can come into the light." But when she eventually mined a story out of the chaos and sent it to a magazine, now it was read at once, and when she telephoned impatiently, only days later, to ask about it, her name was recognized; the editor might even come to the phone.

From *Harper's*, the *Nation*, and the *New Republic* to *Good Housekeeping* and *Metropolitan*, they all bought Yezierska stories that year. The raw, shocking ghetto emotion in her writing, once distasteful, was now esteemed by editors of highbrow, middle, and lowbrow magazines. Anzia had notebooks, large manila envelopes, and boxes full of scribbled notes on scraps of paper with ideas for more stories. The prod of being wanted made her prolific. She couldn't write fast enough. Even her half-finished work was accepted. *Good Housekeeping* asked her to write something about herself. She wrote a thousand-word exclamation about the hardships she had known and was still enduring; it was called "The Immigrant Speaks." In it she told how hunger had forced her to work in a sweatshop soon after she got off the immigrant ship, and how, after she was at last earning enough,

> . . . the landlady came with the raise in rent. . . . The loaf of bread that was five cents became ten. Milk that was eight cents a quart became eighteen. Shoes, clothes, everything doubled and tripled in price. I felt like one put on a rack — thumb-screws torturing my flesh — pay — pay — pay!

She condemned this land of profiteering in which "men . . . create poverty where God has poured out wealth." She had the right to demand more of America, she wrote; her demands were part of the energy that had created America. "Were not the Pilgrim Fathers immigrants demanding a new world in which they could be free . . .?"

Good Housekeeping's editor expanded Anzia's thousand words to two magazine pages with illustrations of a beautiful immigrant girl in a shawl — first, getting off a ship and, then, surrounded by working people in a factory. W. T. Benda, the noted illustrator, received a larger check; but the editor devoted a preface to explaining who Anzia Yezierska was:

> The author of this remarkable appeal to Americans of older lineage came to this country at the age of nine, one of a family of ten children. . . . The longing for an education was already keen in her heart. . . . It is to her credit and the credit of American opportunity that she nursed her longing, got her education, and finally won an enviable distinction as a writer. "The Best Short Stories of 1919" is dedicated to her, and publishers are bidding against each other for her work. *Good Housekeeping* is glad to give this recognition to an American of foreign birth.

Adding to the exhilaration of getting such praise was the constant thought that now Dewey would surely read about her. And just in case he didn't, each time one of her stories was published she mailed a copy of the magazine to him care of the YMCA in China, the address his office had given her. She had talked over with him her first ideas for most of these stories. Now she was working steadily, intensely, through days as long and grueling as those in a sweatshop, but with the growing confidence that she was on her way back to him again as an equal, a recognized writer, the artist he himself had created. She wrote those stories for him to read, as she had done since their first meeting.

Once a week she interrupted her Spartan routine to spend Saturday with her daughter. One of Annie's girls brought the child by subway to visit Anzia amid the piles of manuscripts, occasionally to stay overnight, sharing Anzia's bed. The little room was starkly plain: pale cheesecloth curtains pulled away from the one window; the bed was also the sofa; the only table held a portable typewriter engulfed in worked-over, scribbled pages and large manila envelopes. Books were piled against the wall next to the table; and a shawl-covered trunk served as chair or eating space.

"Who cares about furniture or tablecloths?" Anzia shrugged, as one confidante to another, the first time her six-year-old daughter saw the room. "Let your grandmother have them; all she knows is cooking and cleaning. This is how I live! Like a nun's cell! I'm working for something important, for both of us."

She would talk to Louise about her work in the same confiding tone — how hard it was to create a real story out of mixed-up feelings! The confusion of words in a second language! She showed the little girl the scraps of emotion interrupted in her typewriter, and sometimes the glamorous rewards; the name Anzia Yezierska (not Hattie Levitas) in the magazines.

Anzia and Louise might take a walk to the park when it was nice weather; they always looked in the neighboring bookstores. And then, back in the room, Anzia would seize the hot plate from under the bed, eggs and butter from the windowsill, to scramble an onion omelet in the unwashed frying pan, or spread peanut butter on thick pieces of bread. And before Louise had to leave that afternoon with Annie's daughter, Anzia might say, urgently, to impress the words on her daughter: "We'll be together again as soon as I can make enough money. Maybe very soon." Or: "You and I have each other. Even when we're apart, you keep me company. Often I'm thinking of you — especially when you're thinking of me. Remember that."

Louise was old enough to understand, though adults didn't. Mama had to work day and night and be lonely. Her hard life in that bare, lonely room was a secret Louise carried back with her to her father's Bronx apartment, where his mother cooked and cleaned and didn't understand anything. Through the week, until the next Saturday, the little girl kept that persistent, secret compassion for her mother like a palpable, sharp taste in her mouth, diluting her joy in the candy and cake and other treats her father gave her.

Yet for Anzia, now that whatever she wrote was valued, each morning brought a new, thrilling possibility. The morning of March 4, 1920, brought the most a new writer could hope for: a letter from Ferris Greenslet, senior editor of the highly respected Boston firm of Houghton Mifflin & Company. Anzia's impassioned stories about illiterate ghetto starvelings had reached America's publishing aristocracy.

An editor for a magazine that had bought a Yezierska story had told Greenslet that Anzia would surely write "an important novel." If so, Greenslet wrote Anzia, "this house" would be delighted to consider publishing it. In the meantime, he wrote, he would like, when next he visited New York, to talk with her about her "future literary plans."

4 E. 41 St.
N.Y. City, March 4

My dear Mr. Greenslet

I just received your note of March 3. I shall be very glad to talk over with you my literary plans. Please write me when you come to the city, so I can arrange to meet you.

Sincerely yours
Anzia Yezierska

4 E. 41 St.
March 30, '20

My dear Mr. Greenslet,

Some weeks ago you have written to me, asking me about my future literary plans and I have answered you asking to see you when you come to N.Y. but I have not heard from you.

Sincerely yours,
Anzia Yezierska

You may be interested in one of my short stories appearing in Harpers for April — "Hunger".

Anzia could never bear waiting. The effort to control her impatience with this Brahmin made her uncertain of her tenses; but Greenslet answered the next day with easy self-assurance that he was just starting for New York, hoping among other things to meet her, and would read the

Harper's story on the train coming in. Could she perhaps "look in" at Houghton Mifflin's New York office the following day?

The office, on East Fortieth Street in the Murray Hill section, was a temple of hushed gentility, complacent with tradition and the odor of old wood. Anzia must have felt a certain stage fright as she walked into this sanctum to meet the first book publisher of her experience. She would have had to remind herself that she no longer needed to peddle her manuscripts.

But when at last she faced that important and imposing man, Greenslet, she couldn't help herself. She had brought with her seven published short stories and a long manuscript she was writing called "My Own People," which she said could be the first chapter of a novel. Greenslet had already read three or four of the published stories and was impressed. She was an original, with a new story to tell and a style of her own — a rude, abrupt style, perhaps, but obviously there was a market for it. He glanced at the bundle she placed on his desk and remarked it was almost enough to fill a small book. Anzia jumped at his words. With such a stimulus, she was certain she could quickly produce more. The editor backtracked immediately: unfortunately, there was only a small market for books of short stories. Haste might be unwise. A novel would be a better beginning.

Anzia, as if unhearing, rushed ahead to speak for her short stories. "The Fat of the Land" and "Hunger," for instance, were really like parts of a novel, she said; her stories together made a narrative about the immigrant's dream of America and the sometimes bitter realization of those dreams. The book could be called *Hunger.* The hunger for more than bread was the basic theme of her writing.

As she grew more excited, she thought of a sure-fire idea for selling the "small-market" book. Greenslet could invite Herbert Hoover to write the preface. The great humanitarian had just returned from Belgium, where he had been feeding millions of starving war refugees.

Greenslet didn't say no. He just said pleasantly that before discussing such particulars, or even proposing to publish a book of short stories, he would have to consult other Houghton Mifflin editors.

Two days later, waiting for the decision, Anzia sent him a poem "which would go well with the suggested volume of short stories." It was "Generations of stifled words reaching out / Through you. . . ." She must have hoped that John Dewey's tribute would impress this aloof Anglo-Saxon and perhaps thaw him out. She added:

> Since I have spoken to you I have gone over the notes of my novel My Own People and I feel confident that if I were free to concentrate on this work alone, I could finish the book in about five or six months. That means that I would need about $1000 or $1200 advance royalties. If you were to publish the short stories you could announce at the same time that it was to be followed by a novel in which many of the people of the short stories meet in their search for America.
>
> Sincerely yours,
> Anzia Yezierska

It took Greenslet ten days to answer and smoothly turn down her bid for money. He had discussed her work with other Houghton Mifflin editors and now offered to publish a book of her short stories with her title, *Hunger*. Did she have one or two more stories to fill out the collection?

At the same time, he reminded her in this four-page letter that a book of any writer's short stories was always harder to sell than a novel. Perhaps the "excellence and striking quality" of her writing and all the publicity she was getting just then in magazines might help to increase the sales — maybe even enough to support her while she wrote her novel. Without saying it was the reason for not giving her an advance, he confessed he wasn't sure "the quality of your genius which shows most characteristically . . . in intense flashes" was as well suited to a longer work; that could be seen only when she completed the novel she had begun.

Finally, Greenslet observed that Herbert Hoover was obviously busy that week (his name had just been presented to the Republican party as a presidential candidate), but when the book was in proof, Greenslet might approach the great food dispenser about *Hunger*.

Anzia's next letter crossed Greenslet's in the mail. She had changed her mind about her future novel.

> Since I have spoken to you I met Mrs. Mary Austin who volunteered to be my literary advisor. She wants to help me plan my literary career with a view of the entire future and not for the immediate gain. Mrs. Austin does not think that mss. which I gave you is the best material for my first novel. She thinks the public would be more interested in Hanneh Breineh [the ghetto mother in "The Fat of the Land"] than in a fictionalized story of my life. And I think she is right.

She had reason to be swayed by Austin's opinion. About fifteen years older than Anzia, Austin was an eminent Houghton Mifflin author with an international reputation as a poet, novelist, short-story writer, and mystic. Perhaps Austin felt a kinship with Anzia because she, too, was a strong-minded woman who had long before quit her marriage and turned to writing. In her powerfully lyrical books, Austin had established herself much earlier as a champion of women's rights and the dignity of another ethnic minority, the American Indian. Recognizing Anzia's talent and the career choices she was just then facing, Austin volunteered her counsel as an older, more experienced writer. ("Mrs. Austin suggested that I tell you she would 'see me through' any work that is decided upon," Anzia added in her letter to Greenslet.) Austin's books — *The Land of Little Rain, Lost Borders, A Woman of Genius* are the best known — had by this time become classics; she was at the summit Anzia hoped to reach.

Flattered by this important writer's interest, Anzia rushed to write her a letter:

> I cannot begin to tell you how much that talk with you on Saturday has helped me — it only made me hungry for more — And now your letter this morning — . . . Please see me soon — very soon.
>
> The longing for friendship — for the stimulus of intellectual association which I had to choke in me — you have roused in me again.

I walked away from you weeping. It was the first time an American woman spread for me a table in the wilderness and filled my cup with all she . . . had.

But the handwriting — Anzia's bold, positive, oversized script — keeps contradicting the tremulousness of her words. Two days later, she wrote again regarding her idea for a joint Austin-Yezierska writing venture for a popular magazine: a series of articles titled "The Immigrant Woman Speaks and the American Woman Answers." Anzia then discussed it with a magazine editor, but nothing came of her proposal.

When she wrote to Greenslet at this time, accepting his offer to publish her short stories, she now shrugged off Herbert Hoover, who had just been rejected by the Republicans. "Perhaps it would be best . . . to let the book stand on its own feet." She added: "Please return the poem which I gave you . . . as I must first get Prof. Dewey's permission to use it in any way." She had planned to place it at the front of her book, with or without Dewey's name. Some adviser (perhaps Mrs. Austin) must have warned her against it. (Twelve years later, however, she used it without crediting Dewey in *All I Could Never Be*; no matter what others advised, she felt the poem belonged to her.) On one point, she stood firm. Greenslet wanted to discard the story she had written and published with Dewey's help, "Soap and Water and the Immigrant." Greenslet thought it was "hardly a story in the ordinary sense of the word." Anzia, who remembered Dewey's delight in it, insisted that the essay be included in the book. "This was the first thing that I tried to write and it's more [important] to me than the other stories."

Until the book was published, testing her privileges as author, she kept changing her mind about the title, the cover, the contents, even the dedication. She wrote to Greenslet so frequently in that oversized script that her handwritten letters, now in the Houghton Library at Harvard, along with the company's typed replies, are a virtual diary of her erratic moods that spring and summer — her boldness not altogether covering her self-doubt.

"Going up to the Houghton Mifflin offices to find out when you would be in N.Y.," she wrote in the postscript of an early letter about *Hunger*,

> I came across your advertising representative & we talked over [other] titles which I put down for your consideration:
>
> The Hunger of the Heart
> Hungry Hearts
> Hungry Souls
>
> I also suggested for the . . . cover an idealized picture of a hungry-souled immigrant girl.

And in another postscript on May 3, 1920, "Of the titles that I sent you, I like best — Hungry Hearts — It seems to me this not only expresses the contents of the book, but [is] a vibrant catchword for the masses." Greenslet replied that "all of us here" liked *Hungry Hearts* and would print that title. Nevertheless, two weeks later, on May 20, she proposed a different one:

> Mrs. Mary Austin and others with a keen literary sense have told me that Hungry Hearts gives the wrong note to the book. Mrs. Austin suggested — *They that Hunger.* That is part of a quotation from the Sermon on the Mount — "Blessed are they that hunger & thirst after righteousness."
>
> Do you not think — They that Hunger — a much better title than Hungry Hearts?

He did not. The dies had already been cut for *Hungry Hearts*, and besides, he considered it a more salable title. Anzia capitulated; Greenslet knew best. Anyhow she had become somewhat disenchanted with Mary Austin, who apparently was not giving Anzia the kind of help she had expected. Anzia had a knack for making, but not sustaining, immediate friendships such as that with Austin. The originality and intensity f Anzia's stories were more than matched by the startling vividness of er conversation at a first encounter — she had *no* small talk. But soon af- :r the delightful initial exchange, the two writers' personalities must ave clashed. For example, whatever Austin might recommend, Anzia, ot at all malleable, would not have been willing to reject a pulp maga- ine's money in order to appear only in low-paying literary publications. .lso, she usually brought her current manuscript into her conversations, ıveigling any new but instantly understanding friend to help her out of a ıomentary impasse. No doubt Austin had slipped out of such traps, for .nzia wrote to Greenslet: "I find Mrs. Wengler [a Houghton Mifflin ınior editor] an invaluable help. She really helps with her heart and her ead. But Mrs. Mary Austin — well — I couldn't somehow connect — ."

.NZIA WAS ENCLOSING her fresh-from-the-typewriter drafts in ıany of her letters to Greenslet. Although she had spent years on her rst stories, to meet the increasing requests from magazines she was now /riting stories almost as fast as she could type them. (Her work ap- eared in March, April, June, July, September, and November maga- ines that year. Despite Mrs. Austin's advice, it was impossible for Anzia ɔ turn away an easy sale while she was still poor and hungry.) She sent ach new manuscript to Greenslet, ostensibly for inclusion in the book. ut to get some money as well as to keep her name in print, she needed ɔ publish the stories first in a magazine. So she was in fact asking for ·reenslet's editorial advice before submitting the stories elsewhere.

Attached to an April letter, for example, was the first half of a sketch," as she called it, titled "America Discovers the Immigrant." ight days later she sent him the second half, warning that "there are ıany rough places in it but the [*Red Cross Magazine*] editor rushed me ɔr it and said he would edit it for me." Later the same day she wrote ·reenslet that she was "ashamed of the second half" and did not want ıe story in her book. "As I read it over now it strikes me [as] a runaway team engine of blind passion."

When Greenslet, whose opinion she respected above others, wrote that he liked "America Discovers the Immigrant" and thought it would fit nicely in the book, Anzia changed her mind again and permitted him to keep it. "But I am still working on the last part," she added, "and will send you the improved mss. just as soon as it is done." She sent it to him three months later, retitled "How I Found America." She had changed magazines too, selling it to the prestigious *Century* instead of the magazine that had been expecting it.

Growing more confident, she tried out on Greenslet another idea for her first novel: it was a manuscript in free verse, "The Deported," which she said expressed the future novel's theme.

I am the deported.

The ship on which I stand is leaving the harbor.

The foaming waves converging at the . . . stern . . . are pushing me irrevocably away.

This America whose mountains I dashed myself against . . .

These rock barriers on which I beat out the anguish of my protest and rebellion . . .

Behold! . . . the barriers of prejudice and hate are dissolving in the mist.

These very waves that are separating me, somehow seem to link me with the land I am leaving.

Through the transfigured distance, I see the spires of the great buildings, temples of achievement, landmarks of men who built and created while I tore down and destroyed.

Oh God! Why do I just begin to see America, now that I am torn away? . . .

Now I see that America was a dream to be realized, a potential love to be fathomed . . . an uncharted world to be explored. . . .

Oh America! Though now I am cast away — branded — exiled . . .

I, the deported, go forth . . . to spread among the peoples of the earth the faith in the better world to come — the deathless dream — America!

The subject came directly from the front pages of the daily news-aper. That year, 1920, and the year before, the fear of a "red tide" reeping westward in the wake of the Russian Revolution had provoked iass hysteria in the United States. Led by U.S. Attorney General A. Aitchell Palmer, federal, state, and local police in major cities across the ountry had rounded up thousands of suspected radicals, jailed them vithout trial, and deported many. Rose Pastor Stokes was one of those rrested. Emma Goldman, the anarchist heroine of liberal Lower East ide circles, was deported to the USSR with a shipload of other eportees.

Although Anzia's sympathies were with the deported, she was polit-ally always a bystander, agreeing with the arguments, but too absorbed 1 her own fierce struggle to participate in a movement. And just then, vith her modest rise in fortune, she must have been feeling more opti-iistic about America as a land of opportunity.

Her letter explained to Greenslet: "I would like to show the soul of iese deported rebels — their dreams that brought them to America — ieir uncompromising adolescence — their inability to adjust [to] things s they are — and only as they are being exiled from America do they be-in to see the real meaning of America and the chance they missed. How oes this strike you?" Greenslet replied that it was an "impressive" idea nd could make a novel if she "put a great deal of imaginative meat on its ones" to avoid writing a tract. "This, I doubt not, you could readily do." nd he encouraged her to try.

The *Nation* published "The Deported" as a poem the following ionth, but Anzia seems to have forgotten her idea of turning it into a ovel. She no longer needed to write it: in that undigested jumble, per-aps unconsciously, she seems to have worked out for herself once more ie mystery of her connection with and separation from John Dewey, ho to her was *the* Plymouth Rock American from whom she sought ac-eptance. As if with sudden insight ("Now I see that America was a ream to be realized, a potential love to be fathomed"), she had discov-ed the fault ("uncompromising adolescence") for which she had been anished. Or perhaps a friend who was more involved politically after reading the poem, had pointed out the nature of the activity for which people were being deported. She never mentioned the subject to Greenslet again.

The early months of her correspondence with her Boston editor kept to the same comfortable level — Anzia confiding her waxing and waning literary intentions, asking for advice and favors and getting them; Greenslet, amused, sometimes faintly patronizing, but willing to oblige her. The first rift occurred when she received Houghton Mifflin's legal contract for her signature:

> May 11, '20
>
> My dear Mr. Greenslet,
>
> I cannot sign clause three of the agreement. The best publishing houses such as McMillans do not request their authors to give up any motion picture rights. As to the dramatic rights & rights of translation — those ought to be *subject to agreement,* not "equally divided."

She was obviously getting advice from more experienced writers.

"I am sorry that you don't consider us one of the best publishing houses," Greenslet replied. "We will try to improve." Anzia was mortified, although he was accepting her claim and allowing her to retain the film and dramatic rights. "I have been unfortunate in the wording of my last letter," she wrote back meekly, "and shall be miserable till I can see you and explain."

Thereafter, always signing his letters "Faithfully yours," the Brahmin kept to his pedestal. Most of the authors he enjoyed working with, one understands from the memoir he wrote years later (*Under the Bridge*), were members of the British nobility. He traced his own ancestry back to a courtier of the first Queen Elizabeth. Many titled Britons wrote memoirs published by Houghton Mifflin: Lord Tweedsmuir, Lady Asquith, Lord and Lady Baldwin, Lord Carlisle, Sir William Osler, Sir Ernest Shackleton. Their names are the highlights of *Under the Bridge*; in fact, they were his reward for dealing with ignoble and more grasping authors.

Anzia's intensity about nonliterary details must have been a jarring distraction from Greenslet's customary editorial duties. "I have ideas that would help the sale of the book that would interest you," she wrote him just before *Hungry Hearts* was published, asking for an appointment in New York. As her letters said repeatedly, she had ideas for publicity and advertising, bookstore window displays, department store appearances, and more. Evidently, she could not understand Greenslet's lofty view that a book of short stories was not supposed to make money for the author.

She was equally absorbed in the book jacket. She sent Greenslet two proofs for the picture that would appear on the front of the jacket; the photo was provided by an aspiring photographer whose work Anzia liked. "Better proofs will follow as the man is still experimenting," she wrote. But after nudging Houghton Mifflin again to buy the photo, and after Houghton Mifflin said yes and asked for negatives, she switched abruptly to another choice: one of the Benda illustrations for her story in *Good Housekeeping*. "It has exactly that mystic immigrant face that Mr. Scaife [Houghton Mifflin's advertising manager] was looking for. Those photographs I sent do not come within the shadow even — of Benda's face."

The editors and sales department agreed with her, but "it is utterly out of the question for us to pay [*Good Housekeeping*'s price for the Benda illustration], and at the same time pay anything to the photographer for his trouble," wrote R. L. Scaife to Anzia. He asked her what "in justice" they should pay for the photo she had selected and was now rejecting. Anzia cut right through that delicate problem:

> I called up Mr. Rabinovitch and told him that his photograph good as it is cannot be used for the jacket of the book. I made it quite clear to him at the beginning that he had a *tentative* order and payment depended on the success of the photograph. He therefore expects no remuneration. . . . I hope you can get the Benda drawing.

She had herself received no payment from Houghton Mifflin up to then. The advance royalty check for *Hungry Hearts* — $200 — was not to be mailed to her until the day of publication, October 22. So in July, in

the midst of revising short stories and reading proofs for the book, sh
had to move from her midtown furnished room to a much cheaper on
uptown in the tenement neighborhood of East 101st Street. She chose
also because it was across the street from her sister Annie and, in a sens
more comfortable emotionally; but it meant she was moving away from
"nice" neighborhood, returning to the ghetto crowdedness she had onc
escaped.

In that period of upheaval, early July, Houghton Mifflin's publicit
department sent Anzia a blank form to fill in with facts about her lif
The form was too constrained for her voluble style and too concerne
with unattractive facts. Instead of filling it out, Anzia, after returning th
galley proofs late in August, handwrote a brief, imaginative sketch of he
life, once more revealing only too graphically her distance from Houghton Mifflin's gentility.

> My dear Miss Forbes,
>
> I was ordered to take a rest cure and that is why I delayed in answering your letter and even now I cannot write fully, but shall send you items of interest from time to time.

She drew a line across the page to separate the first item of interest:

> No Don Quixote ever went fighting windmills more wholly unprepared than I as a writer. What is that Amer. saying: "Fools plunge where the wise even fear to approach?" Well I am a case in point. I began my schooling in the sweatshop. During the slack season I did housework & cooking. In time I became proficient enough in cooking to get a free scholarship in a domestic science school. Before the term was half-over, I went to the head of Dep't. and said, "I had enough of cooking — I want better to learn to be a writer."
>
> "A writer?" the woman stared at me. "My dear child — you might as well want to be dean of the university. There are native-born writers who do not earn their salt. What chance is there for you with your immigrant English?"

"If I can't get a chance to learn the American English, I'll write in 'immigrant English,' I answered, " — but write I must."

And without guide or compass I plunged into the sea of the short story and have been earning a living writing before I had a chance to learn American English.

Spinning this and other fairy tales about herself was one of the pleaures of authorship Anzia was just beginning to appreciate. As she ntended, Houghton Mifflin's publicity department used the letters veratim as press releases, and for years afterward the same words reapeared as quotes in newspaper and magazine interviews recreating the easant Cinderella. The fact that people actually wanted and believed uch tidbits about her life — the publicity department's interest, like the *ood Housekeeping* editor's questions — was to Anzia an agreeable foreaste of the even greater attention she might enjoy after the book was ublished.

She was also receiving letters from admiring readers, many from ormer immigrants or children of immigrants who were thrilled to recogize in her stories something of themselves. Anzia wrote Miss Forbes of Ioughton Mifflin's publicity department about them, to explain why she vas going out of town:

> Friends whom I have never met, but who have written me in response to the articles and stories that have recently appeared in the magazines have invited me to visit them in Chicago and have arranged for me to give three readings of my stories — at the Evanston Dramatic League, Hull House, and the Chamber of Commerce. . . . My host is not primarily a literary man, but a businessman, an efficiency engineer. . . . He is getting a [lot] of people interested in the publication of Hungry Hearts. More of this when I get to Chicago.

Basking in their admiration and bountiful hospitality, part of her ompensation for years of rejection and Spartan living, she spent over a nonth with her Chicago "friends." When she returned, she gave a rapurous verbal account, at Houghton Mifflin's New York office, of how she had been feted. The following month her Chicago host came to New York and celebrated the publication of *Hungry Hearts* with another feast. Anzia described that, too, for Houghton Mifflin's publicity department:

> Mr. L. B. Moses made a . . . dinner party at the Waldorf Astoria at which I was the guest of honor. As I listened to the inspiring music and took in the glitter and the glamor of the magnificent hotel I could not help telling [him] that no more than two years ago I begged at this very hotel for a job.

In the period after Dewey, the winter of desperation, she had indeed looked for a job as kitchen manager or even waitress in that establishment.

> I went through the dark, underground employees entrance, that none of the guests who enter through the front door know anything about. . . . All I asked was for a job as a scullery maid, dishwasher or scrub-woman. And even this was refused me. What else was there for me to do but go back to my writing with the courage of despair.

Hungry Hearts was published at the end of October. Anzia asked her publisher to send the first copies to Professor John Dewey, at the YMCA in Peking; Henry L. Mencken, at the *Smart Set*; Max Eastman, at the *Masses*; Louis Untermeyer; and Amy Lowell. She attached a note to the copy for Dewey: "See! I've done the impossible for you. . . . I've plucked out the chaos of my soul."

Then she waited hungrily for applause. The "impossible" achievement, a book of her writing, demanded the world's attention. The wait became painful. A month after publication, the *New York Evening Post* printed the first review of *Hungry Hearts*, giving the new writer qualified praise: "When one considers her own struggles to become an American, her detachment strikes one as little short of miraculous." Two weeks later, William Lyon Phelps, a professor of literature at Yale, ventured further in the *New York Times*: "Many realistic tales of New York's ghetto have been written, but in point of literary workmanship and in laying bare the very souls of her characters, the superior of Miss Yezierska has not yet appeared."

The first faint notes of a prelude. Not numerous enough to gratify Anzia, or for that matter to sell many books. Then silence. Plainly the Houghton Mifflin publicity department, despite Anzia's energetic prodding, was not calling attention to *Hungry Hearts*. Through bleak November days, she suffered this stunning letdown. Her books had appeared and disappeared, virtually unnoticed even in the bookstores. Not a word from Dewey. Anzia, who wrote and lived by her emotions, was again in despair:

> Shivering with cold, I walked up and down the shopping district of Fifth Avenue. I caught a glimpse of myself in the mirror of a passing shop window. . . . Worried, haunted eyes under a crumpled hat. Faded, ragged old coat. . . . All about me . . . windows glittered with ball gowns and gorgeous wraps.
>
> In one window a dazzling Christmas tree blinded me with rage. Why should there be Christmas in the world? Why this holiday spirit on Fifth Avenue . . . why these expectant, smiling faces of the shoppers buying useless presents for each other, when . . . I had been writing and starving for years?
>
> . . . People who read a book little know what small reward there is for the writer while he is still unknown — of his often solitary, starved existence. . . .
>
> If I could only throw a bomb right there in the middle of Fifth Avenue and shatter into a thousand bits all this heartlessness of buying! . . . The slush of the sidewalk [snow] creeping into the cracks of my shoes made me feel . . . wretchedly uncomfortable. . . . If I could only kill myself as a protest against the wrongs and injustices I had suffered! . . .
>
> . . . A sense of exaltation stole over me as I went on imagining the details of my death. I could see the beautiful limousine wrenched to a sudden stop. The pale chauffeur lifting my crushed, bleeding body in his arms. The whole world breaking the hush of the crowd:

"This was the author of *Hungry Hearts*, and we left her to languish and die in want!"

. . . I saw the throngs mobbing the bookstores for my book. My last letter and my picture in the front page of every newspaper. . . . Everywhere people reading and talking "Hungry Hearts." The whole world shaken with guilty sorrow for my tragic death — but too late!

In this excerpt from "This Is What $10,000 Did to Me," written for the October 1925 issue of *Cosmopolitan* magazine, Anzia embellished her account with a coldhearted landlady, ready to evict her for unpaid rent. By 1925 she had been recognized and well rewarded, but the feelings she wrote about had been real during that 1920 winter. Although her stories had been in leading magazines and her book had just been published, she was still embattled and alone. Still fighting with her brothers at home because, thanks to her new status as a published writer, they expected her to help support their father. And still grindingly poor.

The only consolation in her bare room on East 101st Street was to read the great poetry of other sufferers, and even try to write it:

DUMB

My thoughts beat in me . . .
And cannot find voice . . .
Smothered in the smoke of my unused fire!

My dumbness hurts me like a hidden wound . . .
I beat in vain against barriers that I cannot break through.
I am driven and destroyed by famine and dearth —
I, with prophesies and revelations seething in my breast . . .

In me are vineyards of plenty and I go about hungry, begging crumbs.
Mine is the travail of those who produce, but my creations die in me —
still-born-dumb!

She sent this cry to poet Amy Lowell, with whom she felt a spiritual closeness, attaching it to a handwritten letter:

116 E. 101 St.
Dec. 9, 1920

My dear Miss Lowell:

Some weeks ago your secretary acknowledged the receipt of my book *Hungry Hearts*. She said you are recovering from an operation and I hope you are well by now.

I wonder if you had a chance to read my book and if you would be interested enough to write an interpretive review of it for the Times. I felt your warm sympathy for the uneducated in your review of Carl Sandburg's poetry and . . . that you would understand my . . . struggle to find voice.

I am terribly lonely here in America. I have broken away from my family and I live alone in a little room like a prisoner in a cell. I never meet anyone to talk out what's aching in my heart. If you would only let me come to you sometime . . . it would be new life to my stifling spirit. And I feel I could bring to you new life . . .

Sincerely yours,
Anzia Yezierska

The nose-pressed-against-the-glass appeal, which had previously won her the sympathies and help of benevolent lady patrons at the Clara de Hirsch Home for Working Girls, of John Dewey and a number of magazine editors, this time failed. "My dear Miss Yezierska," answered Lowell's secretary on December 13, "Miss Lowell is still unable to attend to her correspondence. . . . She has been unable as yet to read your poem and the book. As she is publishing a new book in the Spring, she fears it will be impossible to attempt any further prose writing this Winter. For of course the publication of her book comes first and she has so little time."

But Anzia had not counted too much on Amy Lowell. A few days before writing that gloomy letter, she had turned restlessly in an opposite direction — to the newspaper office of Dr. Frank Crane.

In 1920, before radio and television, Crane, who was a Protestant minister and a popular and widely syndicated newspaper columnist, had as his audience the then vast circulation of Hearst newspapers throughout the United States. Anzia didn't phone or write; she was impelled to see him by the explosive force of her need, hunger, and rage. Despite every obstacle, she had written and published a book. The world must pay attention!

She walked unannounced into Crane's office, prepared for obstacles. But he was not the god she had anticipated. Though he had awesome powers, Crane was only a kind, ordinary man, pale, bandaged, afflicted with a sickness that was soon to cause his death. Suddenly she felt embarrassed for having burst in on him. Phrases she had prepared seemed all at once stilted. Such a man could not be impressed by her emotional exclamations. Halting herself in mid-sentence, as she was describing her immigrant woes, she waited for him to speak; and when, in his surprise, he remained silent, evaluating or simply absorbing her astonishing recital, she blurted out an apology, handed him a copy of *Hungry Hearts*, and walked out.

For days she worried about her stumbling performance. She accused herself of being a fool. Instead of talking to him as one human being to another and eliciting sympathy, she had completely forgotten herself in fear, thrusting the book at him without finding out if he would even read it. This despair was abruptly interrupted on a morning a couple of weeks later by a phone call from Miss Forbes, advising Anzia to run out and buy a copy of any Hearst paper.

Crane had devoted his entire column to their strange encounter, blazoning Anzia's name (misspelled) and the title of her book on the front page of three hundred newspapers across the country:

ANZIA YEZYIERSKA
by Dr. Frank Crane

I got a new slant on America from Anzia Yezyierska

She walked into my office one day and brought the Old World with her. She had not said three words before I saw farther into the heart of Russia and Poland than I had ever been able to do by reading many heavy books.

She was Poland. . . .

She handed me her book, "Hungry Hearts." At first I thought she might have printed it by private subscription, after the manner of the ambitious but unrecognized. But a glance at it showed me it bore the classic imprint of one of the leading publishers.

Then she told her story, told it well, in a way to rejoice the heart of a newspaper person, in a few swift words, of keen beauty, redolent with individuality.

Here was a person, I said.

. . . Here was an East Side Jewess that has struggled and suffered in the desperate battle for life amid the swarms of New York. . . .

Why?

Because she wanted to — write. And that, ladies and gentlemen, is all there is to genius. An undying flame, an unquenchable hope, an inviolable belief that you are God's stenographer. . . .

Anzia Yezyierska wanted to tell what was in her . . . with the passion of a Christian martyr or a Moslem fanatic.

And she did it. Patiently, giving up all things else, she climbed the altar and fed the flame.

. . . With comparatively little education, with no advantages, in a very hail of discouragements, she produced stories that were accepted and paid for by magazines like The Century and The Metropolitan, stories that O'Brien selected as the best pieces of imaginative work for the year, stories that put her at once in the front rank of American authors.

From a sweatshop worker to a famous writer! All because she dipped her pen in her heart.

I kiss your hand, Anzia Yezyierska, for you are more than a queen, you are a Thoroughbred.

Let no man or woman dare to speak or write on immigration that has not read "Hungry Hearts." I have laughed and cried over it, and I lay it down a bit awed, as if I had seen an alien people's naked soul.

First there was the sheer joy of reading that full-length column. "A man who had popularized the philosophies of Plato, Emerson, William James and others in booklets for the masses," she wrote about this moment a long time later, "and he had actually read my book!" He had not only read it, but also, by devoting a column to it, given her instant, money-making fame.

Anzia bought two dozen copies of the newspapers. She tore out the front page of the first one and began underlining certain laudatory passages: "And that . . . is all there is to genius. An undying flame." "I kiss your hand, Anzia Yezyierska."

She sat back briefly to savor the words.

7

FORTUNE

"SINCE THE PUBLICATION of the editorial on Hungry Hearts by Dr. Crane," Anzia wrote to Houghton Mifflin a few days later, on December 5, 1920, "various syndicates have made tempting offers [inviting me] to become a feature writer for their papers. I am not certain if I shall sign up or not but the big money offered has certainly been a terrible temptation to give up fiction for a time . . . become an Ella Wheeler Wilcox and live on easy street for the rest of my days."

Wilcox, a poet and novelist of romantic slush, "the high priestess of platitude," also wrote regularly for Hearst papers and magazines. Syndicate editors may have thought, from Crane's column, that Anzia Yezierska was a sob vendor with similar sentimental fluency. Anzia was not really tempted. Her writing depended on painful emotion recollected. And she constantly reworked the sentences to make them sharper, more painful, the way she felt. Therefore she could not write to order and was terrified of deadlines.

She could never turn out a column a day or a week just by touching the typewriter keys. Crane, who could, had with his ripe prose instantly moved mountains toward her: two Hollywood film companies and the New York Board of Education. The board, which had previously found Anzia too unkempt and too undisciplined to be a certified teacher, now asked her to give a series of readings from her book. The movie companies — William Fox's and Samuel Goldwyn's — were asking about film rights.

"I thought that you and Mr. Scaife would be interested to know," Greenslet read in Anzia's December 17 letter, "that I have been offered $10,000 for the film rights of Hungry Hearts & a contract of 10400 (200 per week) for the next three years to help in the production of those pictures." She must have been remembering — as Greenslet probably was — that she had just in time deleted the clause in her contract that gave Houghton Mifflin a share in the movie rights, if any. Certainly a fortune in those days, the $10,000 offer towered even higher in Anzia's eyes: in the eleven months since she had signed the contract with Houghton Mifflin, the company had paid her two hundred dollars. She was living in a rear furnished room with milk and crackers on the windowsill. "And in the [movie] contract," she continued in her letter to Greenslet, "is a clause that before each film is shown there is to be flashed on the screen the title of the book from which the picture is adapted and author & publisher. As this would add greatly to the publicity of the book, I thought you might see the worthwhileness of increasing the advertising. . . . I have a suggestion . . . that would cost very little and would bring a fortune to both publisher & author."

Keeping Houghton Mifflin informed of the courtship she was receiving elsewhere (sharp contrast to the publisher's meager advance), her letters seemed to prod an indifferent suitor, proving again and again how desirable she was. But Greenslet remained aloof, perhaps because in almost every letter she added a familiar nudge. On December 17:

> Miss Alice Brady [a noted Broadway actress], the star of "Anna Ascends" & Wm. Brady [equally noted theatrical producer] her father have been so impressed by the reading of Hungry Hearts that they invited me to their house to talk over writing a play based on one of the women characters of the book. A meeting has been arranged for me to meet Samuel Shipman the playwright who is to collaborate on this play.
>
> Whether you see your way to take up my suggestion [about more advertising] I hope you or Mr. Scaife will let me talk it over with you when you come to N.Y.

On December 31:

The contract for the film rights of Hungry Hearts is still pending, as there are several picture Co's bidding for it, but I expect to sign up with Wm. Fox, as the enclosed clipping rumors.

In the meantime, I would like to talk over with you more fully Mr. Moses' suggestion for publicity of the book in the Jewish press.

On January 4:

> The proof of the ad for Hungry Hearts which appeared in the Forwaerts is very well done. And I shall be glad to confer with you or Mr. Scaife any time you are ready to take up additional advertising.
>
> . . . Hungry Hearts will be featured at the Wanamaker [department store] book-week which is to take place in April. I have been asked to speak from the platform of the auditorium and to autograph copies of my book.
>
> There's to be a story about Hungry Hearts in next Sunday's *Tribune* by Samuel Abbot and one in next Saturday's Evening Post by Dorothy Scarborough. Also a review in next week's Nation by Carl Van Doren & one in next month's Bookman.

On her own she had distributed these copies of her book and undertaken other impromptu self-promotion to compensate for what seemed to her the inadequate efforts of Houghton Mifflin. Finally, in mid-January:

> I signed the contract for the film rights of Hungry Hearts with the Goldwyn Co. for $10,000. And I start next Thursday for their studio in Hollywood where I shall . . . help with the scenario.
>
> Have you seen the review of Hungry Hearts by Heywood Broun in the Tribune? Dr. Frank Crane has some splendid ideas for advertising the book and he would be glad to talk them over with you while I am away in California.

From his aerie in Boston, the Houghton Mifflin editor unbent enough to send congratulations. He mentioned possible future advertising and made an effort to be charming: "It's two above zero here this morning, and I must confess that California is a pleasant prospect. I envy you!" Then he repeated his advice to this new writer on the right thing to do, implying once more that she ought to stop bothering with business matters. *Hungry Hearts*, benefiting by so much publicity, he wrote, would take care of itself. Now was the time to finish the novel Anzia had been promising. "If we could have the manuscript . . . to publish next Autumn following the production of HUNGRY HEARTS on the screen, you ought to have a really tremendous sale." Since Hollywood had providently given her the wherewithal, he was assuming, her duty now was to art. He urged her to try to produce a preliminary synopsis of her novel immediately so that Houghton Mifflin could take advance orders.

Although working on the novel as requested, Anzia, made confident by her new fortune, stuck stubbornly to the aggressive note:

> . . . I expect the rough draft of my novel to be ready in May. I need not tell you that many publishers and film co's. have approached me with advance payments to sign over to them the book, but you know my awful aversion for signing any contracts that would bind me in any way. Besides I no longer need advance payments. For besides the $10,000 for the film rights, I get 3 times as much for my short stories as I used to get 6 months ago.

> I would be glad to let you have the novel if you take some steps to advertise "Hungry Hearts." Now is the time to do the advertising. . . . Hungry Hearts has received a tremendous amount of free publicity.

She wrote this aboard the train to California at the end of January.

Starting on the four-and-a-half-day journey across the continent — a fast train's time in 1921 — she had a battered old suitcase, a new blue serge suit, and she was riding toward a startling new situation. Prosperity had come too fast to be trusted.

The first approaches from business prospectors and charitable fund drives ready to exploit the new celebrity, the first essays about her in literary magazines, had just begun to appear as she packed for the trip. But from John Dewey had come only silence. Although he was still abroad, she had sent him the book. She was undoubtedly astonished and perhaps angered that, even in China, he could ignore the extraordinary achievement of this book — in a sense, his own achievement — now that its fame had spread so far.

Therefore, when the *Bookman*, aristocrat of literary journals, asked Anzia, as the new authority on immigrants and American democracy, to review three just-published books on the subject, she had taken the unusual liberty of including a book published four years earlier, Dewey's *Democracy and Education*. Comparing it with the other three, she said Dewey's writing was far too abstract. It was the first book review she wrote:

> Since the writing of this book scores of works on democracy have been written, but this solidly packed volume stands out as the source-book of the highest thought on democracy, education and Americanization.
>
> Unfortunately, Professor Dewey's style lacks flesh and blood. It lacks that warm personal touch that would enable his readers to get close to him. He thinks so high up in the head that only the intellectual few can follow the spiraling point of his vision. . . .
>
> One wonders why a man so imbued with the spirit of democracy must use such undemocratic language, and wonders if the reason

> lies in the man himself. . . . Can it be that this giant of the intellect — this pioneer in the realm of philosophy — has so suppressed the personal life in himself that his book is devoid of the intimate, self-revealing touches that make writing human? Can it be that Professor Dewey, for all his large, social vision, has so choked the feelings in his own heart that he has killed in himself the power to reach the masses of people who think with the heart rather than with the head?

Repeating this too-personal criticism, which she had once made to him more gently, she must have remembered his answer — that the book was addressed to philosophers of education and not "the masses of people who think with the heart" — but evidently she believed this would provoke a response at last. At the same time she had written a deeply felt message of thanks to him in a short story, "To the Stars."

This story is about a young immigrant ambitious to be a writer and helped to realize that ambition by a university president who is unmistakably John Dewey. Most of the president's encouraging remarks to the impetuous, adoring young immigrant are either taken from Dewey's published talks on education or seem to be from his letters to Yezierska (which she apparently copied and used again in *All I Could Never Be* and *Red Ribbon on a White Horse*). "To the Stars" was published a few months later in *Century* magazine.

Anzia had sent out these two opposing messages before leaving for Hollywood, expecting to reach him with one or the other. Otherwise, she could not cope with what was happening to her.

Leaving behind the narrow, dark room on the slum street, she had taken the subway to Grand Central. She was carrying a heavy suitcase, and Goldwyn expense money in her purse could have paid for a taxi; but she had yet to lose the old fear of want. At the train gate, until departure time, she kept searching through the crowd of travelers walking by.

> Every man I saw seemed John coming to see me off. If so incredible a thing could happen as my going to Hollywood, surely John . . . could appear. He must know Hungry Hearts was written

> for him. He must sense my need to share my wealth with him even more than I needed him in poverty.
>
> The gates opened. My train was called. I picked up my bundle, started through the gate, still looking back, still expecting the miracle. I could not [believe] . . . that love as great as his had been could ever cease.

Hollywood in 1921 was a small town with palm trees; most of its film people avidly digested their own publicity. Anzia's arrival was a news event created by Goldwyn's publicist, Howard Dietz, an energetic young man who went to the Spanish mission–style terminal in downtown Los Angeles with a couple of reporters and a photographer. When Anzia stepped off the train that sunny California morning in late January, wearing her navy blue serge suit, round felt hat, dark sandals, and with her obvious uneasiness about the porter, she was immediately recognized by the welcoming group.

Although she was about forty, she didn't look it. Disregarding the dark New York clothes, the "sweatshop Cinderella," as Dietz had labeled her in a press release, looked like a healthy young farm woman from Europe, broad-featured, with childlike blue eyes, fair skin, abundant, long auburn hair pinned up in a loose bun, and a strong peasant body. No makeup on her blushing, shiny face, and no apparent social varnish.

She was obviously pleased by this reception. Publicity, reporters asking questions, were recognition and applause. She enjoyed it, she had worked for it — although in a guarded corner of her mind she knew it was artificial and even vulgar. With Dietz prompting, she gave the reporters a dramatic, exaggerated description of the "cockroach boss," her "starved," oppressed fellow workers in the ghetto sweatshop from which she had escaped. She talked in her throaty, emotion-filled voice about years of loneliness ("my poverty had a bony hand") at a typewriter in a dingy furnished room, and the hundreds of "killing" rejection slips that had preceded this moment.

But when a reporter asked, "What are you going to do with all that money?" she stopped talking. In fact, as soon as she had received the check in New York — $10,000 minus the agent's fee, a fantastic sum then, which could have answered her every need — it began melting away. As she placed it in the bank, she was immediately reminded of spoken and unspoken expectations from friends, relatives, even strangers. And there were her own, even greater, expectations.

In the newspapers that night and the next morning, with her picture in the navy suit and hat as illustration, it boiled down to: "FROM HESTER STREET TO HOLLYWOOD" and "SWEATSHOP CINDERELLA WINS FORTUNE IN MOVIES." Below in the text she read with surprise the twists and changes of her own words. Dietz, delighted with Anzia as a news-getter, had brought the newspapers to her office.

Most writers were not as exploitable. More than that, he found her so enthusiastic about the wonders she had witnessed during her first day in the studio that he suggested she write these glowing impressions for magazines, incidentally mentioning the movie they were making of *Hungry Hearts*. Anzia, flushed with first-day excitement, must have agreed. Dietz sent her a memo the next day summarizing, and offering assistance on, three hackneyed ideas he said they had discussed — about the movies versus real life — and "which you are to write and submit in your own name to the better type of magazines." But overwhelmed by her new experiences, she never had time to follow through.

She was carried along, those weeks, on the giddy crest of unaccustomed popularity; she was the newest attraction in the studio commissary. People working at Goldwyn — writers, directors, production assistants — came up to congratulate her and introduce themselves, inviting her to lunch or dinner, or screenings. Everyone she met seemed to be hoping, by getting close, to absorb some of the invisible magic she radiated: Success.

When she wrote about this later in *All I Could Never Be* and *Red Ribbon on a White Horse*, she lingered on the Hollywood luxuries with which she had been tempted. Having lived a Spartan existence for the preceding three years, having made the same cross-country trip to her sister sitting up all the way on a slow train, her time in Hollywood's sun seemed luxurious by contrast. But the laconic telegrams about Anzia between the Goldwyn office in New York and Goldwyn himself in California show that the temptations they provided on the way to Hollywood were budget priced:

DAVIS SAYS YEZIERSKA NOT ACCUSTOMED TO LUXURIES

THEREFORE ONLY FURNISHED HER WITH LOWER BERTH.

ARRANGE HER RETURN TRANSPORTATION ACCORDINGLY

Economy was the argument of Goldwyn's financial partner in New York, a man who was said to have earned his share in Goldwyn Studios as a war profiteer. With his knowledge of the market, he had been against making "a Jewish epic." Goldwyn, who had looked at the book instead, argued that it would make "a great Americanization picture." The New York man, after signing a contract with Anzia, at Goldwyn's request, to help write the screenplay, suggested a modest Hollywood hotel for her stay. The studio put her into a suite at the Miramar, then the luxury beach hotel of movie stars. In the course of filming *Hungry Hearts* (which Anzia innocently believed she would be able to control), the two opposing philosophies collided behind her back.

At first, in the Miramar's glittering dining room, she gloated: "I could treat myself with a full hand because a millionaire corporation was paying the bills." But she soon became uncomfortable at being waited on. Not only by the waiters — there were the doormen, bellhops, chambermaids, switchboard operators, and elevator men, all expecting tips. At the studios there was her private secretary. These unwanted servitors turned her into an exploiter-capitalist, her Rand School friends would have told her. Her father had called it Babylon (his condemning term for Hollywood).

Two days after her arrival, she moved out of the hotel to her sister Fannie's comfortable home on Wilton Place in Hollywood. Along with the soul she may have regained by halting the indulgences, she banked Goldwyn's expenses money, about $200 a week.

Movie-style luxury was not to her taste. But at first she was thrilled by the welcoming friendliness of the film writers she was meeting, eminent successes whose names — Elinor Glyn, Gertrude Atherton, Rupert

Hughes, Alice Duer Miller — she had long seen on magazine covers and book jackets. When she had been living on crackers and milk and struggling for words, she had often read their glittering, seductive stories in the popular magazines at the library, and she had fervently wished for the ease and frequency with which they produced best-sellers. Now she found it unsettling to be accepted by these veteran professionals as a fellow writer. What had she to say to them?

She was of course a curiosity with her book about the ghetto underclass. An exotic taste of reality in a place where fake was usually preferred. A newcomer not yet reeducated by money. Some of these writers appreciated, for the moment, the tonic of her honesty, and so, "For once in my life," Anzia wrote about this happy interval, "I was part of everything." It took her only a little while to lose her euphoria about "these lovely, important people," and the illusion of their comradeship. At the first party to which she was invited, the Olympians turned into hucksters before her eyes. With dismay, she observed them as they relaxed after dinner and a few drinks, boasting to each other about royalties, contracts, business deals they had made, how to sell the same "property" twice and three times, outwitting the studio bosses. "Even if I turned myself inside out, I could not compete with the sharp, shrewd barter of those business authors."

Except for Will Rogers. She found an instant rapport with that kind, warmhearted, honest man, who called her "gal" or "sister — I can't say your name," and who spoke as simply and directly as she did. He befriended her, inviting her to his family ranch, probably because he recognized a fellow peasant. Nevertheless, she and the cowboy star differed widely in their thinking later on, when Anzia (as usual discovering the worm in her apple) started to lecture him and other writers against the Hollywood system of overpaying stars and underpaying her secretary. Rogers reproved her for holding on to her outsider viewpoint, "fiddling the same sad tune" repeatedly. He thought it hypocritical to attack the system that was supporting both of them so lavishly. Reaching the top, where they were, was due not only to talent and hard work, he said, but even more to luck. "Lap up the cream while you can."

Before the end of her stay, Anzia was thus alone again, this time trying to remain honest amid piles of money.

> The familiar feel of the creases in my blouse, my unpolished shoes, the shine of my old skirt reassured me. . . . I was still unchanged. I was still myself.
>
> But can you be yourself with the money from the movies tucked safely in the bank?

And on the other hand, who could turn her back on so much money?

At the end, Anzia could when the issue was forced, in spite of all her contradictory greed, the yearning to escape forever from hunger and loneliness. In fact, her trial in Hollywood was comparatively brief. Although Goldwyn had originally wanted to hire her for "the editorial staff" and his New York agent had talked to her about a three-year contract at $200 a week, Anzia had hesitated, afraid of having to produce stories to order on factorylike deadlines. But she did want to assist on the film of *Hungry Hearts*.

Perhaps because of this hesitation, Goldwyn had changed his mind. If Yezierska, who had seemed to know dramaturgy (she was supposedly writing a play for theatrical star Alice Brady), did not in fact have such experience, there were "no funds for developing inexperienced people." Through his New York office, Goldwyn had asked her instead to come out "immediately" for six weeks, to help with the screenplay of her book. She had promptly reduced it to four weeks because she had begun working on her first novel, for which Houghton Mifflin and other publishers had been strongly pressing her. She couldn't afford to stay away longer. But compared with the loneliness of writing alone, once she got to Hollywood she found herself enjoying the experience of working with Julian Josephson, a sympathetic, veteran screenwriter; and so she was beguiled into trying to find a footing in that quicksand society. She stayed a month and a half longer than she had intended.

All through that time, volumes of Goldwyn publicity were going out to the rest of the country about the East Side Cinderella and about *Hun-*

gry Hearts. In letters to Houghton Mifflin on studio stationery, she enclosed some examples, along with a studio glamor portrait of herself, to suggest more publicity, advertising, and window displays by the publisher. Although still on trial in Hollywood, she was reassured by reviews of her book, most of them highly favorable, which were now appearing in the more intellectual magazines. "She has struck one or two notes that literature can never again be without," said the *Nation*. "It is undoubtedly one of the most brilliant books produced by an adopted American," said *Grinnell Review*. And in March 1921, the appraisal of a more influential literary authority, Edward J. O'Brien, was published in his *Best Short Stories of 1920*:

> When I reprinted "Fat of the Land" last year I stated that it seemed to me perhaps the finest imaginative contribution to the short story made by an American artist that year. My opinion is confirmed by Miss Yezierska's first collection of stories. . . . I know of no other American writer who is driven by such inevitable compulsion to express her ideal of what America might be, and it serves to underscore the truth that the chief idealistic contribution to American life comes no longer from the anemic Anglo-Saxon puritan but from the younger elements of our mixed racial culture.

Such reminders of her stature outside Hollywood, and the bags of fan mail she was now receiving, must have fortified her when she wrote to Houghton Mifflin. While the editors awaited her first novel, their polite answering letters tried in subdued Bostonian ways to placate her. But their repeated queries about the novel could only have made her anxious. Now for the first time she was forced to produce in public, so to speak, and in haste, with everyone watching.

To come to Hollywood, she had interrupted work on the book. She had so far written several scenes and the title: *Children of Loneliness*. It was to be about the children of immigrants who abandoned their parents to become Americans, could find neither friends nor companions of the heart in their new life, and yet could no longer return to the old. While she and Josephson waited for Goldwyn to read and discuss the finished screenplay of *Hungry Hearts*, she tried to go back to the novel — fruitlessly. She wrote and tore up useless efforts. She told herself she couldn't write about Hester Street in the plush Goldwyn office assigned to her and in the glare of the constant publicity she was receiving.

But her sudden failure was frightening, all the more so in that fiercely competitive environment. Everyone at the studio would perceive a loss of confidence. Success and failure, two aspects of the same person, were dramatized every day by the stories one heard or witnessed there. How thin the separation between success and failure — one day you're a star, the next day no one knows you; you can't get into the studio — how false the distinctions made between one day and the next.

Anzia had the rare chance to choose between the two, at the end of her stay. Goldwyn invited her to lunch. She felt the envying stares in the commissary; the others had guessed that Goldwyn was offering Anzia another, richer contract. Perhaps persuaded by his own publicity, Goldwyn wanted to find out what Anzia's next book would be, whether she was really worth a further investment.

In such a situation, Anzia could be a dramatic performer — colorful, forceful, intense. As she had done in her first meeting with John Dewey, and later with Frank Crane and others, she could carry anyone along with her point of view. But she was handicapped just then by a growing discomfort with the moneyed life Goldwyn had to offer. When she tried to tell him about *Children of Loneliness*, she faltered and flunked his test. Still in the chaos of forming the novel, still too mixed up in this story of her own life, she was unable to present it enticingly. "He looked at me from far away, hiding behind his unsmiling business eyes." Goldwyn was used to buying and selling stories. He suggested that, when she had the plot set, she should come to see him again.

A few days later, William Fox, head of a much larger studio, and evidently more of a gambler, offered Anzia a contract without any preliminary synopses. This producer, she recognized, had an East Side immigrant background similar to her own. Even in his magnificent office, she found it easy to talk to him. She didn't have to sell herself. "I know you've got the stuff," he told her. "I know what I can make of you." For the movie rights of everything she wrote for the next three years Fox offered her $20,000 the first year, $30,000 the second, $50,000 the third.

To his amazement, Anzia did not grab his offer. Signing away her writing in advance would invite catastrophe, she believed. But she obviously was tempted. Fox persuaded her to take the unsigned contract with her and think it over. She held on to it for a weekend:

> Twenty thousand dollars, thirty thousand, fifty thousand. Riches! How could I earn all that money working in my slow underground way? I'd have to speed up, cover up with bluff and craftsmanship what I could not create.
>
> To sign or not to sign. To sign and become rich, not to sign and plunge back into poverty . . .

"I can't sign," she told Fox when she returned the contract, and walked out "released from the terrible burden of indecision."

Her visit to Hollywood had not been the triumph she had anticipated. Goldwyn telegrams reveal what happened next to the movie of *Hungry Hearts.* It was, in 1921, a silent movie, the dialogue supplied by intervening "titles." From New York, after she returned in April, Anzia sent further titles to Julian Josephson, which the scenarist incorporated into the script. Subsequently there was a small skirmish in which she was defeated with one telegram: "YEZIERSKA WAS DIFFICULT IN MONEY MATTERS . . . VERY GRASPING," the studio head wired New York; she had already been "generously" paid for her collaboration. Although "WE GLADLY USED" the titles she had sent, "SHE IS NOT ENTITLED TO COMPENSATION."

Having entrusted to Josephson the completion of the screenplay, which she would then edit in New York, Anzia kept nudging Goldwyn's New York office for the finished script. She was shocked to learn it was being edited by others. "I LEFT STUDIO WITH DEFINITE UNDERSTANDING WITH MR. JOSEPHSON I WAS TO BE ADVISED PROGRESS CONTINUITY AND CONSULTED IN DEVELOPMENT SEVERAL PIECES STAGE BUSINESS NOT YET RIPENED OUR MINDS," she wired Goldwyn studio head Abe Lehr:

YOU WILL UNDERSTAND ANXIETY AND SEE DESPITE EXTREME PRESSURE MY OTHER WORK I DO NOT WANT SCENARIO TO APPROACH COMPLETION DIVORCED FROM MY VITAL INTIMATE FEELING ON EVERY DETAIL. IF IT WAS ESSENTIAL FOR ME TO BE CONSTANT TOUCH WITH SCENARIO WRITER CERTAINLY FAR MORE IMPORTANT FOR ME TO BE CONSULTED ON FINE TOUCHES FINISHED CONTINUITY. SURE YOU WILL UNDERSTAND UNLESS POLICY OF MR. GOLDWYN WHICH HAS GIVEN AUTHORS OF STANDING COMPLETE FAITH IN HIM WERE CARRIED OUT IT WOULD ENDANGER ARTISTRY ORIGINALITY AS WELL AS THE MONEY MAKING POWER OF HUNGRY HEARTS.

Lehr sent back a soothing telegram explaining that the script incorporating all her ideas was too long, editing was only for the purpose of cutting it "TO REASONABLE SIZE," and that both versions would be mailed to her for her "VIEWS."

"REASSURE HER . . . NOBODY IS CONTEMPLATING MURDERING HER BRAIN CHILD," Lehr wired Goldwyn's New York partner. For Goldwyn had decreed that this picture was to be "superspecial." That was the earnest intention (though translated differently) of the moviemakers in California and the financial chieftain in New York. After debating whether to film in a ghetto simulated by the studio or the actual site in New York, which would be more expensive, they settled for California. But to get the right director, E. Mason Hopper, shooting was postponed until the fall. Goldwyn meanwhile invited Anzia to help choose most of the cast in New York, many from the Yiddish art theater.

"WE MUST MAKE SUCCESS OF THIS PICTURE ACCOUNT SO MANY PEOPLE HAVING READ STORY," Goldwyn telegraphed Lehr in September, asking him to watch over the filming. "WE WILL BE SEVERELY CRITICIZED IF WE DO NOT MAKE REAL HUMAN AND GREAT PICTURE." Lehr promised to do that, and even after filming began he halted it, at large cost, for artistic reasons — to recast one of the important roles. Anzia, too, offered to travel to Culver City again and help the director, but Lehr advised Goldwyn in New York, "SHE WILL MAKE IMPOSSIBLE A SANE SHOOTING SCHEDULE."

As the work began in late September, however, the filmmakers were dedicated to her story. "HAVE NEVER SCREENED IN ANY SINGLE DAY A FINER OR MORE SATISFACTORY COLLECTION OF RUSHES THAN WHAT WE SAW TODAY," Lehr wired Goldwyn. "OPENING EPISODE HUNGRY HEARTS IS FULL OF BEAUTY AND CONVINCING REALISM." In fact, the movie Hopper filmed of *Hungry Hearts* was deliberately paced, handsomely photographed, the settings somberly realistic. The actors, except for Hollywood-recruited stars Helen Ferguson and Bryant Washburn, looked like ghetto characters. It had a stark, expressionistic, emotional quality, much like the Russian and German art films of that period.

Apparently it was judged too stark by executives viewing the completed work in New York in late January. They ordered a new ending, a telegram explained, to take the heroes and heroines "FROM THE DRAB POVERTY OF REST OF STORY INTO MORE PROSPEROUS SURROUNDINGS WITH THE FIELDS AND FLOWERS THEY HAVE YEARNED FOR IN THE BEGINNING OF PICTURE." Looking at this new ending, filmed to order in California, two other Goldwyn oficials declared it "ENTIRELY UNNECESSARY" and that it "LACKS DISTINCTION OF REST OF STORY." One man suggested, "IF GOOD FORTUNE ENDING ESSENTIAL FROM BOX OFFICE VIEWPOINT" it "COULD BE WRITTEN MORE INTERESTINGLY BY AUTHOR."

The author was not invited to these screenings and conferences. Instead, in March the financial wizard in New York, asking the studio to send him all the "cutouts" of *Hungry Hearts*, announced plans to "polish and trim" the picture. To polish the work of Josephson and Yezierska, he hired a higher-salaried and more commercial writer, Montague Glass, who caricatured Jewish businessmen in magazine stories of "Potash and Perlmutter," "HAVING IN MIND PUBLICITY VALUE OF HIS NAME." It was like hiring the writer of "Amos 'n' Andy" to jazz up *Uncle Tom's Cabin.*

After Glass was signed, Anzia was introduced to him.

> "I hear your book is a great tear-jerker," he said. "With a few laughs to set off the sob stuff, a story like yours could put you on

Easy Street for the rest of your life. It does me good to see some one succeed who deserves success."

Answering the telegraphed objections of the film's director, editors, and producer to what Glass had done, the New York chief said that he and Glass had merely shortened the picture (which he found "draggy and boresome") and inserted some humorous dialogue. He appreciated the feelings of those who had been close to the film, but insisted that "WE ARE CLOSER TO EXHIBITORS."

The craftsmen at the studio still objected. To counter the Glass version of *Hungry Hearts*, they cut and patched together a third version, which they hoped would appease new York. The compromise that was eventually accepted and sent to theaters was a mishmash of opposing ideas. The original, somberly paced film had been cut and chopped up with additional and inappropriate titles to a nervous, jerky rhythm, and then abruptly pulled out of the ghetto at its end to a country cottage with a white picket fence.

Anzia, unaware of all the arguments, saw the film in a private screening room well before its release. Her reaction never reached the American papers, which were then receiving glowing Goldwyn press releases. But she vented her feelings to the interviewer of a British magazine, *Motion Picture Classic*:

> The titles — everyone of them [Julian Josephson and I had] written as carefully as poetry — the dialect that is the heart-rhythm of a people — and they mixed them up, those intrinsic lines, with clap-trap cleverness. . . .
>
> . . . Imagine for me the horror of finding that after my work was done huge Ogres had the power to meddle with the inviolate lines that had been wrought with pain and agony. Little bits of human heart-pictures that took me weeks and months to portray truthfully — *were cut out.* A happy ending was appended. A happy ending! To my story.

The conflict between financial shrewdness and movie art that had squeezed *Hungry Hearts* out of shape eventually squeezed Goldwyn himself out of Goldwyn Studios (later to become Metro-Goldwyn-Mayer). He started his new venture with ads in the trade papers annoucing, as plain Samuel Goldwyn, that he was "no longer associated with Goldwyn Pictures Corporation."

8

S A L O M E

AS SHE SAT AT HER WORKTABLE in New York, trying to bring her thoughts back to her novel, Anzia brooded instead on the phenomenon of Montague Glass, paid richly to put the blight of vulgarity on *Hungry Hearts*.

To Anzia, Glass was "a sleek, smiling man in golfing tweeds and a red-and-black-striped tie" exuding the self-assurance of Success. Whereas Anzia, even in Hollywood, epitomized the terrible self-doubts of Failure. For "betraying" the still unborn story of *Children of Loneliness* to Goldwyn, who had not understood it, she was now struck dumb. "I no longer believed in it. The importance had gone from it." She was, in her gloomy thoughts, also a failure in all her relationships with men, "outside of life. Not a woman — not a writer."

The notes of stern social and self-criticism she had begun to write in Hollywood, while failing to work on the novel, suited her now; she added to them ideas inspired by Glass and other successful writers she had recently met. The notes carried her, suddenly, fortuitously, back to the story she had once outlined for her files and planned to write about her friend Rose Pastor Stokes, the girl who had married for love a man who also happened to be rich, socially prominent, and handsome. Through Thanksgiving Day of 1917, when Anzia was herself despairing, she had listened to Rose's recital of how that much-envied marriage had fallen apart. As Anzia presented it in *Salome of the Tenements*, which undoubtedly reflected some of Rose Stokes's feelings, the failure was caused by a clash of cultures — the husband's cold, repressed, but socially correct behavior colliding with the wife's uninhibited, hot-blooded way of loving.

It was a story Anzia could step into and fill with her own experiences. The ideas she had about Hollywood belonged to this story of Rose Pastor Stokes. Anzia called her character Sonya Vrunsky and began to recreate her as a Salome of the ghetto, invincible in her determination to capture the man she wanted by trickery and lies when necessary, as ruthless as the biblical Salome, who had demanded the head of John the Baptist. Anzia, who had lied to and tricked both her husbands, readily understood the need for trickery and ruthlessness. She had also known the conflicts between Sonya's hope for an ideal marriage and her realization of its falsity.

Long before reaching Hollywood, the failure of Success had been the theme underlying all her writing. The short stories of *Huntry Heart*, each told in a different way of spiritual hunger, the yearning for an ideal love that could not be appeased by money, the bitter disenchantment with "the fat of the land." Because she was nevertheless still ambivalent — rejecting Babylon even while she desired its riches — she fell upon the theme of Salome with a new recognition.

"The deeper, the finer you are the more you realize the vulgarity the sordidness of success." She put this sentiment into the mouth of Sonya's friend Gittel, the unloved, lonely spinster with whom Anzia must have felt some kinship, too. (She was modeled after Anzia's friend Irma Lerner, a would-be actress who had been a fellow student at the Academy of Dramatic Arts and had become a *Variety* reporter. Anzia actually obtained the role of Gittel for her in the movie later made of *Salome*.)

"I'm an American — not a crazy Russian," Sonya replies scornfully to Gittel's dirge. "I want the vulgar sordidness of success."

"Wait . . . till you get a little older," answers Gittel. "What else is there in life but failure if you're deep enough?"

Putting side the novel she had intended to write, *Children of Loneliness*, and goaded by increasing pressure from publishers and editors, Anzia rushed into *Salome of the Tenements*. On this novel she was able to work in a fury of haste, whole scenes emerging with turbulent emotion, almost as fast as she could write them — the way it had been in the beginning, when she was just discovering "The Fat of the Land."

"I am a Russian Jewess, a flame a longing," says Sonya-Anzia about herself, ". . . a soul consumed with hunger for heights beyond reach. I am the ache of unvoiced dreams . . . the unlived lives of generations stifled in Siberian prisons."

Sonya's real-life counterpart, Rose Pastor Stokes, had in common with Anzia a background of poverty as a Jewish immigrant; they both had red hair, an emotional recklessness, and a love of beautiful clothes. Stokes's sensational front-page romance had given her the opportunity for luxury, making her an even more dramatic Cinderella than Anzia. But her continued dedication to social-political causes made her unlike either Anzia or Sonya.

It was therefore only the externals of Stokes's life and mannerisms, but mostly Anzia's traits, that went into the vivid personality Anzia created for Sonya — intent on conquest, brushing past flunkies and secretaries, on her way to reach the important people she needed.

Graham Stokes, renamed John Manning in the book, sometimes seems, in Anzia's portrayal, the prematurely gray-haired Arnold Levitas, who in his Germanic formality and conventionalism was to Anzia virtually Anglo-Saxon compared to her excitable, passionate nature. Arnold had demanded from his wife (as does Manning in the novel) a decorous behavior and a keen, wifely attention to dinner-table entertaining, both of which Anzia had only briefly pretended before marriage. But in many scenes Manning also resembles John Dewey, the Puritan against whom Anzia-Sonya illogically vents her rage when she realizes that "she loved a high-souled saint — a John the Baptist — a man without blood in his veins." This cool-tempered idealist, feeling isolated from humanity, like Dewey, regrets his inability to be warm and spontaneous. Yet, as Dewey had once done, he tries to control his infatuation for Sonya by escaping out of town; and Sonya explodes: "The coward! . . . The milk-and-water philanthropist! . . . He ran away to Washington like a thief in the night — only because he's scared of me — scared of the breath of love."

The rage and lust and need Anzia poured into *Salome* probably came from feelings she had stored up over three years for John Dewey, feelings she had recognized only after his departure. Like her ambivalence toward money and fame, now that she'd had a taste of them, Anzia's attitude toward Sonya seems to have wavered as she progressed in the writing — at first condemning her, but in the end justifying this shameless, shockingly successful Salome.

ANZIA WAS HERSELF in an anomalous situation just then, a modern Midas unable to use her accumulating wealth. The Hollywood publicity kept multiplying the sums she was supposed to have received. She appeared to be highly successful and rich; and so she was besieged with invitations, "nonprofit" requests for her writing, and financial offers. Former acquaintances, old friends, and complete strangers asked for "loans"; and "any cry of justice, any political, social cause tried to get my name," she remembered years later. "At first I didn't know how to say no, because all the offers that came to me interested me."

Although to save her time and thought for writing her novel she had to reject most of the proposals, those offering her more money always gave her second thoughts. In 1921, when a large loaf of bread cost ten cents and a quart of milk about eighteen cents, she had ostensibly earned enough from Hollywood to support herself in moderate, schoolteacher's comfort for eight or nine years, maybe longer if she lived according to her usual frugality. But anticipating a sizable check for the first book sales of *Hungry Hearts*, she had followed the financial advice of her film agent, R. L. Giffen, and as she explained to Ferris Greenslet in a May 2, 1921, letter, all her movie money had been "invested so tightly that I can't draw on it."

She was therefore writing Greenslet to ask for the book royalties reported in a statement he had sent her on April 28. "I did not know that you pay four months after the statement is issued," she wrote in surprise, "and I would appreciate it if you would send me the check now instead of September." It was no use. Explaining "the sound principle upon which the deferred payment of royalties is based," Greenslet answered that the company was sorry to say no in her case, "but in justice to many other authors," he could not oblige her.

The amount, too, had been a shock: $260.95. Even adding the $200 advance she had received on publication, her total royalties for the six months ending March 31, 1921 (for a sale of 3,500 books, according to Greenslet), were startlingly below her expectation. So, while she was receiving letters from all over the country begging for some of her newfound gold, she was living in threadbare poverty in a cheap furnished room in Greenwich Village and rushing to finish *Salome*. Six months later, when it no longer mattered, Greenslet ignored the deferment principle (perhaps because Anzia had just sent him the manuscript of her novel) and on October 27 mailed her a check of $62.25 for the six months ending September 30.

But whether or not her money had been available to her, she would have been equally uneasy. Since adolescence, when she was trapped in ghetto sweatshops struggling against her parents' Old World edicts, money had meant liberation — and also, as her father saw it, the source of sin. Now even relatives, children of her brothers and sisters, had started coming to her for help. She felt threatened; with their importunities, they could pull her back. Yet only a few weeks earlier, at the Goldwyn studios, as she read the first begging letters ("You have been poor yourself—you can understand my desperation"), she had been choked with guilt for being so rich, for profiting so indecently by writing about the poor.

Some of this internal debate is threaded into *Salome of the Tenements*. Anzia had started the novel to show the truth about Sonya-Salome and, in a sense, about herself: Sonya was a bitch; she reaped what she had sown. But in the writing, her viewpoint changed. She depicted Sonya's hardness, egotism, and conquering strength. A woman intent on having her way, contemptuous of weaker creatures, she had seduced Manning; and then, having suffered from his coldness, she discovered his inadequacies and angrily turned her back on him. In the end, however, Anzia justified Sonya as an artist (clothes designer) more honest, more alive and creative than Manning and the other moralists, more generous and, above all, true to herself. Sonya seems to have become Anzia's alter ego, acting more boldly and outrageously than Anzia dared.

Salome of the Tenements, written in haste, turned out to be a novel of strong dramatic scenes, in fact, of melodrama, embracing its ghetto characters—peddlers, housewives, intellectuals—with a rich, lusty gusto and humor, sharpening with enjoyment the collision between Lower and Upper East Side. The writing is uneven—much of it is vivid and forceful; much of it, mixed with overripe bathos, is pulp. But it flows! Once started, the flow of the sentences is so insistent that it's hard to pull one's eyes away. After the manuscript reached Houghton Mifflin, it was read and turned down in less than two weeks. On November 8, 1921, Greenslet wrote to Anzia, expressing the company's regrets and explaining:

> . . . the book is not an entire success. It has undoubtedly many admirable qualities, of intensity, and emotional effect . . . you have not quite succeeded in making Walling [an earlier name for Manning] a convincing person. The portrait of Sonya, self-centered, grasping, and entirely selfish, is unquestionably done with power. But the character is so unattractive, not to say repellent, that it seems to us likely to handicap the success of the book.

Perhaps the letter gave Anzia a painful jolt. She must have been dismayed — briefly. But her mail and phone and literary encounters were effectively counteracting the Houghton Mifflin verdict. Other publishers were jostling each other in the wings. Her career seemed to be booming. Interviews in newspapers and magazines and other mentions in book columns and literary reviews indicated her name could sell anything just then. She had the confidence and the audience to express her impolitic views freely in these interviews:

> Sex is a universal fact. Its manifestations, however, are ignored in the pages of respectable magazines. For myself, when I write about the Oriental woman [Sonya, for example], I cannot depict her as being as sterilized as the Anglo-Saxon.

She seemed to be challenging Greenslet in the strident tone of that flapper era, a tone that would surely offend him. And:

> Poverty is dirty. But dirt is a disagreeable thing that American writers ignore. I cannot ignore it. In describing a child of the tenements, for instance, I want to be free to say that it is bitten by vermin.

There she was turning her back on Hollywood. The disappointments she had encountered in both directions seemed to have sharpened her views. When, a few days after Houghton Mifflin rejected her manuscript, she was the invited speaker at a social workers' conference on "proper housing for working girls," she lashed out at her audience. She told them about being refused help by their agencies when she herself was homeless and poor.

> There is an unbridgeable chasm between living through such a condition and sitting here comfortably and reading it in reports. . . . I suppose there are a certain number of girls you reach through your activities, but it is small in comparison to the number who approach you and find utter lack of understanding. It's like talk-

> ing to dead walls to talk to some of the people in charge of your organizations.

She spoke for a still larger group of the oppressed in other interviews. Perhaps because of the deference she was getting, even from those she scolded, she had come to feel that she was the voice of "my people," and the generations before them, "generations sent to Siberian wastes," or trapped in ghetto sweatshops on the Lower East Side. And sometimes Anzia appeared in print as a young revolutionary, ready to shake up "the old Anglo-Saxon group" in literature.

Writing a long letter to the *New York Times Book Review* (published in two full-length columns), she attacked a prominent academic and writer, Brander Matthews, for his unfavorable review of Ludwig Lewisohn's *Up Stream*:

> To us newer Americans, *Up Stream* is not merely a book . . . it is our struggles, our hopes, our aspirations and our futures made articulate. It is the cry of young America to old America not to confine literature, education and thought to the formula of a small group. *Up Stream* is a dynamic protest against the sanctification of a priestcraft in education, a revolt against the existence of an Anglo-Saxon intellectual aristocracy. . . .

To improve the argument, she borrowed, without credit, phrases and sentiment from one of John Dewey's speeches:

> It is the glory of America that it is not composed of a single race, one single strain like the other nations of the world. . . . No one racial group, no matter how early settled in this country, can furnish more than one note in this vast symphony of nations. It is what lifts America high above all other nations that the least of the last comers have their share to contribute. . . . But the old-minded men in control of many of our colleges still think in terms of . . . that group of Anglo Saxons for whom the colleges were first created.

Anzia's stories were appearing, during these months, in leading magazines — *Century, Harper's, Scribner's.* The stories were actually parts of her earlier, unfinished novel, *My Own People*, which she had broken up into short segments because she needed the money. Meanwhile, she was busy revising *Salome of the Tenements*, with the help of an editor provided by the Boni and Liveright Company.

Almost immediately after the Houghton Mifflin rejection, Anzia had sold *Salome* to this comparatively new, lively young publishing firm. Boni and Liveright was an upstart compared to Houghton Mifflin, but its best-known partner, Horace Liveright, a Jew like Anzia and prominent in literary café society, had been quick to court her and acquire her prospective novel. Anzia was so charmed and grateful for his appreciation and help (what a contrast to Greenslet!) that she dedicated *Salome of the Tenements* to him.

She was not repelled by the character she had created. Whether stung by or indifferent to Greenslet's comments, she was now in a mood of defiance against Anglo-Saxon gentility. As she revised, she continued to depict instances of Manning's rigidity and formalism. His stiffness contrasted with and dramatized Sonya's spontaneity and ardor, the healthy vitality of her instincts when finally she leaves him. But perhaps because of Greenslet, Anzia added a surprising final scene in which Manning comes to Sonya, begging her to return. Although Sonya chooses not to go with him, she expresses remorse and compassion:

> So at bottom we're all alike, Anglo-Saxons or Jews, gentleman or plain immigrant. . . . When we're hungry, we're hungry.
>
> Till now, Manning had been to her a shadow, an echo of a human being — that had no life — no fire from within.
>
> She had thought of him going through the years making speeches in educated language, using handed down words in high sounding phrases that were as empty, as meaningless as the scientific goodness of his settlement work.
>
> Now he was real. He was human.
>
> A newborn sense of humility came . . . to her. . . .

She saw how men and women helplessly and unknowingly destroy themselves and each other in the blind uprising of . . . passion.

THE FILMING OF *Hungry Hearts* was completed in the fall of 1921. Two months later, Goldwyn Pictures held private screenings in its New York offices. Anzia could invite whom she wished. Despite her disappointment over the intrusion of Montague Glass, it was still a triumph to have her work magnified on the screen. She decided, in a sudden inspiration, to invite Dewey, whose return to Columbia University from the Far East had been reported in the papers.

His voice on the phone was cool, indifferent, almost testy. It had been three and a half years since their last conversation. He said politely that he was too busy, he would be giving a lecture at the time of the screening. And then he paused and with a hint of his former voice spoke more softly: "My letters. Will you return them to me?"

She was shocked to realize that he still felt endangered! But she had to keep the letters.

Anzia filled the screening room anyhow with family, friends, and other people she wanted to impress.

GOLDWYN PICTURES CORPORATION
469 Fifth Avenue
New York

Jan. 16

My dear Mr. Levitas,

The private showing of "Hungry Hearts" will take place next Monday afternoon, January twenty-third at three-forty-five, at the private projection room of the Goldwyn studio, 469 Fifth Avenue. I am most eager that Louise should see the picture as it will not be shown in theatres till next Sept. I have purposely had them show the picture after three in the afternoon so as to make it possible for you to bring her down. Would it be possible for you or your mother to bring her to the studio? . . . I feel you will find it worth your while to see this. . . .

Sincerely,
Anzia Yezierska

Louise was nine years old then. Coming down with her father by subway from the Bronx to the sumptuous movie offices, she was of course impressed. Arnold's feelings about the blatant evidence of his ex-wife's success can be surmised. He never told his daughter how strongly he disapproved of her mother's character, but it was easy to read in his face whenever he mentioned Anzia. It must have rankled this honorable man to see misconduct so extravagantly rewarded. And yet, for both Louise and her father, who were rapt, weekly moviegoers, the fact that Helen Ferguson and Bryant Washburn, two clean-cut, handsome, well-known movie stars, were actually speaking Anzia's written words (never mind the unwashed ghetto types and murky ghetto scenes making up the rest of the movie) — this fact was powerful, incontrovertible, overwhelming.

ONE OF THOSE PURSUING ANZIA for reprint rights to her new novel was Bernarr Macfadden, the health-conscious publisher of *Physical Culture, True Story, Movie Weekly,* and other pulp magazines. He was frequently photographed bare to the waist, with muscles glistening. Without seeing Anzia's new manuscript, while she was still writing it — "Your name will sell it," he said confidently — Macfaddden ofered her $5,000 to serialize the book in *Beautiful Womanhood* and another $100 a week to write a one-page article each month for the same magazine and for giving him "the advantage of your viewpoint on . . . any of our . . . publications." He offered her an office "to use at your convenience" but also suggested she could give her viewpoint verbally at a monthly lunch with him. Anzia took the $5,000 and, once the book was out, divided it into six installments for *Beautiful Womanhood*. She rejected the rest of the money offer, probably because she found even such lenient deadlines too demanding; and because she soon lost interest in Macfadden's vigorous pulps.

Salome of the Tenements was published in November 1922, collecting both highly favorable and strongly adverse reviews. Carol B. Schoen, in her recent literary biography of Anzia Yezierska, observed that *Salome* "seemed deliberately to set out to attack" its potential audience.

> As if in reaction to the Hollywood myth about herself as a Cinderella, Yezierska created an antimyth which rejected the sentimentalized vision of the poor but virtuous immigrant girl who . . . marries the kind American millionaire. . . . [She] revised [it] to show the scheming duplicity of a heroine who used every trick she could think of to trap a wealthy husband only to find that . . . they will not automatically live happily ever after. . . . At the same time Yezierska retained many stereotypes that accentuated the less attractive aspects of Jewish immigrants so there was, in effect, something in the book to offend everyone.

Two critics said the book was a work of genius. "An orgy of emotions . . . poetized chaos" but "shot through with genius," said the *New York Tribune* critic. "Handled by any other novelist addicted to Hebrew themes, the [story of the novel] would hardly have risen above the level of light comedy. Anzia Yezierska has passed it through the sieve of her astonishing temperament and produced a work of art — sentimental, illogical, hysterical, and naive, but still a work of art."

Gertrude Atherton, then a highly successful novelist, wrote a Sunday feature for the *New York Herald* ("Fighting Up from the Ghetto") in which she declared that, although the book had many faults, the author "is the most remarkable case of sheer genius fighting its way through an impenetrable thicket and imposing itself upon an unsympathetic world that I have any knowledge of. . . . This flaming and burning of elemental passion is the main characteristic of 'Salome of the Tenements.' It is one of the few in the yearly deluge of novels that one can never forget."

Perhaps it was because Anzia's style of writing and subject matter challenged respected traditions at that time ("an impenetrable thicket") that she received throughout her career such unusual tributes and assistance from honored and established writers. There had been Mary

Austin's generous offer to help. Later there were Jim Tully and, in particular, Zona Gale, who went out of her way to befriend Anzia. Now, on behalf of *Salome*, there was Atherton, well into her sixties and long since famous for the historical novels she had written (for instance, *The Conqueror*, on Alexander Hamilton). Atherton had just finished a new novel, *Black Oxen*, to be published later that year, about an aging woman who regains her youth through rejuvenation treatments. It became a sensational best-seller.

Another important writer who hailed *Salome* was James Harvey Robinson, an innovative and controversial historian who later brought about significant changes in the teaching and writing of history. He had been one of John Dewey's liberal colleagues at Columbia and had left the university to help found the New School for Social Research. His book *The Mind in the Making*, a history of ideas, published a year earlier, had been on the *New York Times* best-seller list since that time. Of Anzia's book, he wrote in the *Literary Digest International Book Review*:

> There is a great gulf fixt between the so-called sciences of human relations and the overwhelming facts. I wish that every sociologist and social psychologist and miscellaneous moralizer might read "Salome of the Tenements" — might not only read it, but put it in his pipe and smoke it, until its wild fumes so beclouded his facile, pompous generalizations and academic abstractions that he would never again suspect them of answering any degree to the actual heartburnings of the creatures which he pretends to explain.

After detailing the plot of *Salome* as an illustration of what actually happens in real life, in contrast to "academic abstractions," Robinson added approvingly: "Miss Yezierska possesses a vivid and colorful style and a varied honesty rarely equaled in our American fiction. Hitherto few of our writers have dared to be quite as explicit as she is."

These critics were contradicted and far outnumbered by the rest, who strongly disapproved of Sonya. Scott Nearing, in the *Nation*, called *Salome* "an unwholesome book" and Sonya "a devouring monster." Conceding that it was nevertheless "vivid" and "in places . . . well done," he added that "Sonya exhibits a depravity of spirit and an incapacity to live and let live that rivals the degradation of Balzac's most admirable villains." The *New York Times* critic was similarly offended on moral and aesthetic grounds and tried to correct Anzia's understanding of her own protagonist: "[Sonya] is an illiterate, hot-blooded little savage, tossed here and there by the tempest of her own whims and passions, utterly unscrupulous, yet with a longing which is often pathetic for the restraint and cultivation she so entirely lacks, and tries to convince herself that she despises."

Other critics focused on the book's artistic failings. The *American Hebrew* critic wrote: "Those who welcomed 'Hungry Hearts' as a work of genius, wrought with understanding, emotion and art . . . and who waited for more than a year after Boni & Liveright first announced the publication of Anzia Yezierska's second book and first novel, are bound for disappointment. . . . In attempting the smooth flow of stylistic construction, [she] has stilted her talent."

The reviews were a harsh blow to Anzia. Perhaps warned by Greenslet's critique a year earlier in rejecting *Salome*, and the opinion of some friends to whom she had shown the manuscript, she had tried to prevent what she considered such misinterpretations. She confided to book columnist Burton Rascoe that, before *Salome* came out, she had personally visited book critics to explain her work to them. Rascoe quoted her in his weekly *New York Tribune* report:

> People in the Ghetto are high-strung, inarticulate. They are so hungry for little bits of sympathy, love and beauty; they are like children; what seems hysterical or overemotional to Anglo-Saxons in them is a natural state, because they feel so deeply and are not educated enough to articulate their emotions. I tried to explain this; but just what I feared would happen did happen. . . . I was nearly driven out of my head by what they said about my book.

Sonya, according to her creator, had been entirely misunderstood by the critics who described her as "coarse, harsh, relentless, cruel."

> She is none of these things. I know that she cheats and lies and does things she should not do. She does them because she is a higher soul, not a lower one. . . . She has touched the heights of love. . . . If she were less big, she would not do these things.

For the sake of her book, Anzia also wrote once more to Mary Austin, despite a break of almost two years in their acquaintance. She wrote of her pain and suffering at the hands of Heywood Broun, the "insensate brute" who had savagely derided *Salome*: "And I suddenly thought of you, I felt that although you're an American, you would understand the language of the people of my book and that you would help me either by answering Heywood Broun or by writing a review."

Austin evidently did neither. But James Harvey Robinson, who had written favorably about *Salome*, was unusually helpful to Anzia at that time. She told Rascoe:

> I was afraid of [literary people]. . . . Then Dr. Robinson, who is so kind and wise, told me that the trouble with me was that I had an inferiority complex and that the reviewers had inferiority complexes, too, but of a different order. They are like little children trying to be grown-ups, he said, and to keep their jobs they had to appear to be all-knowning and all-wise, while I am afraid and taken in by their superior air.
>
> He told me not to worry about what they said, not to pay attention to them, but to have confidence in myself and go ahead and do my best to be myself. That is a great load off my mind.

Rascoe, who thus quoted Anzia, was persuaded by the fairy tale she had woven about herself. "Miss Yezierska is an extremely emotional, acutely sensitive woman with almost no mental discipline or training and only a meager education, who has somehow managed in the stories of hers that I have read to give life and vividness and drama to her pictures of the ghetto."

Whether because of, or in spite of the disapproving critics and their moral objections, *Salome* sold very well. It was so successful after publication and serialization that it attracted movie bids. Famous Players–Lasky, affiliated with Paramount Pictures, paid $15,000 for the film rights — 50 percent more than Anzia had received for *Hungry Hearts*.

Sales of the book had also been boosted by the premiere of the *Hungry Hearts* movie, which opened in New York on Thanksgiving Day 1922 as the holiday attraction of the Capitol Theatre, an opulent movie palace that dominated Broadway. "Widely discussed in . . . the film industry, it is certainly among the notable efforts of the motion picture year," the *New York Tribune* reported in advance. Upon its opening, the film was judged harshly ("tedious" and with "an incredible and mushy ending," the *New York Times* declared), but its faults were ascribed to Hollywood for the product it created "based on Anzia Yezierska's stories." She received only the benefits of the attendant press coverage. A special movie edition of the book *Hungry Hearts*, published by Grosset & Dunlap and including photos from the film, was featured in the theater lobby and in bookstore window displays, along with *Salome of the Tenements*.

In this fresh harvest of publicity, Anzia was still the Cinderella of newspaper feature stories. Her waiflike letters two years earlier to the Houghton Mifflin publicity department, of how she had "plunged into [writing] . . . without guide or compass" and how she had begged for a scullery maid's job at the Waldorf-Astoria, were once more being quoted in full.

During all this public celebrating of her literary achievement, Anzia's correspondence with Houghton Mifflin's Greenslet had abruptly ceased. There had been an eight months' silence following his rejection of *Salome*. Silent or not, since that time, by her publicized triumphs elsewhere, she had been in a sense thumbing her nose at his moralistic judgment. Then on July 15, 1922, she wrote him a terse letter of complaint:

> My dear Mr. Greenslet,
>
> I see by the M.A.B. [*Mainly about Books*, a trade newsletter] that Hungry Hearts is to be published in England. I am surprised I

have not been notified. Will you kindly let me know how it has been arranged, royalties, etc.

Although he had not informed her — an indication of their strained relationship since *Salome* — Greenslet had in fact arranged for the English publication three months earlier, in April. He may now have expected thanks for his efforts, some expression of delight at being published abroad, for he answered her curtly: "After a good deal of difficulty, I finally persuaded Mr. Fisher Unwin to take a first edition of 1,000 copies of 'Hungry Hearts.'" Then he detailed the royalty agreement, ending with none of the usual polite flourishes except for his "Faithfully yours."

Another year passed before Anzia wrote to Greenslet again. She had been working in the meantime on short stories, some of which she had begun before *Salome*, and now she had other editorial advisers; she didn't need Greenslet or Houghton Mifflin. To a new literary star like Anzia, book and magazine publishers gladly provided such help; and besides, although she was still living vicariously through her writing, and frugally too, in the Village, she could readily attract nonprofessional helpers (she always had). It might be a bright young person who lived next door or who worked in the library or the tearoom where Anzia lunched, and who would be thrilled by acquaintance with a fascinating, famous writer. Anzia gave such a person, usually a young woman, small sums for editing or typing (and sometimes also for mending and doing errands). In addition, she would give her tea and free new books (which Anzia received from publishers as a writer's due); she would listen to the girl's problems, offering highly unorthodox advice, and would pull from her by exhausting interrogation the words and insights she could make use of.

"She devoured you," one of these former helpers recalled of her youthful association with Anzia. "She seemed to need to get inside you, to experience your ideas, sensations, mode of living."

From this young woman, for instance, Anzia developed and wrote a pulp story called "Love Hunger," later published in *Metropolitan*, about the girl's search for and close encounters with love. "I am a handsome, American girl of 24," it begins. ". . . Men tell me that I have the innocent face of a child looking out of a woman's body. I am aware of a radiant aliveness . . . born out of the admiration . . . of many men." At twenty-four, Anzia had not been carefree enough for casual flirtation: now at forty she wrote herself into the life of "a handsome American girl."

Meanwhile, the aborted manuscript of *Children of Loneliness*, left unfinished about twenty months before, when she departed for Hollywood, sat in a bulging envelope on her desk. Its theme of a daughter caught between the emotional ties to her immigrant parents, who wanted to keep her back in their enslaving world of tradition, and the equally strong liberating pull of the new world where she was still a forlorn outsider — this theme had range enough for a long novel. But as a novel Anzia could not write it now. She took it out of the envelope and showed it to a new friend, Clifford Smyth, a *New York Times* editor she had recently met. With his encouragement and advice, she now turned the main part of the manuscript into a long, novelistic short story. It appeared in *Century* magazine in March 1923.

Two or three other stories she finished and sold during this period (late 1921 to early 1923) may have been intended originally as parts of that aborted novel, because their themes seem to be related. For example, "Brothers" is about a young immigrant working as a pants presser in a sweatshop, saving to bring his mother and brothers from Russia and depriving himself thereafter to help his younger brothers become educated and thus enjoy greater opportunities. Then one of the brothers, now a rich and successful dentist, and ashamed of his peasant family, arranges to keep both the pants presser and their mother away from his wedding. "The Husband They Picked for Rebecca," similarly contrasting the two worlds, is about two sisters: Minnie, who on the Lower East Side rejected a poor poet in order to marry for money and live luxuriously in California (no doubt an approximation of sister Fannie); and Rebecca, who comes from that ghetto to visit Minnie in California. On the visit, Rebecca (surely a stand-in for Anzia) says no to a suitor much like her brother-in-law, one of the "all rightniks . . . Jews dehumanized by their riches. Glutted stomachs — starved souls, escaped from the prison of poverty only to smother themselves in . . . plenty." Rejecting this "desert of emptiness painted over with money," Rebecca returns to the Lower East Side to seek her sister's East Side poet.

IN EARLY 1922, after finishing *Salome*, Anzia stepped out of the prison in which she had jailed herself for the past four years while driving toward her goal as a writer. Now she was deliberately trying out the social opportunities that had all at once opened up for her. She was accepting the invitations to literary teas, luncheons, and dinners.

Warmed by her pleasing new social contacts, flirtations of a sort, with writers, editors, and even some critics, Anzia was blooming. In the 1920s, when fashionable women were wearing flapper styles, chalk-white powder, "cupid's bow" lips, and rouge in spots, she was disarmingly original with her shiny, unpowdered, strong-featured face, challenging blue eyes, auburn hair still uncut, tucked into a slightly disheveled bun. Physically and intellectually, she was an intriguing foreigner on the literary scene. "There is an intensity about this magnetic woman which conveys immediately a sense of her . . . power," wrote a magazine interviewer. "She is expressive in every word and gesture."

Being a newspaper celebrity and being published in *Harper's*, *Century*, *Scribner's*, as well as popular magazines like *Munsey's* and *Metropolitan*, gave Anzia an instant recognition that made it relatively easy to meet those she wanted to know. New York writers and editors were more bohemian, more accepting, less formal than those she had met in Hollywood.

The post–World War I years were a period of experiment and innovation in the United States — and of violent reactions against them. Women's suffrage, ratified by enough states to become part of the Constitution in 1920, was still being voted on and rejected in some states, whereas the Ku Klux Klan and the fifty-four- and sixty-hour work week in factories were calmly accepted. Prohibition, which had been introduced as a wartime necessity, became law as the Eighteenth Amendment the same year. Young women threw off their corsets and ventured into speakeasies. New York City, where Socialist and Communist philosophies could be discussed and even espoused, was a center for the new freedom. The first birth control clinic was opened there by Margaret Sanger in 1922; and Hannah Mayer Stone, Anzia's niece, the daughter of her oldest brother, Max, became its medical director.

In an era without the easy distractions of radio or television, with few automobiles or roads for them, and with no air travel, books and magazines, plays and movies, were far more important than they are today. Publishers could afford to try out radically different new ideas in writing. The literary scene into which Anzia stepped from her previous isolation boasted Sherwood Anderson, Sinclair Lewis (*Babbitt* was published in 1922), Willa Cather, Scott Fitzgerald. And on Broadway *Abie's Irish Rose* had recently opened. Anzia was possibly still too grave for that buoyant, extravagant time; but the hedonistic, self-centered heroine of *Salome* could speak for her appropriately. Also heralded in 1922 was John Dewey's new book, *Human Nature and Conduct*, which collected the lectures he had given at Stanford in the spring of 1918, when he and Anzia were still in close correspondence.

From Europe that year came the work of T. S. Eliot (*The Waste Land*), Ezra Pound, A. A. Milne, Bernard Shaw, Virginia Woolf, D. H. Lawrence, John Galsworthy (*The Forsyte Saga*). But copies of James Joyce's *Ulysses*, which had just been published in Paris, were burned by the U.S. Post Office when they arrived in New York.

A poem Anzia had once written about freedom ("I am a spendthrift in love / I am thrifty and wise and prudent in everything but love . . .") was published in August 1922 in *Current Opinion*. She must have taken it from her files in answer to the editor's request. Just as it had expressed her joy in escaping from her confining marriage, so now, as she rediscovered it, the poem reflected her newborn romantic feelings about Clifford Smyth, the first softening of her hard heart after years of emotional deprivation.

Anzia met Clifford Smyth when he, as chief editor of the *New York Times Book Review*, was the preeminent arbiter of new books, and she, recently returned from Hollywood, was the controversial new arrival on the book scene — "society's puppy for the moment." Smyth left the *Times* in 1922 to become editor of the *Literary Digest International Book Review*, another influential publication, and Anzia came to know him better. He was a sensitive editor, able to help her not only with advice about her career, but also and especially by sometimes criticizing and editing her manuscripts.

There was probably a long flirtation. He was older than she, fifty-seven years old in 1923, when Anzia was about forty-two. He was also married, with grown children. For Anzia, he was like Dewey, a quintessential Anglo-Saxon. His aristocratic family traced its tree back to a patriot of 1776. In short, he was the attractive opposite of everything she was.

Extracts from a story she wrote, "Mostly about Myself," with which Smyth must have helped her, and which was later published in her book *Children of Loneliness*, appeared first in the monthly Smyth edited, and in its parent publication, the *Literary Digest*, a newsweekly much like today's *Time* magazine; that year, thanks to Smyth, both magazines also carried a special feature about Anzia and, two months later, a literary appreciation of her personality and work.

All this probably helped to promote *Salome of the Tenements*; and in the publicity, Anzia was sometimes assumed to be very like her passionate, love-torn heroine, Sonya. Perhaps Smyth made this assumption, too. Anzia was, for example, quoted extensively in a three-column story, illustrated with a photo of her, by the *New York Evening Telegram*; the reporter called her a "well-known . . . sculptor of souls and dissector of emotions"—that is, an expert on love and how it affected men and women.

> We asked Miss Yezierska why sixty was the age at which the American man must arrive before he could love. And promptly she answered:
>
> "He is afraid to love before. He is afraid his dignity, his business . . . his life's work will suffer. He is an Anglo-Saxon. . . .
>
> "The Anglo-Saxon is scared of personal emotion. . . . He makes a virtue of cowardice. . . .
>
> "Women are bigger than men, and therefore they dare to give themselves up more to love. . . ."
>
> In her tiny studio apartment in West Ninth Street . . . this re-

American Man Must Be Nearly Sixty Before He Really Loves, Says Novelist

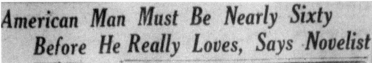

Anzia Yezierska Says His Interest Before That Is Centred in Financial Success.

HIS EMOTIONS ARE GUARDED

Onetime Immigrant Girl Expounds Her Views in Her New Book.

By Elisabeth Smith.

How old is the American man before he really loves?

"At least sixty," comes the arresting answer from Anzia Yezierska, onetime Polish Jew, immigrant girl, now well-known writer of fiction, sculptor of souls and dissector of emotions.

Before he is sixty the American man may climb the heights of financial achievement, but he can never scale the guarded heights of great emotion.

He may sup of success with a big spoon, but he spurns to drink from Eros' magic goblet.

He may clothe [illegible] in finest raiment, but he leaves romance an outcast shivering in rags outside his closely bolted door.

"Love" is a word that has no place in his life's ledger.

At least, so holds Anzia Yezierska who has just offered her public her latest book "Salome of the Tenements," through the medium of Boni & Liveright, her publishers.

We asked Miss Yezierska why sixty was the age at which the American man must arrive before he could love. And promptly she answered:—

"He is afraid to love before. He is afraid his dignity, his business, that his life work will suffer. He is an Anglo-Saxon."

Keynote in Last Sentence.

In her last sentence is found the keynote around which she has built her new novel. In it she holds that love may bloom and blossom in Delancey street, but not in Park avenue. She maintains that romance may ripen in the third floor back of a tenement of the lower east side, while it languishes [illegible]

Anzia Yezierska, onetime immigrant girl and scullery maid in hotel, who, in her latest book, "Salome of the Tenements," declares that the American man must be at least sixty before he really loves.

of the Tenements," and Miss Yezierska turned to certain passages that illustrated the coldness of the Anglo-Saxon with his "paler passions." The plot of the novel is concerned with a beautiful [illegible]

could so sterilize out of their hearts the hunger for men that makes life?"

Critics have spoken of Sonya as coarse, harsh, relentless, cruel. This has grieved Sonya's creator.

Clipping from the New York Evening Telegram, *January 6, 1923.*

markable woman who once worked as a scullery maid in one of New York's biggest hotels and who learned to write English almost as soon as she spoke it, talked of the man of sixty and of love. . . .

"Perhaps occasionally a man may find love when he is younger. He may if he is a poet. A poet knows no age."

"And how old must a woman be?" we asked her.

"Not as old as a man," she replied. "She may be younger, say, forty, the so-called dangerous age. She may be even younger than forty, but no woman under thirty every really loves. The flapper has not an idea of what love is. She is playing at [it]. . . ."

We asked . . . if it were possible to love in the great sense of the word more than once.

"It is possible to love many times," she answered, "and each love may be deep and sincere. It is only by these first, destroying loves that the one real love is born. It rises from the ruins of the earlier loves. . . ."

John Dewey had reached sixty-two by that time, and Smyth was "nearly" sixty.

9

LONELINESS

39 W. 9 St.
May 27 [1923]

My dear Mr. Greenslet,

I am going to England in about ten days and I do not know any people there. I wonder if you would care to give me a letter of introduction to Mr. Haveloc Ellis or anyone else?

Sincerely yours,
Anzia Yezierska

Havelock Ellis, British writer and physician, whose career combined literary and scientific interests, was best known in the United States for his revolutionary *Studies in the Psychology of Sex.* The first volume, published in 1897, had provoked a legal action during which the judge called it a "filthy" book; and in this country, until 1935, sale of the seven volumes was restricted to physicians. Much later Ellis, who was also an early advocate of women's suffrage and birth control, received credit as the pioneer who "tore the veil of ignorance and prejudice from the subject of sex." His was a fresh-air approach, which Anzia herself had espoused in *Salome of the Tenements.* But in the 1920s discussion of sex was still daring in most social circles. Anzia's interest in Ellis was in keeping with her stance as a radical and a rebel, so well exemplified by *Salome*'s freethinking Sonya.

Anzia's request for introductions was her first letter to Houghton Mifflin in almost a year. But Greenslet must have been reading the frequent reports in the literary and daily press about the author he had discovered and the commercial success of the novel he had rejected. He answered promptly and amiably, enclosing a letter to Havelock Ellis, but none for any of the other British authors on the Houghton Mifflin list. However, her publisher in Britain, Fisher Unwin, was ready to supply her with more.

Anzia sailed for Europe, a week-long trip by ship, "to end the turmoil and confusion of my soul," and to meet "real writers." In Europe, unlike in the United States, it had seemed to her, writers would be less dependent on and not so responsive to the marketplace. The U.S. marketplace, for which she had been working assiduously over the past five years, had rewarded her with money, applause, fame, and the accompanying fear of losing it all. Until then, therefore, she had continued to live frugally in a tiny room on Ninth Street in the Village, not yet pausing to spend what she had earned; she still mistrusted her good fortune. As editors pressed for more of her writing, she had been experiencing increasing periods of anxiety about her ability to keep producing stories away from the scenes she was writing about.

Probably it was Smyth who, as her fatherly adviser, had then encouraged her to take the trip. He was himself a member of PEN, a worldwide association of writers. *Hungry Hearts* and *Salome* now gave her admission to that select European circle. Once she got there, however, she was distinctly uncomfortable:

> In London, at the invitation of the English publisher of "Hungry Hearts," I met John Galsworthy, an ardent internationalist, who had started . . . P.E.N., poets, essayists and novelists, dedicated to the post-war dream of peace and good will, regardless of . . . nationality. . . . [The members'] friendly interchange of ideas about what writers can do for one another and for the world [gave me a sharp] feeling of not belonging. They were real people who belonged together in their real world, so sure of themselves that they could think of others.

Anzia, wrapped in herself, had no interest in such an international movement. Meeting George Bernard Shaw, Israel Zangwill, H. G. Wells, John Galsworthy, and others, she hoped not for comradeship, but to learn their secret. How did they write so smoothly, even elegantly, without showing the seams of effort and uncertainty? As a writer, she felt little connection with them at the London gatherings she attended, until she saw the bearded vegetarian, Shaw, at a resplendent dinner table take out and one by one peel three bananas, which he ate casually while everyone else stopped talking.

When she was taken to the home of a fellow Pole, Joseph Conrad, she glimpsed, but did not quite believe, that anguish might afflict such writers, too. Conrad was then an old man, confined to a wheelchair. "[He] pointed to the clutter of manuscripts on his table, and wailed: 'This, on which I have spent long years of labor, will never see print because I won't live long enough to take out the knots.'"

In Paris, where she visited a fellow American, Gertrude Stein, Anzia asked her question more directly, honestly. "Gertrude Stein, in her blunt, brusk way, laughed at me and said, 'Why worry? Nobody knows how writing is written, the writers least of all!'"

Perhaps because she had felt out of place for so long, perhaps out of homesickness, and certainly to save money, Anzia decided abruptly to return to America third class, the way she had first made the trip. "Only by going back to my own people [in 3rd class] could I hope to regain . . . the soul that I had lost with my sudden good luck." But revisiting the lower depths turned into a characteristic Yezierska fable, as reported nationwide by the *New York Tribune* syndicate:

> "You can't be an immigrant twice!" This is the positive assertion of Anzia Yezierska, the Russian immigrant girl who rose from a sweatshop to the position of one of the distinguished fiction writers of the day. . . .
>
> . . . "All the time of my vacation in London and Paris, I was inwardly disturbed by the notion that I was having things so much better than many of my own people. That, first of all, is why I tried to come back in the steerage. I belonged to these people once."

Third class now had tablecloths and other conveniences she hadn't known when she was a nine-year old immigrant thirty-odd years earlier, but it made little difference. As soon as she descended the ship's stairs, Anzia could not overcome her revulsion at the dark, smelly staterooms crowded with travelers who hadn't bathed for weeks, much less the unpalatable conditions in the dining room:

> "Supper was the first meal. And just to see it coming towards me killed my appetite. Plates thrown at you. . . . Bread cut so thick that it took your hunger away. Think of the suffering, if you have sensitive nerves, to see sausage and sauerkraut . . . coffee from big coffee pots. Thick chunks of meat for sandwiches. . . . It was . . . a repast for people from famished countries. . . . There was no attempt at any civilized refinement. . . . But when I gradually took note of the people, and their ways at table, well — . . . I think that table manners are the beginning of culture. . . .
>
> ". . . I felt like a failure. Here I wanted to be one of the steerage and . . . my sense of smell and my sense of sight hampered me."

She was transferred, after one night below, to second class. Comfort and cleanliness, privacy, salads and fresh vegetables daintily served had become necessities — and she had the money for them. "But when I paid the additional fare, the terrible consciousness of life's injustice came upon me. Just because I had the money to pay the difference, I could have all this loveliness, this civilization. . . . Between meals I was down below with the people of the third class . . . much the most interesting people. . . ."

Soon after her return to New York, Anzia reported in another article, written for *Cosmopolitan* magazine: "I moved boldly into a hotel on Fifth Avenue." In *Red Ribbon* she recalled:

> For once I treated myself to the fine expensive things I had always wanted. I . . . transformed the overstuffed hotel apartment into its present austerity . . . bare, unpainted floor, scrubbed to show the grain of the wood, pale-gray walls, plain unpainted furniture: a desk, a chair, an open bookshelf, a low couch covered with monk's cloth. Except for the flowers, it might [be] a nun's cell.

It was a spacious, airy one-room-and-bath apartment on the eleventh floor of the Hotel Grosvenor, at the corner of Tenth Street. In a time when there were no other skyscrapers to interrupt the view, sky and sunlight came from the windows on two sides; below, the windows looked down on a long sweep of lower Fifth Avenue.

But Anzia had not renounced the habits of frugality. When her eleven-year-old daughter, Louise, came to visit on Saturdays, if she stayed overnight she slept on a floor pad, and although they sometimes lunched grandly in the hotel dining room downstairs, they usually ate in modest Village tearooms or cafeterias. Supper or breakfast consisted of food kept illegally on the bathroom windowsill, cooked on a forbidden hot plate, and served from the pot on the only two dinner plates. As a compulsive, habitual rule breaker, Anzia naturally regarded the hotel's doormen and elevator men as tip-hungry spies from whom she occasionally tried to hide these activities.

Her intention to enjoy, at last, a little of what she had earned was always in conflict with the imperative of holding on to pennies. The stark poverty of her childhood and the hungry years when she was becoming a writer still pressed her. Although new books — to read and learn from the work of contemporary writers — were as vital to her as food, Anzia couldn't buy a book or even a magazine. She scrounged them, if possible, from publishers, or else from friends or relatives — often carrying away a volume without even mentioning it.

Accustomed to the embarrassments created by her mother's behavior, Louise never lost the terrible feeling of shame — especially at the Grosvenor, where the uniformed staff was so proper. One Saturday Louise suffered even greater mortification waiting outside a florist shop while Anzia went inside to return a small bouquet; she insisted on getting her dollar back because the friend they had planned to visit was not at home.

But the times Louise stayed overnight at Anzia's were often quite happy. Usually it was a Saturday night when her father had a social engagement. (Her grandmother, now too old to climb the apartment house stairs, had moved to a daughter's home.) Enjoying this respite from solitude, Anzia treated Louise as another adult. Like a farmer, Anzia went to sleep when it grew dark (so that she could take up her manuscript again before sunrise), but she allowed Louise to stay up as late as she liked and read the new books or magazines in a corner under a lamp.

Her daughter had become a nurturing companion, a junior mother. Their conversations might start with Louise's school situation or some secrets (about a boy, perhaps, or a forbidden excursion) she kept from her father, but they always went on to discuss Anzia's troubles, which were mostly about writing. Louise was starting to give admonitory advice. This was because Anzia even then gave her that freedom — in their discussions and in allowing her to read the unexpurgated books (*Jurgen, Ulysses* etc.) on her shelves — that would have shocked and angered Louise's father.

A few times Louise was permitted to listen silently when a newspaper reporter or magazine writer came to interview Anzia — someone who, for instance, really believed that Anzia had once scrubbed floors for a living. Louise would smirk to herself. Not only because Anzia was obviously indifferent to the dust curled under the bed or in corners, but also because she had always found ways to get someone else to do any dreary domestic chores.

BY THIS TIME the interviews were about Anzia's third book, *Children of Loneliness*, which, thanks to Clifford Smyth, was on sale in the fall of 1923, soon after Anzia's return from Europe. It contained most of the short stories Anzia had published in magazines during the preceding two years and, in addition, a preface, "Mostly about Myself," which Smyth had suggested and helped her to produce, and an epilogue, "You Can't Be an Immigrant Twice," a reprint of the newspaper interview. These two pieces filled out what might otherwise have been a skimpy book. Smyth, along with being editor of the *Literary Digest International Book Review*, had become Funk & Wagnalls' literary adviser; his job was to find promising books for the company to publish. So it was Funk & Wagnalls, just then branching out with general trade books after establishing itself as a publisher of dictionaries, that published *Children of Loneliness*.

All the stories or essays in this, her third book, show Anzia's growing sophistication in theme and viewpoint: her immigrant characters have left the ghetto. "The Song Triumphant," originally published in *Munsey's* magazine half a year before Anzia's trip to Europe, seems to foresee her stab at being a steerage passenger; she was already hoping for this way out of her loneliness. It may have been prompted also by the marriage of Anzia's niece and confidante, Cecelia (Fannie's daughter), to a highly successful composer-songwriter, Milton Ager (some songs he later wrote were "Happy Days Are Here Again" and "Ain't She Sweet"). Anzia both enjoyed and condemned Ager's obvious wealth. Her story is about a young Jewish poet angry and tired of poverty on the Lower East Side, who becomes a successful lyricist of popular songs, then repents for having succumbed to materialism, renounces his riches, and returns to the ghetto to regain himself among his own people. But the poet's story is immediately followed and contradicted in *Children of Loneliness* by "You Can't Be an Immigrant Twice."

"An Immigrant among the Editors," a humorous essay in the collection, satirizes Anzia's experiences with political-intellectual magazines such as *Free Mankind* (a pseudonym perhaps for the *New Republic* or the *New Masses*):

> . . . a thin, white educated looking magazine, without covers, without pictures, without any advertising. . . . It gave me the feeling when I looked through the pages that it was a head without a body. Most of the articles were high words in the air . . . but some of the editorials talked against paying rent. This at once got me on fire with interest. . . . If this magazine was trying to put the landlords out of business, I was with it.

Mocking the editors ("I found myself face to face with a clean, cold, high-thinking head"), she also mocks herself as the impulsive, untutored immigrant whose brain was "a sort of Hester Street junk-shop, where a million different things — rich uptown silks and velvets and the cheapest kind of rags — were thrown around in bunches," and reports the verdict of another magazine editor: "Such a chaotic mind as yours would be useless to an intellectual journal."

In sum, *Children of Loneliness* is a collection of pieces gathered together by Smyth to produce a salable book for that fall, while Anzia set to work on her next novel. The title story, however, was a major piece of work, a novella more skillfully written than any of her previous fiction. This most critics seem not to have noticed. Although more approving than their reviews had been for *Salome of the Tenements*, they gave this book much less attention — tempered praise mixed with impatience. Anzia was already losing her magic. That her writing was "vivid" and "dramatic," conveying memorable scenes of life in the ghetto on the Lower East Side, was immediately conceded by all the reviewers. But — there was usually a but — "her gift is not creative; she is a reporter and an autobiographical rather than a fiction writer," said the *New York Times* critic. "She would win [more] respect if she would show in her work more of the self-control, the restraint that art demands," was the opinion of the *Literary Review*.

Jewish critics were offended by her characterization of poor, uneducated ghetto Jews and their uncultured, ungrammatical speech, which some evidently believed was due to Yezierska's own illiteracy. The only reviews giving *Children of Loneliness* unclouded praise were the *London Times Literary Supplement* and the *Literary Digest International Book Re-*

view (of which Smyth was editor). "While all these tales have the touch of creative imagination, they are desperately true to life," commented Yale literature professor William Lyon Phelps in the *Review*, contradicting the *New York Times*. Repeating the familiar story of Anzia's struggle as a sweatshop worker to learn a new language and become a writer, Phelps added that "long before she had attained . . . mastery of the English language . . . there was in her work a core of fire. . . .She was even then better off than those who have had every advantage, but lack central heating." Her only problem, he pointed out gently, had been to control herself, because "every time she sat down to write, it was as tho her heart would set the paper aflame."

THAT SHE NEEDED an authoritative blue pencil Anzia knew only too well. Being told repeatedly, even by critics who admired her work, that "Miss Yezierska has real power which needs greater restraint" (Edward J. O'Brien's summary) only reinforced her sense of crippling handicap because she had learned English as a second language and learned literature chiefly at night after working all day in a factory.

She had always reached out for reassurance — at first to her sister Annie, who knew less than Anzia about grammar or literature, but could often remember more vividly the Yiddishisms of their neighbors. Annie and the friends or acquaintances whom Anzia persuaded to listen as she read them her manuscripts were each like a familiar crutch enabling her to step out more boldly on her own as a writer:

> . . . the club-leader of the settlement, a college student, the druggist on the corner, the doctor on the block, anyone she met with a gleam of intelligence . . . she would stop and make them listen to some little scene . . . that she happened to be working on. Their comments somehow helped her get a truer word, a deeper stroke in her picture.

In her relationship with John Dewey, she had discovered the ideal editor, one who admired everything she wrote but could gently correct a misused word, restrain some effusion, or even suggest the precise word she was searching for. It soon became her habit to seek such editors or friends who would self-effacingly read her unfinished, still shapeless pages and try to propose restraints or better words. She needed someone, amateur or professional, anyone against whom she could bounce her own ideas. Always she started out by herself in chaos, striking out boldy in every direction:

> I envy the writers who can sit down at their desks in the clear calm security of their vision and begin their story at the beginning and work it up logically, step by step, until they get to the end. With me, the end and the middle and the beginning of my story whirl before me in a mad blur. . . . I can not sit still inside myself till the vision becomes clear and whole . . . in my brain. I'm too much on fire to wait till I understand what I see and feel. My hands rush out to seize a word from the end, a phrase from the middle, or a sentence from the beginning. I jot down any fragment of a thought that I can get hold of. And then I gather these fragments, words, phrases, sentences, and I paste them together with my . . . blood.

Her emotions could mislead her into bathos. Then her stories might be ripe pulp. As examples, "Love Cheat," about a Russian-born woman painter who discovers after a brief affair with a New York newspaperman that he is "an empty sensualist, a love-cheat," and "Love Hunger," equally vapid and yet magnetically readable, both appeared in *Metropolitan* magazine (six months apart) at the same time Anzia was publishing major stories in *Century, Harper's* and other literary journals.

Friend or editor helped her to distinguish between the sentiment and sentimentality in her first raw drafts. But that was only a small part of the arduous writing process for her and whoever assisted her. For she had discovered that to write honestly about what she knew, at least during the first years of her career, she had to sacrifice the refinements in the American language she had acquired with painful effort and to relearn the ghetto idiom that had been her own speech as a child. She had to reenter emotionally, as an almost innocent, the immigrant world of poverty and greed and frustrated wanting. If she found upon later rereading that the paragraphs or pages resulting from these forays into her emotional depths failed to match her feelings, she would ruthlessly abandon them and start again. She was always rewriting.

No matter who helped her in the selfless task of reading, editing, and bouncing back to her her own ideas in different words, the manuscript would evolve unmistakably hers, because she vigorously attacked it afresh the next day, by herself or with another helper, and slashed away pitilessly whatever now seemed stiff or foreign to her. Her instinct as she hacked away at the words she didn't like, to get closer to her own truth, was usually infallible. But "dirt and disorder" returned with each new story, and her devouring need for hand holders, as she groped her way out of her chaos, consumed friendships and family relationships. For she confronted almost everyone she knew sooner or later with her manuscripts, including her young daughter.

> Writing is ordinarily the least part of a man. It is all there is of me. I want to write with every pulse of my blood and every breath of my spirit. . . . I burn up in this all-consuming desire my family, my friends, my loves . . . my very life.

Smyth was for a long time her editor and friend and, probably for a short time, her lover as well. Departing for Europe, she had left a key to her safety deposit box in an envelope with Funk & Wagnalls, "to be kept until called for." Underneath that notation on the envelope she added "Dr. Clifford Smyth, International Literary Review" as the one who might call in her absence. For Anzia, who trusted almost no one with her financial or personal secrets, this indicated a close relationship. It was also a revelation of the sparseness of her friendships. Smyth had been unusually helpful, almost fatherly, to her. As editor of the *New York Times Sunday Book Review*, and later, of the *Literary Digest International Book Review*, he had published lengthy, admiring reviews of her books. During this period (1923–24), when she was working on her next novel and publishing few short stories, he helped to keep her name in public view with feature stories relating to *Children of Loneliness*.

At the time Anzia was developing this friendship, she was experiencing the sweet-bitter mixture of success without assurance; she was alone in a strange, exhilarating place. Being a celebrated author attracted people to her; she could have all the editorial help she wanted, but while enjoying such popularity with newfound well-wishers (critics, editors, publishers, professionals who made money from her achievements, as she did from theirs), she would sometimes wake at night with the frightening feeling of being lost — the terrible aloneness an immigrant knows on first arriving in a new country.

BECAUSE OF HER HARSH, ascetic, priestlike devotion to her vocation, Anzia had had no time for friendships unless they helped her work. Her sisters Annie and Fannie, who had been selfless substitute mothers, could no longer help. She had outgrown Annie's capabilities, and Fannie was too far away and too immersed in her husband's business problems. Fannie's brilliant daughter Cecelia Ager (who later wrote movie commentary for *Variety, Vanity Fair,* the *New York Times,* and other major publications), although eighteen or twenty years Anzia's junior, was the confidante who best understood Anzia. The two had an on-and-off relationship over the years; when Cecelia would impatiently refuse to read her latest manuscript, Anzia, rebuffed, would angrily reject all contact with her niece for months.

But toward most of her family Anzia had always been a critic looking down from a mountain peak. She had distanced herself from her parents not only by her aspirations and achievements in this new world, but even by the table manners and sensibility she had acquired since quitting their home when she was about seventeen. She had never been close to her brothers. A few rare times after she moved to Fifth Avenue and had the leisure to feel lonely or sentimental, she had gone to see Max, the oldest of her nine siblings, the first to come to America, and the first of the brothers to become a pharmacist. But she didn't care for his wife and was soon bored with Max's bourgeois mentality.

After *Salome* gave her a comfortable income, Anzia undertook to share in the financial support of her father, now widowed. In fact, she became the collector by mail of the monthly contributions from the three brothers who lived, and had drugstores, in other cities (Isadore in Denver, Dave and Gus in the north and south of California). Bill, the youngest in the family, who was born in this country and was livelier and better informed than the rest, had become a career army officer. Anzia had enjoyed talking to him, until his departure for China. In China he married and seemed to forget his monthly obligation. Infuriated because a dunning letter she sent him had not been answered (he may have been on his honeymoon), Anzia wrote to army headquarters in Washington, D.C., to complain of his dereliction. This scandalous letter became part of his army record and earned her Bill's enmity for the rest of his life.

There remained Henry, a high school mathematics teacher. Also born in this country, he was about ten years younger than Anzia, plump, blond, blue-eyed, sweet-tempered, loyal and kind to all the family. He was proud of Anzia's success and glad to help her in any way he could—withstanding her difficult temperament, reading her manuscripts, giving her the fountain pen in his pocket or the magazine he was carrying, sometimes taking her to lunch. While making use of such services, Anzia felt a gentle contempt for his stodgy, good-natured "all rightness" and that of his schoolteacher wife.

Anzia's father had married again soon after his first wife died. Anzia couldn't stand the new wife; compared to her dead mother, for whom she now felt warm filial love and remorse, this woman was coarse. So, although she sent her father the monthly check, she seldom saw him. She brushed aside softer sentiment because in her view he had remarried in too much haste. No matter how helpless he was, an old man living alone, how could he have married such a woman?

She had thus freed herself from the small, time-wasting social occasions of a family; but also from the cushion it provided against stark loneliness. Sometimes, when she relaxed, she had moments of regret for her failures toward her mother and her separation from the family. She had to harden herself against these moments and go back to her work.

But when she returned from Europe, she was determined to enjoy life more. In Paris she had had her long red hair cut in a fashionable, carefree bob. She was, after all, the model of a liberated 1920s woman.

She moved into the splendid, sky-high apartment in the Grosvenor, ready to live a freer, happier life. Clifford Smyth, the alluring opposite to which she was magnetically drawn, was working with her, making the final arrangements for *Children of Loneliness*. Perhaps she was more ready to accept him as a lover because she had so bitterly regretted her failure with Dewey.

In a story published a few years later, "Wild Winter Love," Anzia wrote about such an affair, blending aspects of Dewey and Smyth into her portrait of the lover for whom a middle-aged, foreign-born woman writer had left her husband and daughter. She was, in fact, fictionalizing someone else's experience — the story of Rose Cohen, whose autobiography, *Out of the Shadow*, was published in 1918 — but, as usual, Anzia filled the story with her own memories:

> They lit up the street with their happiness. The world seemed to sweep away before their completeness in each other. . . . How shameless, at their age, to get so lost in their love!
>
> But a rich power for work was in that love. It put a new appeal, a deeper humanity, into her writing. . . .
>
> . . . For the first time in her life, she found a lover, an inspirer, and an audience all in one — a man of brains who understood the warm rich muddle of her experience. . . . His calm Anglo-Saxon face was like a background of rock for her volatile, tempestuous, Slavic temperament.

The affair in "Wild Winter Love" ended when it was discovered by the man's wife and he deserted his new love to return to his wife and daughters. The woman writer in the story committed suicide.

> A lonely losing fight it was from the very beginning. Only for a moment, a hand of love stretched a magic bridge across the chasm [separating Jew and Gentile]. Inevitably the hand drew back. Inevitably the man went back to the safety of his own world.
>
> In the fading of this dazzling mirage of friendship and love, vanished her courage, her dreams, her last illusion. And she leaped into the gulf that she could not bridge.

Anzia, her long, red hair cut short, about fall 1923.

Rose Cohen, forty, attempted suicide, according to a *New York Times* report of September 17, 1922, by jumping into the East River. She was rescued and taken to Bellevue Hospital. "God didn't want to take me," she said. For Anzia, the desperation of that story relates to her own momentous separation from John Dewey. The affair with Smyth, though it also furthered her work, was not as central and affecting in her life. When they became lovers, she was imediately disillusioned by Smyth's lack of physical tenderness and his insensitivity. Anzia once confided to her niece Cecelia her distaste for and disappointment in that sexual experience. Perhaps Smyth, like Dewey, had misread Anzia's temperament; she must have seemed more sophisticated sexually than she actually was — indeed a "volatile, tempestuous" Slav. These experiences with clumsy lovers evidently confirmed her observation that "Anglo-Saxon" Americans were repressed, ashamed and afraid of their own emotions, for that is how she portrayed them thereafter in her writing.

Two women she knew at this time were also involved with married men. One was a girl from an upper-class Boston family. She had cut loose from those restraints and was enjoying her freedom in Greenwich Village, as well as Anzia's exotic bohemian ideas. Anzia's unkempt manuscripts amazed her. She was delighted to read them and offer suggestions, but her help was usually too superficial to be of much use. Anzia nevertheless enjoyed listening to the problems of this girl from a different world, a happier, Bostonian world. When after several years the girl's love affair had to end, she closed down her apartment to return to New England and gave Anzia some of her beautiful antiques. Her former lover was going to pay her expenses through medical school. The other woman, twenty years olders, a friend from Rand School days, had been the mistress of Clarence Darrow, the great criminal lawyer and defender of civil liberties. He, too, had recognized an obligation toward his former mistress and was sending her a monthly check. Anzia felt a natural bond with each of these women. They talked to her more freely than they could to anyone else — and yet she could not lower her own defenses with either. But when each for a different reason moved out of New York, she missed them.

Her disappointment in Smyth did not end the friendship; he continued to help her while she worked on *Bread Givers*. The book's dedication reads:

To
CLIFFORD SMYTH
To Whose Understanding Criticism
And Inspiration I Owe More
Than I Can Ever Express

Self-protecting as Anzia was in some matters, as for instance when, for the sake of her writing, she rejected a glittering contract in Hollywood, she was always frankly exploitative.

In her self-centered dealings with others, compelled by the urgency of her need, Anzia somehow expected everyone to appreciate her dedication to a higher aesthetic than ordinary people knew. Just as her father, a rabbi, had exacted such deference, she always expected Annie and Fannie and their children to wait on her with food and lodging or whatever she required, and, similarly, those who had the editorial skills she lacked to contribute to the same noble cause. Without even asking, she would also appropriate from a relative's or friend's home pens, books, magazines, writing pads, a clock she'd seen on the coffee table or mantel — whatever object she suddenly decided was essential to her work. She was somehow above or beyond the standards of politeness of ordinary people.

That brazen self-absorption was one aspect of her behavior; at the same time she fought a sometimes paralyzing self-doubt. This loneliness was different from that she had known before. She had virtually reached the goal for which she had forfeited family and friends — she was a recognized writer — and still she had not gained the emotional comfort she had expected from association with artists and intellectuals.

Fame warmed her in its artificial sunlight while she worked on her second novel. In that time, almost two years, she wrote no new short stories, but her stories in *Hungry Hearts* and *Children of Loneliness* were now being reprinted in textbook anthologies, alongside stories by de Maupassant, Poe, Chekhov, and Hawthorne. She was one of the models for other young writers to follow.

AFTER SHE CONSECRATED her life wholly to writing, probably as far back as her desperate year of poverty in San Francisco, Anzia gave up idle, time-wasting pleasures, such as plays, movies, even parties; she wouldn't stay up at night for them, except on a very rare occasion. She ignored cosmetics, beauty parlors, frilly dresses. Despite her passion for beautiful clothes in brilliant colors (which she revealed sometimes when buying a gift for Louise), she chose to wear virtual uniforms — finely tailored navy blue suits or shirtwaist dresses. (When she was older and her hair turned gray, the suits were gray.) Even in these uniforms, with her vivid coloring and explosive personality, men found her strikingly attractive; but perhaps because of her repeated disillusionments, she no longer seemed to care whether she attracted them.

She had also renounced the distraction of soft-cushioned chairs, rugs, and draperies in her home, choosing to live in "a nun's cell." These choices were not just to save time and money. They were her way of coping with the chaos she faced every day, trying to find the right words. Above all, they created the ordered simplicity she needed because of the crowded, dirty, disordered ghetto flat in which she had grown up and could never entirely escape.

So after she could afford whatever she wanted, she persisted in this self-imposed discipline. She had an impressive address now, a lofty Fifth Avenue apartment, furnished with expensive simplicity, stripped for writing: aside from a bed, a few Windsor chairs, and bookshelves (the Boston antiques), she had a large monastery table and a typewriter, the best portable phonograph available (music was her consolation), and see-through curtains to let in the sun.

Yet in this simplified splendor she would often find herself on a Sunday morning staring from her high windows at the bleak emptiness of Fifth Avenue below, the city hushed from up here in the Grosvenor, and feel homesick for the noise and warmth of the poor neighborhoods she had lived in and the ghetto friends who were now envious strangers. Even Annie's oldest son, whom she had known since he was a baby, had threatened a lawsuit because the first two stories Anzia had published, "The Free Vacation House" and "Where Lovers Dream," were about Annie's experiences.

Annie had relived these experiences in confiding talks with Anzia; and Anzia, transforming them into fiction, had often worked over the manuscripts with Annie. When each story appeared in a magazine, it had been an incredible, gloriously happy event for Annie as well as Anzia. Magazine payment then had been minimal, not enough for a month's rent. But when Anzia came back from Hollywood, supposedly affluent no matter how frugally she lived, Annie's oldest son, just then trying to establish his own small business, asked Anzia for money to buy equipment. He believed Annie's contribution deserved payment. Anzia's explanation — that she couldn't touch her money, it was all tied up — only angered him. His threats had come to nothing, but for a while it had been difficult for Anzia to see Annie or the other children.

> Now I am cut off by my own [people] for aquiring the few things I have. And these new people with whom I dine and to whom I talk, I do not belong to them.

That she should be alone again, here in the midst of plenty! She felt an irrational anger at her newly acquired friends, "promoters, talent scouts for the book trade," whose "business was booming best sellers," the "gospel of the cash register." She was ready to discard her own false front, the personality she had assumed with such people. She knew that someday, perhaps soon, she would be found out; the friendly critics would discover that she wasn't the genius or literary wonder they said she was, and she would lose this high-rise apartment, along with all her unmerited wealth.

Work had always been the most effective remedy against such depression. But as Anzia worked on *Bread Givers*, she had some reason for these moments of panic: her last book, *Children of Loneliness*, had received markedly less attention than her first two. She seemed to be losing her audience.

Her correspondence with Houghton Mifflin also suggested this decline. When in December she wrote on the stationery of Boni and Liveright (publishers of the successful *Salome*) asking for a "review copy" of Kate Douglas Wiggin's *My Garden of Memory*, she was answered by a Houghton Mifflin junior editor. Instead of sending her a free publicity copy, a courtesy that might be expected for a well-known author who might review the book, he wanted to know in which "periodical" she intended to review it. He said the company was "short" of copies. Anzia didn't reply to this small snub. A year later, she wrote again to the Houghton Mifflin Company rather than to an editor, and to the same faceless entity six months after that, asking about her royalty statements. Greenslet answered correctly, fastidiously each time, citing the figures to show she had been sent whatever was due her. Rebuffs. Sitting at his editorial observation post in Boston, self-assured in his manners and in his business practices, he seems in his letters to be the model of a Bostonian gentleman dealing with a mercenary, untutored peasant. In the years since publishing *Hungry Hearts*, his genteel and sometimes patronizing affability had gradually diminished to bare politeness as Anzia kept asking, even greedily demanding, more ads, more publicity, more favors.

He and his colleagues had undoubtedly observed the rise and fall of many ambitious writers. If her books had turned out to be consistent, really impressive money-makers, her raw manners would surely have been overlooked. Or if she herself had been appropriately appreciative, or perhaps had learned the manners of a nouveau (apprentice) WASP, that too might have made her acceptable. But Anzia, ever hungry, actually famished for recognition, applause, love, trying to feast after (and before) a long famine, could never be temperate. She couldn't help suspecting and questioning the royalty statements. She had fought too hard; it had required "brutal self-absorption" to reach this place in the world. It was even harder to stay there. She was still in combat, and lonely.

WHEN LOUISE TRAVELED downtown by subway to visit her mother, it often seemed like a visit of mercy. Coming from a fifth-floor walk-up apartment with fire escape on a busy Bronx street to the carpeted plush of the Grosvenor lobby and gliding to its upper reaches with the uniformed elevator man — that is, from economy to elegance — one would expect the opposite. But the quality of the visits depended on Anzia's moods.

Louise and her mother were first-name comrades rather than just family. Since the time when they had escaped together from Arnold's home to try their fortunes in California, Anzia had been confiding her desperate problems, as one friend to another. Louise had thus become sensitive, like a finely tuned instrument, to the weather of Anzia's feelings as Anzia called on her for understanding and help. At the age of three or four, this understanding required a subdued "grown-up" behavior, *not* crying or even complaining while living in someone else's house (as, for instance, Aunt Fannie's or the boarding home in San Francisco). But as Louise grew older, and Anzia could afford her own quarters, which had gradually improved over the years, Anzia's problems seemed to grow more complex.

There were of course wonderful, exciting Saturdays, as when they walked over to Wanamaker's and saw one of its large windows devoted entirely to Anzia's *Children of Loneliness,* with a photo of Anzia above a great pyramid of books; or when they went to the tea honoring Anzia in Doubleday's garden on Long Island and met other writers and critics; or when an important *New York Times* editor stopped them on Eighth Street to tell Anzia how much he enjoyed *Children of Loneliness*; or even when a larger than usual check provided for a feast in a glamorous tearoom like Mary Elizabeth's or Alice McCollister's.

Although Anzia always felt herself to be basically poor, she had, after the movie version of *Salome,* discovered the means to pay for Louise's orthodontia and her piano and dancing lessons. She must have derived a virtuous pleasure in volunteering to pay for such middle-class luxuries, which she herself had never known.

Nevertheless, Louise experienced a lot of Saturdays with Anzia that were gloomy or at least clouded. It might be a very bad review of Anzia's latest book; a shockingly poor royalty statement (where would the Grosvenor rent come from?); demands from close relatives like Annie's son; disappointments in new friends; or just Anzia's ordinary malaise, when she was struggling with a manuscript or feeling lost and alone in the world. Louise came downtown on these Saturdays, fresh from crass, material comforts — a full icebox in a scrubbed Bronx apartment — comforts to which she would of course return. Louise's father liked to bring home a box of candy on the weekend, and he especially liked to take Louise to the movies on Saturday night when she returned. So as she left Anzia toward dusk on a sad Saturday, Louise could feel all the more heavily the weight of Anzia's aloneness in that empty space she lived in.

But compassion would get mixed with annoyance or even anger. When she was dissatisfied, her mother created scenes with waiters, salesladies, repair people. Anzia always wanted things done differently than anyone else; she always called attention to herself. She returned merchandise after she had used it. It was embarrassing to a child who wanted only to be a normal sheep like everyone else. Anzia also sometimes butted into Louise's small personal relationships — gratuitously, as if to make up for not being with her all the time. She might telephone Louise's friend's mother and rearrange some private plan the two little girls had secretly plotted; or she might speak to Louise's father about something Louise had told her in confidence. It was startling, upsetting.

So although at the bottom of all her mixed feelings about Anzia there was love and sympathy, Louise knew — she had known since the age of four, when Anzia had abruptly sent her back across the country to her stern father — that Anzia could never be entirely trusted. Once on a school day Louise walked back into her classroom after lunch and found the name Anzia Yezierska written large on the blackboard. She naturally assumed her mother had been there, butting in once more, trying to influence the teacher for some embarrassing purpose, leaving her name in large letters. But when Louise asked about it, Miss Goldfarb started telling Louise enthusiastically about "this well known writer."

What bothered Louise most was that, after she got to be twelve or thirteen, Anzia would usually bring out a manuscript on Saturday mornings. Anzia would be stuck at some crucial point — she just needed a word, a phrase, a transition to get her over the impasse. Louise would have to read it out loud while Anzia, holding the carbon copy, listened, batted out a too-sentimental phrase, which Louise rejected, offering another instead; Anzia might accept it happily or ask for another — and so it would go through half a dozen pages of grueling word hunting. These work sessions occurred regularly as Louise's vocabulary and perception increased, but the manuscript, any manuscript — which had displaced her to win her mother's primary attention — was always an onerous burden to Louise. Sometimes Anzia, up since early morning, in her haste to get the pages written, would have skipped washing her face and the breakfast dishes. For Louise, the unmade bed and dirty dishes added aggravation to the disorder of the scribbled pages.

WHEN ANZIA encountered flare-ups of anger in her once-adoring daughter, she felt guilty — not for interfering in her daughter's affairs or for imposing the manuscripts on her, but for what she had done, helplessly, years before in giving her up. Remorse and loneliness, but also the comforts of being a successful writer living at the Grosvenor, must have been the gritty mixture Anzia felt as she worked on *Bread Givers*, the novel based on the events of her own childhood and youth. In spite of the torment of writing, now she was realizing a growing power in recreating her past and understanding it better.

Recalling the crowded, dirty tenement, the flat overflowing with clothes, rags, dishes, pots, her father's books, and assorted litter in which she had lived with her family when she was ten years old, and the loud, bitter fights they'd had, she discovered an unexpected happiness there: however they had argued, despite the hunger and the constant fear of being evicted into the street when her sisters were out of work, they were all together.

Although the novel was based on a part of her life, it was far from a factual account. She sharpened the drama of real events by eliminating muddy contradictions, adding or exaggerating incidents where she felt compelled to. So, while portraying intensely believable scenes of her family's daily existence, she left out of the novel her six brothers and many extraneous (to her) aspects of her sisters' lives. She focused on the "wasted lives" of these three "bread givers," submitting to their father's pious tyranny. Anzia had been the only one of the four girls to quit the sweatshop, defy this biblical patriarch, and escape.

In *Bread Givers*, the other three sisters ended their sweatshop bondage by marrying men her father chose for them. He had forced them, the novelist wrote, to give up their own choices and had found their husbands through a professional matchmaker. In reality, the marriage of the oldest daughter may have been so arranged, but not Annie's and Fannie's. Perhaps they had rejected suitors whom Anzia would have preferred, but each seemed to be reasonably content in her marriage. Anzia wrote biting portraits, virtual caricatures of her three brothers-in-law (and often expressed similar ideas about them in private conversations); but her judgments were not those of her sisters. The core of the book, however, which is the youngest daughter's fight to free herself — the harsh conflict between her Old World father, stubbornly maintaining traditions thousands of years old, and his equally stubborn child — is profoundly true to Anzia's early life. "Blood-and-Iron" her father called her.

No one in her family, not her sisters, mother, brothers, or father, ever understood why she had to fight so fiercely and often, why she was always the storm center in their tenement flat. In their world, women had always waited on men; it was the universal, immutable law of life. The injustice, which stung Anzia unbearably, had never occured to them.

CONSIDERING it a prestigious book, Doubleday gave Anzia a garden party to celebrate the publication of *Bread Givers*, and in advance printed five hundred numbered copies, to be presented to important people. One of these Anzia sent to a friend from her drama school days, Marcet Haldeman-Julius. It was a mark of her great affection, or an indication that, to Anzia, Marcet was a person of special importance.

"To Marcette-Haldeman Julius," Anzia wrote in the flyleaf, misspelling her friend's name and misplacing the hyphen, "Long, long years ago, you knew of the turmoil & confusion of my soul that shaped this book. Anzia Yezierska." She added an afterthought: "Here you will also recognize Helena & her brute bread giver."

Helena was Annie's European name. Marcet had been Annie's, rather than Anzia's, special friend. The inscription suggests how truthful the book seemed to Anzia. Affected by the force of her own creation, she often could not remember what was real and what invented in this or, for that matter, her other stories and books. Even in conversation, describing actual incidents, she seldom bothered to stick to the plain facts.

But both true and false, *Bread Givers* is piercingly convincing, as its 1925 reviewers testified. "One does not seem to read," said William Lyon Phelps in the *International Book Review*, "one is too completely inside. . . . I feel . . . as if looking not at the picture of life, but at life itself." The *New York Times* critic wrote: "The Smolinsky family and the flat in which they live is almost painfully actual." And the *Springfield Republican* echoed: "They are living, breathing persons, this family."

She had also improved her use of the ghetto idiom. "It has a raw, uncontrollable poetry," the *New York Times* remarked. "Miss Yezierska has accomplished for the Yiddish what John Synge has done for the Gaelic," said Samson Raphaelson, in the *New York Herald Tribune*. "She has rendered its beauty in English without losing any of the color of the original." For example, this moment, when ten-year-old Sara (Anzia) tries to earn her share:

> On the corner of the most crowded part of Hester Street I stood myself with my pail of herring.
>
> "Herring! Herring! A bargain in the world! . . . Two cents apiece."
>
> My voice was like dynamite. Louder than all the pushcart peddlers, louder than all the hollering noises of bargaining and selling, I cried out my herring with all the burning fire of my ten old years.
>
> . . . People stopped to look at me. . . .
>
> "Also a person," laughed [a woman shopper], "also fighting already for the bite in the mouth."

"How old are you, little skinny bones? Ain't your father working?"

I didn't hear. I couldn't listen to their smartness. I was burning up inside me with my herring to sell. Nothing was before me but the hunger in our house. . . . Like a houseful of hungry mouths my heart cried, "Herring — herring! Two cents a piece!" . . . And before the day was over my last herring was sold. . . .

It began singing in my heart, the music of the whole Hester Street. The pushcart peddlers yelling their goods, the noisy playing of children in the gutter, the women pushing and shoving each other with their market baskets — all that was only hollering noise before melted over me like a new beautiful song.

It began dancing before my eyes, the twenty-five herring that earned me my twenty-five cents. It lifted me in the air, my happiness. I couldn't help it. It began dancing under my feet. And I couldn't stop myself. I danced into our kitchen. And throwing the fifty pennies, like a shower of gold, into my mother's lap, I cried. "Now, will you yet call me crazy-head?"

With this book, Anzia had reached maturity as an artist. *Bread Givers* seemed to regain for her the literary attention and respect she may have lost after *Salome of the Tenements,* and even to go beyond that. In its time, 1925–28, the novel was admired as a colorful, suspenseful narrative of family tensions in the ghetto — the Old World versus the New — written with unusual veracity. Many women must have agreed with Anzia's heroine; but in those years each fought her own real-life battle alone. Within a few years, there was the Depression. *Bread Givers* went out of print and was forgotten.

A half century later, ten years after Yezierska's death, a young social historian, Alice Kessler-Harris, rediscovered this antique in a library and brought it to a publisher's attention. It had become contemporary in the meantime. Because of the women's movement and the consequent changes in women's perception of themselves, its story of the war between father and daughter has taken on a larger significance than it had in 1925. Its picture of the immigrant society in which that war was fought is now better valued as history. The book has a vigorous, much longer new life in college classrooms and feminist bookshops here and abroad; and Anzia, a stormy individualist whose work was completely forgotten in her lifetime, has gained more enduring status as a pioneer.

That winter of 1925, soon after *Bread Givers* appeared in bookstores, Anzia decided, as if planning to make peace with another warring power, to go to see her father. At the exhausting end of a major project, she was experiencing the letdown, almost a feeling of loss. But she must have been pleased by the good reviews.

> I felt I had justified myself in the book for having hardened my heart to go through life alone. . . . My sisters, who had married according to my father's will, spent themselves childbearing in poverty. I too had children. My children were the people I wrote about. I gave my children, born of loneliness, as much of my life as my married sisters did in bringing their children into the world.

So after the birth of this last child, *Bread Givers*, there was a necessary pause. While she was waiting and perhaps anxious for the push toward the next story, loneliness came back, enfolding her in its cold. She wanted to be again with people who were "real," her own kind, in the heart of the crowded Jewish neighborhood where her father still lived.

In *Bread Givers* Anzia had written out her anger at her father and the guilt he forced on her. The writing freed her. She had come to understand and sympathize with him as a zealot like herself, alone in a world of compromisers. She was ready to make peace with him to whom for years now she had been sending only a check. Perhaps she wanted his forgiveness.

This time she carried the check with her to his dingy, jumbled apartment. But there was no answering warmth or greeting when she entered his room and found him with his books. He accused her immediately. She wrote about it twenty-five years later:

> "What is it I hear? You wrote a book about me?" His voice and the sorrow in his eyes left me speechless. "How could you write about some one you don't know?"
>
> "I know you," I mumbled.

"Woe to America!" he wailed. "Only in America could it happen — an ignorant thing like you — a writer! What do you know of . . . history, philosophy? What do you know of the Bible, the foundation of all knowledge?"

He stood up, an ancient patriarch condemning unrighteousness. . . . "If you only knew how deep is your ignorance — "

"What have you ever done with all your knowledge?" I demanded. "While you prayed and gloried in your Torah, your children were in the factory, slaving for bread."

His God-kindled face towered over me. "What? Should I have sold my religion? God is not for sale. God comes before my own flesh and blood. . . ."

"My child!" His eyes sought mine as if something in me had touched him. "It says in the Torah: He who separates himself from people buries himself in death. A woman alone, not a wife and not a mother, has no existence. No joy on earth, no hope of heaven. . . . Your barren heart looks out from your eyes."

No communication was even bearable. Anzia had ended *Bread Givers* with a tenuous truce: the father grudgingly accepted his daughter's invitation to live with her "if you'll promise to keep sacred all that is sacred to me." But in real life a truce was impossible, and not only because Anzia could never have given him such a self-sacrificing invitation. She had forgotten the noise and dirt and smells in his apartment, his never-ending condemnation of her, and her renewed anger for past grievances.

She fled back to her isolation cell at the Grosvenor, where it was clean and quiet.

III

FAILURE

10

LOSING

LIKE A WOMAN TRYING OUT SUITORS, Anzia had changed her publisher with each book, seeking more appreciation with each change, or at least more advertising and publicity. She had moved from Houghton Mifflin (after their rejection) to Boni and Liveright, then to Funk and Wagnalls, and with *Bread Givers* to big, commercial Doubleday, Page & Company.

But after completing her newest book, *Arrogant Beggar,* she turned back for one more flirtation with Houghton Mifflin, the Boston aristocrat. This time, perhaps because Ferris Greenslet had lost his "ever-faithful" humor with the temperamental and demanding author, R. L. Scaife wrote Anzia about their acceptance of her manuscript, congratulating her on the "advance . . . we think you have made" over past work. Houghton Mifflin would be glad to welcome her back to their list, he wrote, if she would agree to a 10 percent royalty rate along with a "comprehensive advertising appropriation," which the company understood she would expect.

Answering promptly in January 1927, Anzia asked what the advertising appropriation would be. Greenslet met her in New York the same week to discuss the terms, but evidently she didn't like them, for two weeks later she wrote him a terse, one-line letter asking him to return the manuscript. She gave it to Doubleday instead.

After that the correspondence with Houghton Mifflin turned sour. In April Scaife reprimanded her for attempting to sell the right to reprint "The Fat of the Land" in a forthcoming anthology. Houghton Mifflin had retained reprint permission rights in their contract, Scaife reminded her, and so would set and collect the fee, which he said was thirty dollars. Half of it would be sent to Anzia with her royalty statement six months later. She wrote back that she owned all the reprint rights of her other books, but realized now after rereading the Houghton Mifflin contract that "in my ignorance I've signed away half the proceeds of such [*Hungry Hearts*] sales."

The next source of irritation was a $2.50 item in her October 31 royalty statement for "use of copyright material." Scaife explained that it was half the fee for reprinting five and a half pages of "How I Found America" in a textbook Houghton Mifflin was publishing. In the same letter, dated November 7, he frankly expressed the company's annoyance with Anzia. Rejecting her request for half the advance payment that Houghton Mifflin had already received for permitting Grosset & Dunlap to publish another edition of *Hungry Hearts*, with photos from the movie, he admonished her: "This seems to us a little premature [the new edition had not yet been printed] in view of the fact you did not let us have your new book but recalled it."

The critical success and quality of *Bread Givers*, a book Houghton Mifflin might have published if the editors had been more receptive to her earlier work, no doubt had whetted their taste for her new manuscript. But *Arrogant Beggar* was not as well written as *Bread Givers*. Like all Yezierska's writing up to that time, it is an intense, dramatic, rapidly flowing, easily readable protest — in this case, against organized philanthropy. It attacks uncharitable ladies bountiful who dispense their bounty as a self-gratifying social activity.

Yezierska is recounting in *Arrogant Beggar* with fictional variations her own youthful experience of winning a scholarship to Columbia University, but she has altered characters and episodes, forcing the narrative to push her message. Adele Lindner, the Jewish immigrant salesgirl who is Yezierska's "arrogant beggar," is thrilled by the opportunity to move out of her dark tenement room into the comparative luxury of a well-furnished home for working girls. Despite the rigid rules and hours for waking, eating, and returning at night, she is delighted with her new life in this home, with the sunlight, cleanliness, better food and furnishings, until she loses her sales job and, to avoid being expelled from this heaven, is persuaded to enroll in the home's training course for domestic service.

Because most of the girls in the home, like Adele, do not aim to be servants, this training course, a pet project of the home's board of directors, is so badly in need of students that Adele's rent is forgiven while she studies hated kitchen skills. But she remains a reluctant and backward student, doing so poorly that she is once more in danger of losing her place in the home. To recover, she undertakes the mammoth task of cleaning and polishing the huge kitchen single-handedly one night while all are asleep. The overnight miracle, plus an effusive letter of gratitude she writes to the board of directors, deeply impresses these ladies, and they decide to pay her tuition to an outside training school so that she can become a domestic science teacher and thus help "her people." The home's founder, Mrs. Hellman, offers Adele further help: Hellman clothing discards and a part-time job as waitress at the Hellman table while attending school.

Adele is swiftly disillusioned. She discovers she is being paid less than the usual hourly rate for waitressing, and she realizes the true nature of Mrs. Hellman and the other directors by eavesdropping on their discussions at teas and luncheons far more lavish than the meals provided at the home. Similarly, her early romantic interest in Mrs. Hellman's son has turned to cold disdain.

At a public ceremony in which New York City's mayor and other dignitaries celebrate the home's achievements, Adele reveals her real feelings. Throwing away the speech of gratitude she was supposed to give, she shouts out:

> I hate this Home. I hate myself for living here. I hate the hand-me-down rags I wear on my back. I hate every damned bit of kindness you've ever done me. I'm poisoned with the hurts, the insults I suffered in this beastly place. . . .
>
> Hypocrites . . . boasting of your kindness. . . . Feeding your vanity on my . . . misfortune. . . . You had to advertise to all — "Remember, beggar, where you would have been if it hadn't been for us!"

With that satisfying denunciation, Anzia must have avenged herself for her own years of forced docility. In her case, she had left the Clara de Hirsch Home for an uptown furnished room in order to spend four years at Columbia University Teachers College. Accepting the tuition, the hand-me-downs, and other "humiliations," she had retained her relationship with her chief benefactor, Mrs. Henry Ollesheimer, for years thereafter and even dedicated her first book, *Hungry Hearts*, to her. (A letter she wrote to Houghton Mifflin suggests that she was under pressure to do so.)

Anzia's conception of true charity is exemplified in this book by Muhmenkeh, the shrunken, toothless old woman who takes Adele, homeless and sick, into her basement flat after the girl has run away from her previous benefactors. Muhmenkeh barely sustains herself as a sometime kitchen worker and door-to-door peddler, but she treats Adele to the best she has, caring for her solicitously and expecting nothing in return. After Muhmenkeh's death, Adele transforms the basement flat into Muhmenkeh's Coffee Shop, a pay-whatever-you-can restaurant rendezvous for artists and others in the heart of the ghetto. A patron of the coffee shop is a pianist-composer who, like Adele, is a former protégé of, and refugee from, the Hellmans. He provides the romantic happy ending Adele had previously hoped for uptown.

In the words of Ralph Waldo Emerson, which Anzia chose to keynote the book, "We do not quite forgive a giver. The hand that feeds us is in some danger of being bitten. We can receive anything from love, for that is a way of receiving it from ourselves; but not from any one who assumes to bestow. . . . We ask the whole. Nothing less will content us."

This undemanding generosity was the behavior Anzia hoped for or expected from others. She had always acted on the assumption that members of her family, no matter how distantly related, owed her help — not charity — when she needed it, because she was a struggling artist. From her viewpoint, the Jewish tradition in which she had been raised — that those who are well off are duty-bound to share with those who aren't — imposed this obligation not only on members of the same family, but even on those of the same East European village, the same ethnic background, in fact on all Jews.

The contrived ending she wrote for Adele, however, was the opposite of Anzia's own choices. For Anzia there was no way back to the ghetto; nor could she, who rarely felt "well off" and was always in fear of losing what she had, behave with the generosity of Muhmenkeh, the character she admired.

Arrogant Beggar did not improve Anzia's situation. She had written it in a lean time emotionally. The new friendships including Clifford Smyth's, were fraying. Perhaps she felt her sources of creative energy drying up in the Grosvenor's arid air. In her letters and conversations, she sometimes expressed her homesickness for the comparative poverty and comradeship of the unrecoverable past. So she moved, as she was finishing the book, to a cozier, less expensive three-room apartment on Waverly Place in the Village.

Bread Givers may not have sold as well as she had expected, and she had published only one short story in the interval. But it was not only to save money that she was moving; she was hoping the new apartment would offer a happier, more comforting and creative environment. In the next five years, a period of increasing disappointments, Anzia countered setbacks by changing her surroundings several times again — as if in the next place she might regain the self she had left behind by mistake on Hester Street.

There was no housing shortage then; many New Yorkers changed apartments yearly, enticed by the opportunity to live rent free for a month or more, which some landlords offered just to fill their buildings. The Waverly Place apartment was two flights up, low-ceilinged compared to the Grosvenor's sky-filled room, but it had a mantled fireplace in the living room, a Dutch door and built-in cupboards in the kitchen, and a tiny bedroom — old-fashioned rooms with Village charm. Anzia decided to furnish them appropriately (this would not be another "nun's cell") with such touches as turkey-red-checked kitchen curtains and brightly painted pottery. She devoted herself to remaking this home, a new mood for a new place. After living in an ivory tower at the Grosvenor, she would be able to warm herself again, closer to people.

Louise, who was still her Saturday visitor, was now fourteen years old and enthralled with dance. Anzia enrolled her in a Saturday morning class at the Dalcroze School of Eurythmics just down the street from the new apartment. Sometimes they lunched in its raw-vegetable-and-vitamin-conscious tearoom. Anzia had become a permissive, understanding parent. Almost everything Louise was forbidden to do at her father's was allowed downtown at her mother's; she could try cigarettes, read Henry Miller or Vina Delmar, even meet a boy.

Anzia was also cultivating new friendships, young artistic types who came to tea at Waverly Place, especially those who would read and criticize her manuscripts. *Arrogant Beggar* came out with appropriate advertising the following spring. She was hopeful again — until the reviews. As they slowly appeared in October, November, December, and January, they were dismaying. There were only a handful, and these hidden in the middle pages of the Sunday sections. Most of them pronounced evenly pro-and-con judgments to the effect that the plot was obvious, the characterizations thin, Yezierska lacked "good taste," but nevertheless she told her story with marvelous color and dash.

They were not the kind of reviews to sell books. Because the rest of 1927 therefore promised to be bleak, Anzia was furiously thrashing

Frontier woman, valiant pioneer, determined, belligerent — this was the character of Anzia discerned by Willy Pogany, a noted painter, who made this portrait at the time Arrogant Beggar *was published. Courtesy of Yivo Institute Archives.*

about, seeking alternatives. For almost ten years writing had been her temple, as much her shelter from the world as religion had been for her father. Now that this temple was becoming inhospitable, she was looking for a way to replenish herself as a writer. If not the ghetto, where else was there to go?

She decided suddenly to get an ordinary nine-to-six job. Any kind of work, in a factory, in a shop as a salesgirl, would be better than trying to write without conviction. In a fury of determination, after rapidly discovering how few jobs she was qualified for, she found work as a waitress in a Village restaurant on University Place. Perhaps the owner knew her and was willing to oblige her briefly. Or perhaps she had conned him into believing she would wait on customers. But to her friends and relatives who came to see her on the job (and to leave tips, of course) it was obviously a stunt — a way of getting publicity or something to write about. No one believed that Anzia, still living in the cozy apartment on Waverly Place, would actually persist in such meek, drudging anonymity. In fact, she kept the job for about two weeks.

The another way out, or at least the possibility of finding one, occurred to her. She received a request to contribute toward a gift for John Dewey. Associates and former students of the philosopher-educator had formed a gift committee; James Harvey Robinson, Anzia's former friendly adviser and booster, was committee chairman. The gift was to be a portrait bust by the eminent British sculptor Jacob Epstein, who was then visiting the United States. Although the request was not from Dewey, it seemed like a sign of acceptance, a token that, thanks to her literary achievements, she had reached the status of other prominent Dewey friends and former students.

It was almost ten years since she had last seen him, but she read about him often. The *New York Times* had reported in July 1927 the death of his wife, Alice. He was about sixty-eight years old, still highly active and publicly visible in professional and political causes (the crusade to save Sacco and Vanzetti, for example), still writing on such subjects for the *New Republic*.

This man, who had always been in her thoughts, had given her a certain education, even during his absence. Reflecting on their past conversations and the seminar sessions, and reading his books, she had absorbed many of his ideas — political, philosophical, and literary — and used them in her writing. She was no longer the romantic of ten years ago. A middle-aged woman, forty-five years old, she was not only wiser, more understanding than when they had known each other; she was also, at least in the eyes of others, the successful writer he had made possible. At this moment she had the strongest motive for trying to see him again; she was lost. She had lost the purpose of what she was doing (as her father had warned) by making so much money. Ten years earlier, Dewey had given her a direction to follow; she must have convinced herself that she could get back that certainty if she saw him again. In any case, she hoped to erase the gracelessness of their last encounter. No longer a beggar, she could at least meet him now on equal terms.

When she wrote to ask for an appointment, he sent a brief note setting the day and hour, and so for the first time in ten years she arrived at his office once more. This time she had to wait outside his locked office door, inside the philosophy library at Columbia.

He was almost half an hour late. Their reunion, as she described it in *All I Could Never Be*, was for her a disaster. He showed up with a brief apology and remained as aloof and polite as if he were encased in glass. Against his cool, distant smile, she stumbled through an explanation for coming to see him. "The whole object of her quest — he — she — the very thought of any comradeship between them turned into a phantom. . . ." A telephone ring interrupted her embarrassed effort, and while he answered it she discovered her first book, *Hungry Hearts*, on his bookshelf. Pleased, she picked it up to look for her inscription and found that the pages were uncut.

In spite of all she had professed to herself in advance, she had actually hoped to regain his boundless kindness and a milder version of the friendship she had once had without asking. Although this account of their final meeting — a harsh experience for her — is based only on her fictional recollection, written at least a year or two later, it is probably reliable. She did embroider and change the truth of many events in her life when she was writing or talking about them, but about Dewey she seems to have been a careful reporter. Dewey associates have recognized him in her several fictional portrayals of his appearance and personality. Her report in *All I Could Never Be* of the Dewey research project in Philadelphia is corroborated by information in Dewey correspondence and other documents. She must have needed to recreate him believably for her own sake.

It is therefore reasonable to wonder about Dewey's calm detachment during their last meeting. Why, after keeping himself unavailable to her for so long, did he agree to see her? Out of curiosity? Or apprehension? (She still had his love letters.) Perhaps only to show her the futility of her dreams about him. But then why — a contrary signal — did he keep her uncut book prominently visible on an office shelf?

Anzia did not comfort herself with such questions. She was shocked by his indifference and struggled to say anything plausible as she picked up her purse and gloves "to escape from the horror . . . of two ghosts making dead conversation. 'Good afternoon,' came the dead monotone, holding open for her the door. 'I wish you all the success in the world.'" She had never foreseen, during the years of his absence, that the god she had enshrined far above all other men, the most understanding, most generous being she had ever known, could become this impersonal stranger.

Now she saw herself failing, as a woman and as a writer, wherever she turned in this completely heartless, competitive world. She had personally discounted the value of her success, but she had also become used to the applause and the money; and now she was losing it all.

The bruising failure with Dewey pushed her more firmly toward the idea of getting away, not to her sister's this time, but to a place where she could work. The retreat she chose was the lakeside campus of the University of Wisconsin. Several years before she had been invited and well paid as "woman of the year" to speak at another midwestern university, Ohio State. This time she was offered the privileges of a Zona Gale Fellowship, which meant that all the university classes were open to her; she could consult their faculty; she could browse in the intellectual company of noted scholars; and all her expenses for the year would be handsomely paid.

Wisconsin, with the La Follettes, was noted for its progressive politics and liberal labor legislation. Well-known university scholars had helped to draft that legislation. The new president of the university was Glenn Frank, who had previously been editor of *Century*, when that literary magazine published Anzia's "The Fat of the Land" and other stories, boosting her career at its beginning. So, besides presenting her with a feast of educational opportunity, the university seemed to Anzia a place where she could get new assurance and help while she began working on her next book.

The fellowship was intended for young, aspiring writers; it had come to Anzia because of her friendship with Zona Gale, who was a university trustee. In unpublished notes, Anzia once tried to explain the baffling (to her) nature of their encounters. She described Gale as a beautiful woman, elegantly dressed, ash-blond hair coiled in a high bun, gracious, friendly, untouchable—"a saint in cellophane"—by which Anzia expressed her admiration, envy, and frustration at not being able to get close to the other woman. Zona Gale was older and far more successful than Anzia. A novelist and playwright at the top of the literary world, she produced a new book every two or three years—such highly praised, best-selling novels as *Faint Perfume, Preface to a Life, Miss Lulu Betts, Papa La Fleur,* and over a dozen more. Gale had also won the Pulitzer Prize for her dramatization of *Miss Lulu Betts*.

The friendship began as a literary exchange. Anzia interviewed the Pulitzer Prize winner for a magazine piece about her because she greatly respected Gale's work, especially for "the restraint I lacked." Gale said at their first meeting, "I've been wanting to meet *you*. I feel I have known you a long time," and added her praise for Anzia's stories. After that they met on Gale's initiative whenever she visited New York from Wisconsin.

With Gale, as with everyone else, Anzia was an arresting conversationalist, even abrasive, cutting through pleasantries to reach her own point of interest, forcing the other person to match her own pace in pursuit of insight, always demanding the sharpest, deepest truth. There was even generosity in the challenging way she spoke. She blazed with emotion. A discussion with her was never ordinary. People who enjoyed this stimulus, Gale included, found Anzia exciting. But, then, they might also experience a sudden disillusionment (as happened to Dewey): the discovery, in this brilliant, daring woman, of a child.

Anzia shared with Gale the same dedication, the understanding of what it means to be alone. Gale always professed a keen, affectionate regard for her; and yet, despite Anzia's yearning for this friendship, it could not grow, it fell apart in the face of Anzia's devouring need. A word of sympathy and she spilled over. They were having tea at an early meeting, talking about their common writing experiences, and suddenly Anzia put down her cup and demanded: "You are so clear about life — tell me, *how* can I go on? Nothing is real to me but the past. *How* can I learn to be like other people?"

Each time in their conversation Anzia pounced, making such a demand, she wrote in these notes about Zona Gale: "there was a swift click of silence," — her supposed friend withdrawing. "The violence in my voice, the violence of my gestures must have opened the gulf between our different worlds. . . . I always felt her fear of me, her fear of my being too emotional. And I resented the kindness that cloaked that fear."

As she had earlier with Mary Austin, Anzia was doomed to reencounter that barrier throughout her life. Except with John Dewey, the only Gentile who had given her a deep and patient understanding. *He* had not felt threatened by her anxieties, her demands, her excess. Until she herself had turned off the current.

But setting off for Madison in the summer of 1928, she could brush aside such pessimism. She was going to the University of Wisconsin fortified by her acquaintance with its president and with Zona Gale's promise of introductions to its leading thinkers and doers. Her dream of immersion in the curriculum of a great university had returned: that its education could magically free her from insecurity and change her into a fluent, polished stylist.

"Something unripe, unfinished in me," she wrote in a supposedly formal letter of application for the fellowship (which Gale had already given her), "keeps me from living up to what I know. I feel if I could have a year's time to work out my problems under the guidance of trained minds, I'd be able to grow as a writer and become a saner, more useful human being."

She enclosed a carbon of this application in a letter to Gale on May 31, 1928, a month before her departure. "Zona — dearest friend," she wrote, inventing an intimacy that, it seems clear from her later notes about Gale, did not really exist, "this moment — I feel closer to you than to any human being I have ever known." She also felt sure of Gale's understanding, she wrote, "in spite of the unreasonable things I may do and say to shut myself out from you."

"You are Vision — Revelation." This friendship, the love it offered, if only Anzia could have believed in it, might have alleviated the hurt of her repeated failures with others. Zona Gale was magical — beautiful, successful, unfailingly generous. Yet, as she got closer, Anzia, like the child who denies love in order to be more tightly held, insisted there was a "chasm between your world and mine. . . . You say there is only 'one world.' If there is only 'one world,' show me — help me see it!"

In several unpublished chapters she left in her files, Anzia reported many years later her experiences at the university. She inserted the chapters tentatively into her fictional autobiography, *Red Ribbon on a White Horse*, but removed them because, she said, "I felt my criticism of education wasn't ripe enough." These chapters relate her startled reactions to some traditional university customs; for example, to a droning lecture on Shakespeare's literary sources for *Hamlet*, even to this lecturer taking off his watch and setting it on the lectern in front of him. She was naturally contemptuous of "sources" and any set procedures for analyzing literature, believing that the study of great books should be inspiring and uplifting rather than factual and scholarly. She was therefore offended by the "stale hash" and pedantry of some professors of literature and amazed at the joylessness of literature students enrolled "not for an education but to cram required courses."

She also wrote about a scholar who enlightened her, Max Otto, the philosopher to whom she came after her disappointments with the English department. Challenging him with her biased view of the university ("I thought at a University I'd learn to be whatever I was meant to be . . . at least I thought I'd learn how to write — "), she received a logical answer: "The miracle has to come from you, not the teachers. But we can help you formulate your questions."

She saw his point and calmed down. The freedom she enjoyed with Otto to speak freely and to be understood, not reproved as an outsider and ignorant critic, was a restorative. She returned several times for such healing conversations, and one day when she was in the midst of a fresh attack on "this petrified forest of dead knowledge," he commented on her extraordinary intensity. "You're Jewish, aren't you?" Instantly offended, she lashed out at him: "Did I ask you if you are Catholic or Protestant?"

He walked away from her in silence and brought back a glass of water. The water, and a book he took from his desk and gave her, dispelled her anger. It was by Spinoza, the ostracized Jew who, he said, had been his inspiration. "Other people met darkness with darkness," she wrote about this incident. "He turned on his light."

IN THE FALL, Anzia's daughter, now sixteen years old, came to join her, entering the university as a sophomore. Although Louise moved into a university residence for girls, and Anzia lived in a frugal furnished room a trolley ride away (as was her custom, she was saving most of the expense money for future need), they met more frequently than they had in New York. Each time they met Anzia carried along her current manuscript. They had lived apart for twelve years now, but with the comparative proximity Anzia got interested in her daughter's everyday problems. About the middle of the first semester Louise suffered adolescent heartbreak; the classmate who had been her attentive suitor suddenly stopped calling. It was a dark tragedy for Louise. Anzia, seeing a simple solution, telephoned the boy herself and *asked* him to call — so outraging Louise that she told her mother she would never look at her manuscripts again. Eventually, perhaps several weeks later, as the dark lightened, they were back to their normal arguments over a manuscript — Louise resuming her critic's lecturing role (she had grown vehement), Anzia meekly accepting the lectures.

When confronted with Louise's anger, Anzia would recognize, for the moment, that her behavior had been inexcusable. It never prevented her from behaving the same way again, and again, because she was fueled by an irrational, explosive need to protect — and of course manage — her daughter.

At the university, Louise was studying in the College of Arts and Letters. Anzia, with her taste for unfettered learning, preferred the classes of the university's new Experimental College. Its director was Alexander Meiklejohn, a philosopher and educator to whom she had been introduced early in the year. In the new college's unstructured program, students were free to question and argue with their professors as equals, a freedom Anzia applauded. The classes were lively. She participated in at least one classroom discussion — not enough to become disenchanted — and she invented the setting of such a class, with Meiklejohn as its instructor, for a chapter she wrote about a student struggling with a question of ethics.

This strident, redheaded young debater declares in class that he intends to change his name from Weinstein to Winston in order to be admitted to medical school. After becoming a doctor, he says, he will take back his Jewish name. Meiklejohn argues with him, citing Spinoza's courageous way of facing ostracism, which the student angrily rejects (Why must all Jews be crucified?). Then Meiklejohn turns to the narrator (Anzia) for her opinion. She answers with a supposedly personal story: she had once obtained a stenographer's job in a bank by hiding the fact that she was a Jew. "But I couldn't get away with it. . . . The day I gave up my Jewish name, I ceased to be myself. I ceased to exist. A person who cuts himself off from his people cuts himself off at the roots of his being; he becomes a shell, a cipher, a spiritual suicide — ."

Writing this chapter years after she left Wisconsin, Anzia borrowed the experiences of two young people with whom she was then involved — a nephew trying to get accepted by a medical school in San Francisco and her nineteen-year-old daughter, getting her first job in New York — to illumine her own remorse for having run away from her ghetto heritage. But in fact neither she nor Arnold Levitas, both assimilated Jews, had ever introduced their daughter to Judaism.

THE FELLOWSHIP year ended. Anzia returned to New York and began working on *All I Could Never Be* in the fall of 1929, the time of the stock market crash. She was writing about John Dewey.

All I could never be
All men ignored in me,
That I was worth to God

are the lines from Browning's poem she quotes on the title page. "I was a prisoner of an experience from which I could not escape till I saw Browning's lines," she told critic William Lyon Phelps in a letter about this book. They expressed for her how Dewey had, godlike, changed her life, rescued her, a would-be writer and substitute teacher, from a chaos of anger and self-doubt, and pushed her toward her greatest possibility. She was writing the story of this love that had once touched her, to free herself and also to preserve it from the ashes.

But New York in 1930, the year of confusion and panic following the crash, was a frightening, disturbing place for a writer. Anzia lost most of her small fortune as stocks became worthless, and her royalties were dwindling. Book publishers, fearful, were retrenching; magazines, suddenly losing circulation and advertising revenues, were not buying stories. Many failed, and their editors, Anzia's friends, were out of jobs. She had to escape, not only to be able to work, but also — an urgent need for her now — to live more cheaply.

In *Red Ribbon on a White Horse,* Anzia said that she took a train to the mountain village of Fair Oaks, New Hampshire, because she saw a photo of its best-known villager, a woman writer, in a promotion pamphlet issued by the state. The Anzia of *Red Ribbon* arrived one day, without previous acquaintance or warning, at the other writer's doorstep, was nevertheless welcomed, and then returned to New York only to pack for New Hampshire. Anzia's migration to Arlington, Vermont, may have happened like that. In the spring of 1931 she moved to Arlington because Dorothy Canfield Fisher lived there.

Fisher was another writer Anzia admired and greatly envied for her polished, unruffled prose in neatly plotted magazine stories and novels.

Her best-known books — *The Bent Twig, The Deepening Stream, Seasoned Timber, Rough Hewn* — distill the essence of farm families and landscapes in Vermont or the Midwest. Fisher herself, confronted abruptly by Anzia, was as generous and kind as her books suggest she would be.

"She arrived, weeping and distraught," Fisher later noted for the record in a folder containing Anzia's letters to her, "to try to live here — and I think to get some new materials to write about."

With this Vermont writer's help, Anzia rented a farmhouse for about twelve dollars a month. The furniture was donated by Fisher and Fisher's friends and neighbors. On the day Anzia moved in, they also put homemade bread, milk, butter, and eggs in the icebox. The backyard of this house, close to the only street of the village, had been planted with stringbeans and yielded a boundless supply all summer long.

Anzia's surroundings were farmland and mountains. Most of her neighbors were the farmers from whom she bought milk, eggs, and vegetables — busy people, laconic in speech, insulated from newcomers by their hard work and excluding customs. What could be more alien to them than an overemotional, East European Jewish New Yorker?

So for Anzia living there was lonely, lonelier than she had expected. She consoled herself with the enfolding mountains and the extremely low cost of food and rent. For about a year and a half she tried to adjust herself to this strange place. She had the example of Dorothy Canfield Fisher, who in this landscape kept producing stories and books.

Anzia had hoped for more companionship from Fisher. She still had the dream of what a writing friendship could be — an exchange in which Anzia could offer her wild, unsorted inspirations and scraps of stories, and in return absorb Canfield's neat, well-modulated style. "How could I have been fool enough to imagine," she wrote later in *Red Ribbon*, about a character named Marian Foster, "that my need for her would rouse in her a responsive need for me, that our differences would be a creative stimulus to each other!"

They were in fact extraordinarily ill suited even to understand each other. Unlike Zona Gale and other writers Anzia had previously sought out, Fisher, though willing to be charitable, did not feel she had much to gain from the exchange. She summed up Anzia, in the abovementioned notes, as "a Russian Jewess of little education and a very emotional temperament who had written a few intense books about (I think) Jewish immigrants in New York."

Over the year and a half of Anzia's stay, they never reached first-name familiarity; but they did meet now and then sociably. Judging from the letters Anzia wrote to Fisher after some of the meetings, their discussions were often held at Fisher's home and consisted mostly of Fisher enlightening Anzia. An articulate woman, Fisher had traveled widely, earned a doctorate at Columbia University, and done post-graduate work at the Sorbonne. Anzia appreciated Fisher's superior knowledge, sometimes just her explanation of Vermonters (the local shopkeeper, her landlord, the dairy man, her farm neighbors), whose reactions to Anzia's New York manners frequently upset her.

"You put the searchlight of your wide sympathy, your deep understanding on the dark muddle of my narrow experience," Anzia wrote at the end of her stay in Arlington; it was a letter of gratitude for "the countless talks on internationalism, the hours . . . of your precious time [spent] making clear to me my own story." Nevertheless, this letter and the others they wrote to each other reveal two obviously opposed points of view.

Fisher was happily married, well rooted in her family and community, confident and successful in her work, a leader in the village in charitable efforts and holiday celebrations. Her life seemed serenely lived with her husband and adult son in a large home, comfortably filled with heirlooms. Anzia's rootlessness (a middle-aged woman, about fifty-one then, and still looking for a home!) must have puzzled her at the same time it elicited her compassion.

To reciprocate for Fisher's many favors, Anzia volunteered a criticism of a story Fisher was writing:

> Your chief character . . . is too subjective for the ordinary reader. The average person hates such selfless goodness . . . [the reason] Christ was hated & betrayed. . . . It would help to make her more real if you can show how some of the people whom she is *trying to*

help & has helped find flaws behind her back. Little human vices such as watching her time when she is with someone.

Not a viewpoint Fisher would care for or adopt.

ANZIA ENLISTED editorial help in June 1931 from another unsympathetic source. After graduating from the University of Wisconsin, Louise, just turned nineteen, came to Vermont to spend the summer working with her mother on *All I Could Never Be*. It was a difficult and stormy time for both of them. Anzia's method of work — starting with rough typed pages (all her unsorted ideas emotionally crowded together) and working toward clarity — was hard on any helper because it demanded from that person a tolerant creativity without offering any sense of accomplishment. The helper had to suggest or rephrase words and ideas that Anzia would naturally change or discard in the final version when she had, by means of such help, finally sorted out her own intentions. But it was doubly hard on an immature daughter to whom her mother's manuscript had always been a misshappen intruder.

Louise was impatient with her mother's sentimentality and Jewish colloquialisms and was certain that she (Louise) was right. She agreed with her mother on the one fact: that Anzia wasn't really a professional writer. Figuratively gritting her teeth, the daughter set about cleaning up the manuscript like a necessary chore, ruthlessly insisting on cutting out whatever she believed was excessive or "crude." Anzia, always perceiving editorial wisdom in native-born Americans, and also weighted by feelings of guilt toward her daughter, would yield momentarily and then later try to restore her own healthy vitality and subversion. In appreciation of that summer's work, she dedicated the book "To my daughter Louise." Nevertheless, *All I Could Never Be* was probably devitalized by the smoothing out, wherever Anzia had permitted it.

The book was further handicapped by its virtually irrelevant, obviously tacked on ending. In this Anzia had been influenced in part by publisher George Palmer Putnam and, later on, by Dorothy Canfield Fisher.

Anzia was probably more willing than in earlier days to please a publisher; it had been five years since the publication of her previous book, *Arrogant Beggar*, which had fared poorly in the press and in bookstores. In a period of hard times, she was no longer in great demand. Putnam was the executive editor of the oldest and most distinguished publishing house in the country, G. P. Putnam & Sons. He was a grandson of the original 1837 founder and was also prominent as an explorer and author of books about his explorations. Along with his *Mayflower* heritage and adventurous career, which must have made him especially charming to Anzia, he was obviously an admirer of strong-minded women. The proof was his interest in Anzia's writing and, more particularly, in Amelia Earhart, whom he had also brought to his publishing house as an author and whom, in 1931, he married. Earhart continued her daring solo ocean flights after the marriage, evidently with Putnam's encouragement.

As a publisher, Putnam had had considerable success with the books of some outstanding writers of the period, but his influence on Anzia's book did not turn out well. Her novel *All I Could Never Be*, in telling about her encounter with Dewey, was also an explanation of how Anzia had reached her present situation: the end of love, the emptiness of success, the confusion of middle age, and even her effort to deny the need for sex while her body spoke insistently for it. She told of the blight that was impeding her work because of her loss as a woman: "The power to express had vanished. Without Henry Scott [John Dewey] she was dumb — impotent . . . bound to earth for want of [the] transforming breath of love." And she ended her novel with a planned return to the place where she knew she belonged: "Bathed in the poetry of ancestral memories, it seemed to her there was only one way to go on — to go back to her roots — back to the ghetto."

Putnam had persuaded her that this ending was unsatisfactory. Perhaps he pointed out how far Anzia was from that solution. But the two-chapter epilogue she tacked on to the manuscript was equally unbelievable for so strong-willed a woman. She wrote about a New Hampshire village to which Fanya (the writer in the book) had escaped from the dead end facing her in New York; about the kindness of the villagers and then her surprised discovery of their intolerance and even hostility toward the outsider or the eccentric. In particular there was a deaf old woman, a dairy farmer, who was ostracized by the rest of the village because of the queerness brought on by her disability. Into this setting, a strong, tall Russian-Polish commercial artist comes looking for work. Because he is, in a sense, Fanya's countryman, the librarian sends him to the writer, and Fanya befriends him with food and shelter when the villagers, fearing a stranger, shut their doors on him. He turns out to be a sensitive, intelligent man, as well as an artist. The act of sheltering him despite the village's disapproval warms and comforts Fanya. And so, at the end of the novel, they became lovers.

When Dorothy Canfield Fisher, at Anzia's (and Putnam's) request, read the manuscript with the appended ending, she was disturbed and strongly urged Anzia to make changes. Above all, she asked Anzia to disguise the New Hampshire villagers, especially the deaf old woman, because they were too recognizable as actual people of Arlington. It would cause them pain, Fisher said.

She advocated another change that, she said, was a matter of artistry. Without intending it, she matched Anzia's one-time criticism of a Fisher story — from the opposite vantage point:

> Their becoming almost at sight, actual physical lovers, will make your readers think . . . they have been mistaken in thinking that Fanya is a rare personality, will make them feel that she is only a common phenomenon a woman looking for a lover to satisfy her heart and body, rather than that rare one a human being looking for some meaning in the wretchedness of life that will satisfy her mind and soul, as well as her heart and body.

"That is the kind of people they are," Anzia insisted. "That is the whole tragedy."

In fact, her heroine had something of Anzia's temperament. "A Russian Jewess could never achieve the heroic power of restraint of an Emily Dickinson." And Anzia admitted in another letter: "The girl might have been a nobler character if she had learned restraint. But it wouldn't have been true to life. . . . Reality — the truth as I see it is to me more than art."

Despite Fisher's repeated arguments, Anzia was unwilling to transform the portraits of impoverished villagers she had depicted so believably in her novel. ("Those sordid details . . . are as vital to the sincerity of my picture as . . . beauty and idealism [are] vital to your "Hillsboro People.") She did change her mind about her heroine's behavior, however. Writing Fisher a few weeks later, Anzia conceded "The full meaning of what you said about that last scene suddenly hit me between the eyes." And so she replaced a frank, passionate embrace with a "delicate intimation" (Fisher's words) of a love to blossom in the future.

In *Red Ribbon*, published eighteen years later, Anzia was more honest, relating that the reason she went to Arlington (Fair Oaks) was an illusion ("I wanted to make a new start away from the market place where I had lost myself in the stupid struggle for success") and the reason she left it a recognition of the truth that she could never belong there ("The place was beautiful, but the sky wasn't my sky, the hills weren't my hills. It was a beauty that pushed me back into my homelessness").

Until she came to that realization, she tried to steer herself, in this alien environment, into a new writing direction. After Louise left Arlington, Anzia remained for another year, declaring in her letter to William Lyon Phelps about *All I Could Never Be*: "This novel ends the cycle of my experiences as an immigrant." (She must have been deeply affected by increasing comments from some critics that with each new book she was writing the same story over again.) "I have started something entirely new. A play. And I know as much of the technique of playwriting as I [once] knew about the writing of novels. I feel like a person who has set out in an airship across unknown seas — how — where will I come out in this venture? God only knows. But Ah — the thrill of wrestling with the dreams forever beyond us."

The play was probably a false start, as unnatural for Anzia as was her letter to Phelps. He was a man with whom she liked to be on friendly terms because of his importance (he often quoted her in his book column), but whom she didn't really admire. "A hummingbird who flitted from celebrity to celebrity," she described him later in *Red Ribbon*.

DRAMATIZATION of one of her stories may have been suggested to Anzia by Rose Pastor Stokes, who had written to her in a sorrowful mood. Anzia saw her now and then on occasional visits to New York.

Hard times, physical and financial, had struck Stokes. She had cancer, caused, she thought, by the police clubbings she had suffered when picketing a few years earlier. She was about fifty-two years old, and the harsh illness had taken away her beauty.

Her position in relation to Anzia was now reversed. Anzia, although in decline, was the well-known author of five books, with a sixth about to be published. Stokes, having turned her back on wealth when she fell out of love with Stokes — or perhaps in love with another man — had refused alimony and was no longer able to earn a living from her writing. She had a small home in Westport, Connecticut, where she hoped to earn some money by taking in boarders. In 1927 she had married V. J. Jerome, a Communist theoretician who worked as a language teacher. But the financial problems caused by her illness two years later had been overwhelming.

So Stokes had written her autobiography. She told Anzia she hoped to get as large an advance for it as Emma Goldman had received for her book *Living My Life*. Unfortunately, she could not find a publisher. She must have asked Anzia to use *her* influence.

Anzia's letters, full of sympathy, were not helpful. She had holed up in Vermont, she explained, because she could live there on thirty- five dollars a month; and she invited Stokes to come for a visit. George Palmer Putnam, who had published Stokes's play *The Woman Who Wouldn't* in 1916, and was publishing Anzia's *All I Could Never Be*, was unable to publish another book, even Stokes's autobiography; he had in a sense been forced out of his own publishing company.

"As a matter of fact the publishers lost heavily on Emma's book," Anzia wrote Stokes. "Publishing is in such a bad state that Putnam has . . . taken a job in the story dept of the Paramount movies. His name is still with the firm but he is practically out of it."

When Anzia moved back to New York, she discovered that her new book had become a victim of this dethronement: Putnam's uncle, the senior partner of the firm, had died; the man's son contested George Palmer Putnam's share of the inheritance and his authority. Putnam therefore left the firm abruptly, before Anzia's book was printed, taking with him his favored authors, including Anzia and his wife, Amelia Earhart. He brought their books to the house of Brewer & Warren, which, when he joined it, was immediately renamed Brewer, Warren & Putnam. A year and a half later this firm was dissolved and its list taken over by Harcourt, Brace & Company. Putnam then went to Hollywood to continue as story editor for Paramount Pictures.

The upheavals probably helped to depress the prospects for Anzia's new book when it appeared in the fall of 1932. Moving through three different publishing companies, it could scarcely have been promoted with any continuity. The Depression's effect on book sales was still severe; and the reviews of *All I Could Never Be* further damaged her diminishing literary reputation.

Only the *Christian Science Monitor* commended her. A couple of other critics gave the book faint praise in brief synopses. Some misread and completely misunderstood the book. For example, Geoffrey Hellman, in the *Menorah Journal*: "The title 'All I Could Never Be' derives from the fact that the man with whom Fanya is in love, Henry Scott, is symbolic of a bloodlessness, an ability to substitute work for life . . . to which she and her kind can never attain." The *New York Times* was bluntly negative: "From time to time Anzia Yezierska's name crops up . . . with books bearing titles like 'Hungry Hearts' and 'Salome of the Tenements,' and because of her personal background and history they demand some attention. . . . Unfortunately, however, apart from the original story she had to tell . . . her work as a creative artist has so far been negligible. This last book of hers, 'All I Could Never Be,' is no more a new book than a new edition of a previous publication."

Having once been a luminary, she now read obituaries for her decade of success. "This [book] is particularly disappointing," said the reviewer of a New York afternoon paper, "because one expected so much more from Miss Yezierska whose early short stories, which appeared some ten years ago, were fired with revolt and genuine feeling."

11

SILENCE

"SUDDENLY THE AMERICAN FAIRY—whether she is a good or a wicked fairy, who knows? —waves her wand and [Anzia Yezierska] is transported in an instant from Hester Street to Hollywood; from one day to the next . . . suffering is abolished for her. How does she feel? More unhappy than she has ever been in her life. . . . The foreshortening of time which is proper to a dream or a fairy story is a nightmare in actual life.

". . . By snatching her away from Hester Street and the only experience about which she knew, the film magnates effectively destroyed the possibility that their expensive goose might lay another golden egg. In fact, they gave it such a fright that it stopped laying altogether."

—W. H. Auden, from his introduction to Anzia Yezierska's *Red Ribbon on a White Horse*

From 1932, when *All I Could Never Be* appeared, until 1950, when she was close to seventy years old, Anzia published nothing. In 1950 book reviewers were surprised by the appearance of her seventh book, *Red Ribbon on a White Horse*, and the author's newfound skill. Most of them remarked that this book had emerged after an inexplicable eighteen-year "silence." It seemed as if she had been stunned into silence by the last, savage criticisms of her sixth book in 1932; and in *Red Ribbon* she said that, by leaving the ghetto and poverty, she had in those years lost the power to write. But it wasn't true. Throughout the eighteen years she had been, like a frantic swimmer caught in a down-current, fighting and shouting into a void: no one heard.

"The sudden paralysis or drying up of the creative power," Auden continues in his introduction to Anzia's last book, "occurs to artists everywhere but nowhere, perhaps, more frequently than in America; nowhere else are there so many writers who produced one or two books in their youth and then nothing."

Anzia's initial creativity had lasted longer than that of most such traumatized artists. Twelve years of recognition, six books, and scores of magazine stories before reaching the down-current. And then she had continued writing—no doubt in panic, as she discovered that nothing she wrote would sell. She had lost, it seemed very suddenly, her audience and her confidence, yet she couldn't stop writing because she was afraid of the emptiness if she did.

> Without a country, without a people, I could live only in a world I had created out of my brain. I could not live unless I wrote, and I could not write [what editors wanted] any more. I had gone too far away from life and I did not know how to get back.

Although she had come to disdain the circus of fraudulent publicity that had surrounded her for twelve years, a circus she had encouraged, its absence was shattering. At first she was not prepared to be a nobody again. When in a bookshop or restaurant she unexpectedly encountered one of her literary friends, perhaps a fellow celebrity of the recent past, she would start to smile a greeting — until she noticed that, as months, and then a year or two went by, they seemed not to see her. She had turned into Cinderella after midnight. Perhaps it was her own shame for having failed that made such encounters too difficult now. For having written a book that flopped, for stories that the editors didn't want, she condemned herself. She was remembering her father's gloomy predictions.

Walking on Eighth Street in the Village one day in 1934, she almost bumped into a man who ten years earlier had been her most ardent booster. He had been the publicity director of Boni and Liveright when Anzia's *Salome of the Tenements* was its best-selling novel. Now he was gray, less buoyant in his greeting, but he asked with simple curiosity, "What are you doing these days? I haven't seen your name in print." Instantly enraged, Anzia glared at him. How he had fawned and flattered her when she was Boni and Liveright's star! She said that she was working on a book and brushed past, leaving him in mid-sentence.

The silence suffocating her (while she still struggled to be heard) she thought came from the deafness and blindness of former friends and well-wishers, all members of "a society that feeds on the blood of young geniuses, exploits them while they are in fashion and then discards them like last year's models."

Editors, even critics, who had been pressing her only a few years earlier for more of the immigrant stories, relishing the gusto, the flavor of her earthy ghetto characters, now complained that she was repeating herself. When she ventured onto new ground — she tried writing, for instance, about Annie's son Oscar, who had fled to Paris and there had coldly turned away his mother when she came to visit him, a story Anzia called "Bonds of Blood" — her work was promptly rejected. In the confusion of finding herself unwanted, even invisible, without the assurance of writing about people whose gestures, emotions, and vocabulary she knew intimately, she foundered. The stories lacked conviction; she couldn't pull the pieces together with certainty. No longer were there willing editors eager for whatever she wrote, ready to help her smooth out the roughness. She had landed again in a strange new world.

All she could recognize now — and rebuff — were the hypocritical excuses or marked disinterest of people who, in good times, had professed friendship. Rubbed raw by these encounters, Anzia thought she discerned the same change in members of her family — her brothers, their wives and children, sometimes even in her daughter, now twenty years old and working as a secretary.

But from Louise's viewpoint, nothing much had changed. Her mother's frugality and fear of poverty — she never bought a newspaper, for instance, picking up discards from the street trashcans — were no different than they had been in the days of her comparative wealth. Anzia had always lived simply, whatever the address, with a bed and a desk and a couple of chairs surrounded by the same dusty books and manuscripts. Reading Anzia's writing had always been for Louise an unpleasant toll exacted for the Saturday visit. The writing, whatever story it was, was always in pieces, and it always seemed to Louise to have a crude, overemotional, not-quite-nice tone and texture that exasperated her. Louise didn't know, because Anzia didn't tell her, about all the rejections of the manuscripts between rewritings. Whether because of pain or mistrust, Anzia kept such information to herself.

After finishing *All I Could Never Be*, Anzia had taken off to visit Fannie again and recuperate. When she returned to the city, she moved into a furnished room, a ninth-floor front bedroom in a large Riverside Drive apartment house that had lost its grandeur in the Depression. She had decided on the uptown move to get away from what she now perceived to be fair-weather friends in the Village.

Anzia's new landlady was a young, pretty redheaded southern woman, a would-be concert singer who, as a sympathetic fellow artist, reduced the weekly rent a couple of dollars so that Anzia would take the room. In order to afford singing lessons and the long wait for concert offers and fame, she rented out most of her apartment, sharing the kitchen and bath with her tenants, and worked as a tearoom hostess. Meeting Anzia in the kitchen or having tea in Anzia's room, perhaps even suggesting a phrase or two for Anzia's newest page of manuscript, she would linger to discuss the reasons she had left Georgia, her present experiences with men, and troubles with overbearing tearoom customers. Still compensating for her youthful bondage in sweatshops, Anzia enjoyed in this case the glimpse into southern Anglo-Saxon life and once more how it felt to be young and pretty and American-born in New York.

She was in her early fifties then. After the lonely year-and-a-half period of working on a book in Vermont and her most recent disillusionment with the literary world, she was glad for the easy, random encounters with nonliterary people made possible by her reduced circumstances — talks with her fellow roomers, other tenants in the building, even young people she met in the Columbia University neighborhood.

Keeping to the early rising habits of her youthful sweatshop days, she would work on her manuscript from five or six in the pre-dawn till noon, devour a large lunch, and take time in the afternoon to walk out and see people.

The years had not tamed her as much as they do most women, although they had softened the fierce warrior's expression. She had never worn makeup. Now, as her cropped, auburn hair grayed, it looked reddish blond. She still took long walks and that, along with the constant emotional tension she experienced — whether from anger, despair, or exaltation — kept her fair skin flushed with color. She dressed always in the same tailored navy blue serge or gray tweed suits remaining from more affluent times, and in the same flat-heeled sandals. Middle-aged, she was still a handsome, unique woman, still a constantly surprising, exciting personality. She had a way of picking up in an elevator or in a shop someone with an intelligent face, carrying an interesting book, or wearing a dress she liked. She would challenge the person with a question about the book or, if he was carrying a newspaper, about an immediate event ("How do you like Roosevelt shutting up the banks? What does it mean?"), and if she got a worthy response, would pursue it further. She preferred, and seemed to attract, the young.

Vestiges of her former celebrity remained; her stories were still being reprinted in high school textbooks and popular anthologies, which her new acquaintances might have seen. The New York State Regents exam still included a question about her life: "Complete correctly the following sentence: Anna Yezierska (came as an immigrant to America, was the Little Mother of the Russian Revolution, was shot as a spy, is the heroine of a novel translated into English)." She was in fact now supported, though meagerly, by reprint fees, as well as the few bonds still left from her Hollywood wealth. But it was not so much her past fame that attracted young people. They were flattered by her frank interest in their ideas. As a perpetual outsider, advocating rebellion against the entrenched, whoever they were, she had much in common with some of her visitors, those who had recently left home and the restrictions of parents. A number of them were glad to read her manuscripts and offer suggestions. One of her new friends was an English major, a future professor whom she recruited at their first meeting. He didn't mind. He had read Anzia's stories in his classes. Although he himself was subdued by authority, he admired Anzia's fighting spirit so much that they corresponded for years afterward, and whenever he came to the city from his upstate university, he returned to read her manuscripts.

But along with these agreeable social interludes, Anzia suffered periods of deep depression. Her volatile emotions swung sharply from one extreme to the other, and the low periods lasted longer these days. She now had little contact with the editors to whom she still hoped to sell her stories; she had dropped even longtime friends. Offended by perceived slights, she had in one way or another abruptly cut off needed connections.

Sometimes in her gloomy assessment of her situation, she believed she had "written herself out." She lost faith in the stories she was writing and rewriting. In a dark mood, enduring a headache (to which she was frequently subject), she decided that her work had been going downhill, getting thinner and thinner, because she had nothing *real* to write about. She had lost touch with reality by leaving the ghetto, running after false gods. She accused herself of trying to run away from her Jewishness and at the same time defended herself (as if against her father) for wanting to escape him. To be a writer one had to live alone and be free; but once free, how could one write in a desert of loneliness? What was there to write about?

These ups and downs also weighed on Louise, her mother's steadiest visitor and confidante. Louise had always felt she had to rescue Anzia from despair — but how? On the other hand, when Anzia thrust a manuscript at her daughter and Louise faced a familiar, often-worked-over page now completely and devastatingly rewritten, Louise would savagely attack whatever Anzia had changed, or she would refuse to read it any further.

ANZIA HAD DECIDED, from her daughter's first school compositions, that Louise was exceptionally talented; she kept nagging her daughter at the weekly Saturday visits, and in phone calls in between, to devote the spare time after work during the rest of the week to lonely, unrewarding dedication to art. Louise thought, yes, someday she would probably become a famous writer. She made a small effort in that direction, starting short stories, even the first chapter of a novel. But meanwhile there were easier, more attractive ways to spend one's time, and her mother's example was not persuasive.

Unpredictably, shockingly, Anzia would now and again jump into her daughter's life, trying to rearrange it in a more desirable pattern. This time there was the terrible example of Adele, Louise's roommate, a girl Anzia had introduced to her daughter when Louise wanted to halve the apartment rent. But Anzia determined soon afterward that Adele and her boyfriend were wasting too much of Louise's time in idle partying. So she telephoned Adele's Jewish Orthodox parents in Buffalo and revealed to them Adele's secret: their daughter was in love with a *goy*, and if the parents didn't get Adele back to Buffalo right away, she would surely marry him. Louise returned from work that night to find Adele crying and packing. Adele's mother was in a Buffalo hospital in critical condition after a heart attack.

Adele was gone. The outrage Louise felt washed over Anzia like a summer rain. She had accomplished her purpose. She and Louise continued that rocky, fighting relationship, and yet they needed each other. Anzia found Louise often harsh and unfeeling, savage in her criticism of the manuscripts, and, above all, deliberately unwilling to understand her. If Louise hated the manuscripts, Anzia said, it meant that Louise hated Anzia herself. No, Louise said, but she didn't like the manuscripts being thrust at her every Saturday, no matter what. She was angered by her mother's disregard for anyone else's feelings — those of Adele, Adele's mother, and for that matter Louise — as evidenced by, the telephone calls that would wake Louise early Sunday morning or interrupt her at night in a private moment with a friend, and in any case came too often. She didn't know how to ward off Anzia's intrusions. It annoyed her that when Anzia would become politely acquainted with one of Louise's friends, she would later ask for filial service from that friend — editing, carpentry, errands, or some other kind of help. More than anything else, Louise hated being swallowed whole — Anzia taking for granted that Louise liked the same things and felt the same way Anzia did, or that she could act in Louise's behalf.

There were periods when Louise refused to read the manuscripts and prohibited the early-morning phone calls. But that didn't help, because when she didn't see Anzia or speak to her by phone, instead of enjoying the freedom, it made her gloomy. The knowledge of Anzia alone and unhappy — so much more desperate in her loneliness than anyone else — was unbearable. The phone calls, even the manuscripts, were lifelines nourishing both of them.

During that time, the first half of the 1930s, Anzia moved a lot, perhaps because her writing had also become rootless. She was restlessly trying out subjects. It may have been through the Riverside Church, which she attended once in a while because she liked the sermons, and because it was near her room, that she learned about the cooperative house for people of similar backgrounds (middle class, but cast adrift in the Depression). "The Gilded Poor House," Anzia named it when she started a novel about it. By that time she had moved into the brownstone cooperative and discovered its different kind of poverty, so much quieter and more secretive than the ghetto's.

A poorhouse to Anzia had nineteenth-century connotations; it was the dreaded end for the impoverished old when they were no longer able to work on a farm or in a factory. But her housemates were not that old or that destitute; they were ex-professionals, ex-bookkeepers, even a librarian, refined in their dress and manners, clinging to the relics of their former status, but somehow seedy.

After the novelty of their company wore off, and Anzia realized there couldn't be any companionship among people who each pretended to be better off than the rest, she moved out, taking along her notes for the new novel. She wrote several chapters of *The Gilded Poor House* in the following year, but she could not continue it. She didn't sympathize with these people. They were all pretenders.

Then she spent a summer at the MacDowell Colony for writers and other artists in Peterborough, New Hampshire, and a fall and winter in New York's Greenwich Village again, sharing an apartment on Twelfth Street with Louise. Her daughter was now an assistant editor on a subsidized publication devoted to economics. It was the first time they had lived together since Louise was four years old. They were resolved out of necessity to turn over a new page in their relationship.

The apartment was a floor-through. Anzia had the rear bedroom, Louise the front. Between them was the living room, giving access to the kitchen and bath, as well as to the outside door. Theoretically, since they had two shut doors between them, both had privacy. But in fact their opposed routines kept colliding. Louise, coming home with a friend after dinner on a weekend night, laughing and then abruptly hushing her friend in the hall, might wake Anzia from her first sleep. Or Anzia might rush out to the bathroom in her flannel nightgown just as Louise was greeting someone at the door. Anzia, making breakfast at dawn, scraping the pot as she spooned oatmeal from it, annoyed Louise, especially on Sunday mornings.

Louise slept later but she was also tidier, more deliberate (like her father); the daughter was irritated by the food-smeared pots in which her mother cooked. After devouring breakfast in haste, Anzia left the dirty dishes, unmade bed, unwashed face and hands (for a later moment or never) to get immediately to her worktable. That instant she had to go over the notes scribbled at waking moments during the night and add the first fresh thoughts of morning. She couldn't wait; she would write in spurts of ideas as fast as she could, and later try to assemble the parts. She wanted order in her disorder, but she didn't have time or thought for scrubbing or dusting *now*; she had to capture the early morning's vitality.

And although Louise was away at a job most of the week, her irritation with her mother's habits, in fact the very example the daughter set — cleanliness before art — sometimes disturbed Anzia so much (her own daughter an "all rightnik"!) that, if she were not so driven, she would have found it difficult to keep her mind clear for her work. Many times Anzia admitted to herself and to Louise that "if I hadn't left you with your father and your grandmother back then," Louise might not have been so perverted by bourgeois attitudes. To Anzia's dismay, not only had Louise become "crazy clean," but also, when it came to getting a job and pushing ahead of other people, she had had Anzia's aggressive spirit knocked out of her. Anzia's daughter didn't know how to fight, except against her mother. Which was why Anzia felt it necessary to intervene now and then on Louise's behalf.

That spring Louise moved to a clean and tidy apartment uptown and soon after that Anzia gave up the Twelfth Street apartment and took the train to Fannie in California. She traveled west every two or three years during those dispiriting times. After each try in a new direction and its disappointment, she turned back to her older sisters — to the familiarity and comfort of those to whom she didn't have to explain herself. Annie had been a constant refuge ever since Anzia at seventeen had left their father's home, but Annie had died a hard, lingering death in 1928 at the age of fifty. Her sister's long agony of dying (of pemphigus, a rare skin disease) tore away some of the already unstable ground under Anzia's feet. After that she wrote to Fannie frequently between visits, and Fannie, now widowed and still maternal, sent her packages of California dried fruits and cookies.

Anzia would return to her sister's large, comfortable home in Hollywood as if returning to her beginnings. She couldn't go back to the noisy dirt of the ghetto or to the now warmly remembered religious fervor of her father's chanting (he too was dead); but being with Fannie was being "at home" for a while. Fannie gave her a sunny room to herself and quiet; the house was always hushed for Anzia. Fannie's children had long since left, and she was lonely, eager for reminiscences of their youth. She treated her younger sister like a visiting dignitary, waiting on her with food and whatever she wanted. Nevertheless, accepting all this service as her due, Anzia wearied of it fairly soon. She rediscovered with each visit that Fannie's life, and the kind of card-playing friends she had, were "stultifying." From her viewpoint, Fannie, overweight since her marriage, had succumbed too readily to the fleshpots.

She was offended by her sister's innocent "all rightness," her beaming delight over her children's achievements — Fannie's son was a doctor and her daughter, Cecelia, was now a film critic for *Variety* and married to a successful Broadway songwriter. Fannie's constant satisfaction with things as they were, Anzia thought, was disgusting. Her overweight and the overabundant food she put on the table to please Anzia became for Anzia the symbols of Fannie's callous disregard for the suffering that Annie and Anzia and others in the family had experienced. This was the Depression! When Anzia came back to New York after one of her visits and began to worry again about dwindling resources, the memory of Fannie's fat-of-the-land made her angry and she lashed out in a bitter letter, describing how she, Anzia, was living in a cheap furnished room and counting pennies each time she went to the grocer. She accused Fannie of being money-bloated and unfeeling.

Shocked, Fannie sent a check in her answering letter, writing in sorrow and bewilderment. What had she done to Anzia to deserve such venom? By then Anzia had had time for contrition. Her younger brother, Henry, had just arrived from seeing Fannie in California and vigorously enlightened Anzia about her painful, unjust attack on their sister. So Anzia wrote Fannie two hastily penciled letters of apology that managed *not* to apologize:

> . . . and I told [Henry], "Yes. You're right. You're right. You're right." I had to promise to sit right down . . . and on bended knees confess to you my guilt. But even while confessing I was wrong & intolerant with all my intolerable meanness — you know in your heart of hearts what was behind all that. — No use going on talking words. We are different. Let us forget & forgive the past & make the most of what little there's left.

Fannie of course forgave. Perhaps Anzia did. She still went back to Fannie's for reassurance or comfort, although she never stayed as long or returned as often as Fannie would have wished. In late February 1935, she left Fannie's comforts to travel to El Centro in California's Imperial Valley, which had become famous to newspaper readers as the center of continuing farm labor battles. A series of strikes by the migratory fruit and vegetable pickers had erupted at the harvest times of the different crops throughout 1933 and 1934. The lettuce workers' strike had just been defeated.

The fact that poor, uneducated migrants of diverse ethnic strains were able even to band together was due in part to desperation — the wage rate had dropped on some ranches to as little as fifteen cents an hour — in part to more sophisticated strike leaders, some of whom were Communists, and also to the funds raised from sympathizers outside California. One tactic was to rent, in the strike area, some farmland on which the strikers could put up tents and hold out.

Growers had also organized, and had armed forces of police, sheriff's deputies, American Legion volunteers; they had also hired strikebreakers to raid the strikers' camps and battle the "reds." The townspeople naturally favored their farmer neighbors. Farm roads were patrolled against "outside agitators"; food and supplies sent by sympathizers were confiscated; strikers were beaten up, some even tarred and feathered and chased out of town. Many others had been arrested and jailed despite the efforts of the American Civil Liberties Union. One ACLU attorney had been seized in his El Centro hotel room and dropped out in the desert.

At the time Anzia took the train to El Centro, a trial of eight strike leaders charged with "criminal syndicalism" was under way and was going badly for the defendants. Recalling her sweatshop days when, as a girl of sixteen, she had herself defied a boss, Anzia, now about fifty-four, was seeking a subject as worthy as the ghetto sweatshop, exposing herself once again to "reality" after her long absence from it.

But as soon as she stepped off the train and started asking questions, the police chief arrived to take her to the town jail. Who was she? Her Russian-sounding name aroused suspicion. Why had she come to El

Centro? Why had she asked for the courthouse? Anzia said the town librarian might tell him who Anzia Yezierska was. So he telephoned the library and when the librarian instantly identified her and told him, over the phone, the whole Cinderella story, he turned polite and apologetic. It was those agitators, he explained. He had to protect the town from Bolsheviks.

By the end of that afternoon, after Anzia had asked him why he was meeting the trains, his feelings about the strike, and his attitude toward *his* bosses, she had made a friend of him. He was gratified by the interest of an author whose books had become movies. He invited her to his home. When Anzia came to the library, the librarian invited this eminent author to *her* home. In El Centro, among the social circles of the police chief and the librarian, Anzia once more received the pleasant attentions given to a celebrity. She even liked the police chief. He and the librarian and their friends gladly supplied her with the town's official story of the strike and the criminals on trial. They also prevented her from speaking to any lettuce workers.

SO, FOR FOUR YEARS, she had explored avenues that turned out to be dead ends, writing and saving notes, producing chapters with no conclusions. Then, late in 1935, she came back to New York and discovered the connection with life she had been seeking.

In *Red Ribbon on a White Horse*, Anzia later wrote of this time, saying that in the course of job hunting she sat in Union Square park and met other jobless people on the park benches; she joined them again in Stewart's Cafeteria at meetings to organize the Writers' Union, then marched with them in a demonstration to demand government jobs. That was fiction derived from the experiences of Louise's friends, and from the story about them, "Cafeteria Society," written by Louise, which was published in *Scribner's* magazine in 1938. Anzia would have carried a banner, if asked, but she was not in New York during those days of ferment. The WPA arts projects were already established when she came back to the city. The federal government, after initiating the projects for the fine arts and for theater, was starting one for writers—"one of the noblest and most absurd undertakings ever attempted by any state," wrote W. H. Auden in his introduction to *Red Ribbon*. Writers were to be paid a weekly salary, like carpenters or bricklayers. The plan was noble in that the government was for the first time recognizing artists as worthy of support; and it was absurd, Auden comments, because there are no possible standards a bureaucracy can use to choose and assign thousands of artists to create art.

Some of Anzia's younger acquaintances and Louise's friends were already employed and receiving $21.67 a week on the WPA Art Project or the Theater Project. Louise's best friend was a children's art teacher on the first project. Anzia, who in Hollywood had rejected a job paying twenty times the WPA salary, because she would have had to produce stories on demand, now saw the Writers Project as a heaven-sent solution to all her problems: a way out of her uncertainties and, besides that, a steady income.

There was one daunting obstacle. In addition to showing some proof that she was a professional writer, she had to pass a poverty test. Applicants were taken only from the welfare rolls. Proving professional competence was apparently simple. All kinds of writers, including a high school essay contest winner and the author of a typewriter manual, qualified for these government jobs, Anzia discovered after she got on the project. Qualifying for welfare was far more complicated. Anzia, who felt entitled to disregard rules made for everyone else, was accustomed to outwitting bureaucrats. Ever since her schoolteaching days, she had maneuvered her way around official nonsense. For the WPA, though, she took lessons in deceit from younger, more inventive deceivers.

The trick was to seem to be absolutely penniless and yet to be living somewhere on thin air. One needed an address to prove one was a New York resident, also in order to be visited by a welfare investigator and then to receive the eligibility notification by mail. But one was not supposed to have money to pay the rent or for any other needs, nor any relatives or friends who could help. Anzia closed her small bank account and asked a niece to keep the money for her; she answered the investigator's questions like a pauper, produced skillfully altered envelopes from old letters that indicated she had lived at the same place for two years, and after waiting through a period on welfare, became one of the elect on the Writers Project.

It was like being readmitted to the excitement of youth — a kind of rebirth that made her extraordinarily happy. "I feel like a bit of withered moss that has been suddenly put into water, growing green again." She had escaped from isolation and financial worries, from the claustrophobia of writing manuscripts that no one would read or publish. And she had the company of all kinds of writers. Newcomers to literature and survivors from the 1920s — Richard Wright, John Cheever, Harry Kemp, Maxwell Bodenheim, Edward Dahlberg, Claude McKay, Harold Rosenberg — were among those who worked there; also hacks, poets, would-be poets and novelists, ex-newspaper reporters, advertising and cookbook writers. Even the eccentrics seemed interesting to Anzia — like Joe Gould, an elfin alcoholic who, outside the project, was writing the oral history of the world by talking about it mostly in bars; and a delicate New England lady who wrote poems only about flowers.

Most of the writers were required to turn in reports on New York scenes for a future guidebook. Anzia applied for the Creative Writing Section, so she could do her own work. Because her name was recognized by the director of the project, Orrick Johns, a poet and former book reviewer, she was assigned to that section, like others of comparable reputation. These writers received the superior salary of $23.86 a week.

Orrick Johns was a sensitive, sympathetic overseer, considerate even of the nonwriters on the project. His appreciation gave Anzia the tacit support she needed to write with vigor again — and now she had a subject. She had taken a cheap apartment on Morton Street in the Village, a mile or so from the Port Authority building that housed the project. When she finished her early morning writing at home, she could walk to the project "as lighthearted as if I were going to a party."

It *was* a party for her. A massive, high-ceilinged freight elevator, big enough for a public bus, carried the writers up to a great hall — one undivided floor of the building, a square city block of noisy activity, blending voices, typewriters and other clattering distractions — where six hundred worked. Social gaiety was readily available. In the morning, the writers exchanged greetings and gossip as they arrived and signed in. During the day, groups went out for coffee or lunch to share their complaints, and on paydays, after turning in their assignments, there was Tony's bar.

> On the first payday everybody went to Tony's Bar to cash his check. . . . Then we crowded into the smoke-filled banquet hall at the rear of the bar, ordered a feast — a thirty-five-cent . . . dinner. . . . We were as hilarious as slum children around a Christmas tree. Pockets jingled with money. Men who hadn't had a job in years fondled five- and ten-dollar bills with . . . tenderness.

There were also frequent Writers Union meetings at which they discussed grievances and planned protests. "To keep what we had," Anzia reported the union leaders' dicta, "we had to stay on the offensive and persistently make demands for better working conditions and more pay."

Political factions had sprung up within and outside the union, seeking power from this shipwrecked community. The most efficient and best organized were the Communists. Flailing weakly against them were Trotskyites, America Firsters, anti-Stalinists, pro- and anti-Roosevelt groups.

The younger writers, who were more gregarious, were especially friendly to Anzia because, in spite of her past fame and despite being in her mid-fifties, she was happy to be in their company. Joining them over a cup of coffee, she enjoyed a semblance of the comradeship of poverty she had known in her youth. For the first time in years, she belonged. The constant bubbling of conspiracy — of writers against the bosses (editors and supervisors) and against the project hierarchy in Washington — was nourishment to her. Although she didn't participate in the sit-ins and other forms of union protest (because she was home working), she supported most of their causes in principle and put her name on the petitions.

She was required to sign in only once a week for her paycheck and to show some portion of her manuscript once a month, but she would come in sometimes just to catch up on the latest developments in the continuing melodrama unfolding in that great hall. On top of the discords and intrigues naturally developing among such oddly assorted personalities forced to work in supposed harmony, periodic bolts of lightning flashed from Washington. Almost every month someone in Congress or in the right-wing press uncovered scandals among the writers or artists proving that the projects were shameless "boondoggles." New directives came from Washington in response to these accusations, replacing supervisors, tightening procedures, cutting budgets, and ordering the firing of "incompetents." And in response to the frightening new strictures, the union staged increasingly vigorous protests.

Writing about these events in *Red Ribbon on a White Horse*, Anzia described the project largely in comic terms, as a carnival; one could both laugh at and grieve for her heroes. She understood the high-intensity exhilaration of Richard Wright at the beginning of his career, winning the *Story* magazine prize, which meant publication of his first book. She believed that "he had the intelligence to take what he could get wherever he went and build with it. He would . . . not become rattled by [success] as I had been." For him and for Anzia, toward the end of her career, the project was the vital support (intellectual as well as financial) they needed to keep on writing.

She also sympathized, in *Red Ribbon*, with the fantasies of the nonwriters and long-finished writers for whom the project, although it gave them the illusion of professional work, was actually a dole. From the puckish middle-aged Joe Gould, Harvard graduate and ex–Boston aristocrat, who kept talking about the book he never wrote, she created the character of Jewish scholar Jeremiah Kintzler, "a caricature of genius," whose life of Spinoza turned out to exist only in his conversation, adding to him aspects of herself and of her father.

In 1938 the Dies House Un-American Activities Committee staged a highly publicized hearing on the WPA projects with testimony from a right-wing writer-informer. Soon after that an army engineer was put in charge of the WPA and he appointed new project directors. In New York Orrick Johns was replaced by a more efficient bureaucrat and the

Creative Writing Section, in which Anzia had enjoyed complete freedom, was terminated. All writers were ordered to turn in a certain minimum wordage daily. The end of the project was in view.

> We . . . were forced to keep up the bluff of "honest work" . . . shoveling meaningless words from one dead pile to another and then back again. . . .
>
> Every day it became harder to blind ourselves to the cold fact that we, like the privy-builders and road-makers of other public projects, were being paid not for what we did, but to put money into circulation.

Soon after that, Anzia quit. She was already immersed in the book that would become *Red Ribbon on a White Horse*. Writing it occupied most of the next ten years. The manuscript kept changing shape as she wrote and then removed chapters. In the end it was a comparatively brief book — less than two hundred pages. She submitted it, in various shapes and with different titles, to many publishers during those years; it was repeatedly rejected.

"We are sorry to have to tell you," wrote a Houghton Mifflin editor (*not* Ferris Greenslet, to whom she had sent it), "that we do not feel sufficiently certain of finding a market for 'Sing O Barren' to justify us in making you a publishing offer." This was in October 1943.

Anzia had absorbed other blows earlier in 1943. Fannie, her ultimate refuge, died of cancer in the spring. Hearing the terrible prognosis, Anzia had traveled to California to be with her sister at the end, but she became so angered at slights she felt she had received from Fannie's two children, Cecelia and Victor, that she left Los Angeles abruptly, before Fannie's death. Then she suffered months of remorse, haunted, she wrote Louise, by "the tragedy of . . . Fannie's whole life — how she had tried to get hold of life through her children — through overfeeding people tried to appease the loneliness, the hunger. And I who should have known better, left her when she was dying, because I allowed myself to be hurt by Victor's uniform and Cecelia's fine clothes and her snobbery. How could I survive the pain of life that sometimes seizes me if not by trying to put it in the Journal of My Other Self?" (the latest change of title).

In such dark moods, feeling piercingly alone, she forgot that she had herself pushed away many friends because they were not instantly responsive when she wanted them. She saw herself as an outcast, like Spinoza.

> In the life around him he saw nothing but phantoms pursuing bubbles. Everyone aimed at the possession of something outside of himself. . . . Each one sought to be other than he was naturally. And they were all unhappy. I shall strip naked, said Spinoza. . . . I am overloaded, suffocating under the rags of beliefs . . . desires and ambitions. I will go on the quest for something *new* — myself!

These are marked lines in her copy of Benjamin DeCasseres's *Spinoza: The Liberator of God and Man*. Ordinarily she liked reading and studying the more stylish writers — Elizabeth Bowen, Henry James, Katherine Mansfield, Somerset Maugham, Aldous Huxley, Graham Green, Thomas Wolfe, Edith Wharton, and above all, and repeatedly, Henry James, who as a writer was everything she was not. But for companionship in her loneliness, she derived comfort from writers who had suffered as she had. She marked lines to read again and again in Oscar Wilde's *De Profundis*, Walt Whitman's *Leaves of Grass*, George Santayana's poems, and the reassuring psalms her father had once chanted from the Bible. She had fled from her father's stern, masculine religion, but she was still a believer urgently seeking God. She had tried out Christian Science, Theosophy, Baha'i, and other non-Jewish deviations. But it was the Old Testament she reread most often.

She wrote about these feelings to Louise during the wartime years 1943 through 1945, when she couldn't pick up the phone to reach her daughter (Louise, a volunteer with the American Red Cross, was in the southwest Pacific): "I've been going through the most awful feeling of lostness . . . like one dead among the living. . . . I can no longer delude myself with attempts at writing." But a day later Anzia might be in a buoyant state. The Village was like a small town; she met acquaintances as she walked out on the street after her morning's writing. Young people who had worked with her on the WPA, neighbors, many of them aspiring writers or artists. Often she met one or another of Annie's children. Annie's youngest daughter, Ruth, who lived nearby, might be out with her four-year-old daughter, Kathy, Anzia's special delight. "I'm going to read to her Alice in Wonderland. Someone lent me the book and I'm reading it for my own benefit as well. I never read it before." She was writing to her daughter as often as her simmering emotions dictated. "You don't know how much I enjoy your letters!" Louise wrote back from Australia. "Because you write them as if you'd just stopped talking to me — and without premeditation."

At a distance, she and Louise were more tender toward each other than they could ever be in the same room. Anzia wrote most of the time about the book, around which everything else revolved. "I'm still at the William Fox chapter," she said in a May 25, 1943, V-Mail letter. "My, is it hard! But I'm at it." And ten letters later, on June 25:

> I blew up at Celia the other day. In one of my impulsive moods of resentment, I returned to her by special delivery some [worn] clothes she brought. What is this terrible feeling of resentment and hate that blows up between us . . . ? After it's over I always regret it . . . too late. Thank God that when everything fails me and I make a mess of the few remaining relatives, I have this book to go back to — I'm doing a chapter on which I have worked on and off for a year and a half.

On August 19:

> Yes, I feel I've at last got the title for my book if I *ever* get it done.
>
> *Hymn of the Homeless*
>
> How do you like that . . . ? It [speaks for] the Jews in the present state of society and [for] me.

She didn't mention Houghton Mifflin's rejection of the manuscript in October. Instead, she wrote to Louise:

> I still can't get over the miracle that you & I are such genuine friends. It's not what we write to each other, but so much of what we don't have to write. . . . In fact, I often feel closest to you when I let the drunken preoccupation, the crazy obsession with my infernal, endless book crowd out my letter to you.

"Somehow I feel that . . . distance has brought us closer together," she repeated later that month in a letter of expiation, starting with "the criminal things people do . . .

> When you understand all that led to the commission of the crimes you cease to condemn — I'm talking of the time I left you with your father and your well-meaning ignorant grandma — and you were exposed to . . . harsh experiences before you were old enough to cope with them. If you could understand all that led to that seeming irresponsibility on my part, you would . . . forgive me. And I feel that you . . . do forgive even if you can't see why I did it . . . by the natural way in which you write me of all that is happening to you. . . . Your letters make up for everything — for loneliness, for illness, for guilty conscience and death itself — everything is evened out with your letters.

When Anzia proposed taking those letters to a literary agent or at least to the newspaper (*PM*) where Louise had worked as a second-string movie reviewer ("All your letters are priceless impressionistic records," she kept nudging, "which you can incorporate in your coming novel"), Louise said a firm but gentle no. Anzia had been proud of her daughter's byline on *PM* — she had, unknown to Louise, nagged Cecelia into getting Louise the job as Cecelia's assistant — but she seemed even more delighted when Louise quit the job to join the Red Cross and send letters back from the Pacific, an experience she thought was turning Louise into a stronger, deeper person, in fact a writer. Her daughter kept denying the exaggerations ("I don't think I'm being reborn, as you do. . . .I don't transform myself with each new experience"), but in the mail she never flared into anger, as she had always done in reaction to her mother's overpowering, insistent pushes when they were together.

ANZIA WAS STILL WORKING on the book, now called by its final title, when Louise came back to New York soon after the war's end. The new title came from a proverb Anzia said her father had taught her. Or she may have invented it herself: "Poverty becomes a wise man like a red ribbon on a white horse."

Through a series of agents, the manuscript had been rejected numerous times. Depressed and once more fed up with the literary folk of the Village, Anzia moved to a furnished room uptown near Columbia University. Then she trudged with her manuscript to show it to some of the distinguished university scholars nearby, including Henry Steele Commager, Lloyd Morris, Reinhold Niebuhr (whose class in Applied Christianity she had started attending). Although none of these people could get her book published, they gave her extraordinary encouragement. Urged by Niebuhr, these eminent men read and admired her manuscript and promised to praise it in print once it was published. Niebuhr, who had introduced her to the others, now also arranged for Anzia to meet his friend the poet Wystan Hugh Auden, and Auden, at her request, agreed to write an introduction for the book.

That promise may have been enough to persuade a publisher. Late in 1949, Charles Scribner's Sons accepted *Red Ribbon*. "My dear Mr. Wheelock," Anzia wrote to the editor that November in a hallelujah of delight,

> Can you thank the sun for shining or the rain that falls on parched ground for making it live again? No more can I thank you for being the poet-editor that you are — for picking up a downtrodden, crushed worm of a manuscript like mine and seeing in it not only the rejected human soul of an individual, but the soul of a race, a people. . . .
>
> The way has been so long and hard and lonely that your acceptance of the Mss. is still like a mirage in the desert. . . . I feel that writing is only the half of [a book]. . . . The creative spark of the editor who feels and knows what you're trying to say . . . makes it come to life.

At the thought of writing again, I'm like Naaman, the leper, bathing in the river Jordan, feeling his flesh grow fresh and clean as a child's.

John Hall Wheelock, a poet and above all a kind and thoughtful man, was touched. "We are proud and happy to be the publishers of *Red Ribbon on a White Horse*," he assured her, while tactfully mentioning in the same letter that there would have to be revisions. He thought perhaps she tended to be "too humble and too grateful to others. An editor is not much. Don't feel that when you have done a fine piece of work you should be too grateful in those who recognize it."

For two or three months after that, while she worked on revisions and submitted them to Wheelock, Anzia enacted the role of a literary Rip van Winkle, grateful, even rapturous, to those who had waked her from a long sleep. Wheelock's unfailing respect and tactfulness must have compensated for years of disrespect and nonentity. She wrote him again on January 15, 1950, about

> the miracle that you've actually accepted my manuscript and [that] my lost world of lost people will have you for their . . . editor.
>
> I go about like one risen from the dead. Cycles of experience long buried . . . leap into life. Stories . . . clamoring to be written all at once. While waiting to hear from you about revisions, I finished one of those short stories. It's still only a rough draft without any literary form. But it would be a great help to know what you think of it. May I bring it along next Wednesday [when we discuss revisions] and leave it for you to read . . . at your leisure?
>
> At seventy [She was probably a couple of years younger], one lives on borrowed time, aware that any day may be one's last day. And tied to this woman of seventy is this over-eager East Side novice, just learning how to write, bursting with stories that would take seventy more years to complete.

Upon accepting her book, Wheelock also wrote to "Dear Auden" to make sure of the promised introduction. This would obviously help to sell the book. He said that "Miss Yezierska . . . is tremendously grateful to you for your interest — indeed, she tells me that the book would not have been written without your kindly encouragement, your counsel." Anzia must have told him that, cavalierly erasing the years of effort and scores of helpers before she met Auden. Perhaps she had also said as much to Auden, who not only arranged with the publisher to accept a minimal fee ($150) for the introduction, but tried to arrange that this would not come from Anzia's advance (the usual source for such fees). Instead, Scribner's paid half the fee, and the other $75 was to be charged against Anzia's future royalties.

But after a few months of these graceful exchanges with her benefactors, Anzia erupted abruptly into outrage. She could not bear the rather stately introduction Auden wrote for her book! She had evidently expected great poetry lyrically saluting her writing (the gesture John Dewey had once made to her art). She wrote Auden immediately after reading it:

> Although I know you must have worked hard on this essay of an introduction, the fact remains that . . . it produces the impression that so much has been written around and about the book in order to avoid any expression of appreciation.
>
> And after all, should not a foreword stimulate interest in the book? This introduction inhibits it.
>
> Could you write about a page or two, about five or six hundred words that express your idea of the book in general without going into such analytical detail as to its matter?

Louise was horrified by Anzia's rude arrogance. She had been helping her mother with the revisions. She tried to explain what Auden's introduction meant; it was in fact an understanding analysis of Anzia's story. He touched on the Faustian problem of all artists tempted by money and success, and he saw her book as reflecting the modern disease of alienation. "The immigrant is coming more and more to stand for the symbol for everyman," Auden concluded, "for the natural and unconscious community of tradition is rapidly disappearing from the earth."

Because his long, formal introduction didn't instantly translate into emotions, Anzia felt cheated. To check her mother's irrational anger, Louise suggested asking Auden to cut parts of the introduction, to make it simpler and more direct; and Anzia seemed to accept the suggestion. Then, embarrassed, but fearful that Anzia might do worse, Louise spoke to Auden on the phone, broaching the compromise. He readily agreed to do it. Anzia, however, was still simmering. She arose from sleep the same evening and shot off another letter:

> My daughter's attempt to translate your essay into words simple enough for me to understand, her standing back of me on the phone and forcing me to apologize and her editorial advice to you, is the end of the hoax, the climax of the comedy. . . .
>
> After all my attempts to compromise with common sense, the *dybbuk* burst loose in me again, crying, Better to go back to dishwashing and scrubbing floors than to the faking literary world where a highbrow like Auden is king. Let them all go nuts singing the praises of the king's fine clothes; the dybbuk in me kept shouting, the king is naked! The king has no clothes and Auden doesn't even know that he doesn't know, and never can know what Red Ribbon on a White Horse is about, or he wouldn't have filled fifteen pages of abstract Audenia — . . . spinning words upon words, only to widen and deepen the gulf between his English gentility and my Hester Street. One page of simple, honest writing, one poem from the heart could have bridged the gulf. But you keep your poetry for Igor Stravinsky, for Isherwood, Cocteau, Bernstein. For Hester Street you only have the pedantry of a head without a heart.

At the same time Wheelock, wanting to smooth over the unpleasantness, sent Auden two letters. The first hoped that Anzia wasn't causing him too much trouble. "I have come to be very fond of her, as doubtless you have — she is pure emotion without the bridle rein," he wrote, and went on to suggest cuts in Auden's introduction that followed Anzia's (Louise's) proposal. In the second, written after reading a carbon copy of Anzia's outburst about the naked king, Wheelock apologized for his inability to prevent it, but thought from his experience with many authors "the whole thing" would blow over.

He was right. Anzia turned meekly agreeable through the reading of proofs and galleys over the next month and a half—until she came to the introduction again. This time she flared up briefly, cutting a few more of Auden's paragraphs, and then wrote to Wheelock: "Tell Auden I got out of a sick bed to bring in those cuts in person *to make sure they're cut.* If I die from the heart attack caused by reading Auden's introduction, the guilt will be yours as well as Auden's because you as editor could have told him in all *sincerity* what havoc his murdering malice has caused." But once the cuts were made, she subsided into humility.

> My dear Mr. Wheelock:
>
> Do you remember your own poem, *Exile from God*?
>
> I do not fear to lay my body down
>   In death to share
> The life of the dark earth and lose my own
>   If God be there . . .
>
> And when I read that Introduction, I knew the death of exile from God. I was plunged back to the despair of thirty years ago in Hollywood when Montague Glass was hired to add slap-stick laughs to Hungry Hearts.
>
> But this morning I got up realizing, where is the gratitude for all the months of patient work you've put in editing my book, if I cause you so much trouble over that Introduction? Now, for the last time, I submit to anything you think best. Never again will I cling so stubbornly to my idea of my life or my book. What is the good of having written it if I haven't learned by now to be humble at all times, in all things.

Red Ribbon on a White Horse was published in the fall of 1950 and was applauded by a large number of critics. The response of these professional readers was far better than any Anzia had received since *Bread*

Givers, twenty-five years earlier. Those who remembered her from the 1920s welcomed her back from her eighteen-years "silence." It seemed that in the interim she had progressed in artistry and could now resume an up-to-date place in the literary world with this late flowering of her talent. Some remarked also on Auden's "penetrating," perceptive introduction. "How much he has been able to say and to suggest in eight pages!" exclaimed the *Saturday Review of Literature*.

And yet, in spite of the fine reviews, the book died almost immediately. Scribner's sales department, perhaps disagreeing with its senior editor, had found the book unsalable; it was unadvertised, unavailable in most of the city bookstores. Most of the first printing was remaindered. With the resurgence of red hunting in the United States, 1950 was not a good year for a book of its sort. That year Senator Joseph McCarthy told President Truman that the State Department was "riddled" with Communists; the McCarran Act, passed over a presidential veto, ordered severe restrictions against suspected Communists here or trying to get into the country; Alger Hiss was sentenced for perjury; Truman sent troops to Korea to fight the Communists of North Korea; and Miltown came into wide use as a tranquilizer.

TODAY IN PAPERBACK reprintings, *Red Ribbon* reads differently than it did in 1950. Current readers are apt to be more involved with this writer's search for truth as a Jew, a woman, and an artist. From today's perspective, the book is a small work of art, cleverly and subtly designed, encompassing vivid pictures of America's social history — the Lower East Side ghetto, Hollywood, New York publishing in the 1920s, the Depression, the WPA, a New England farm village — in less than two hundred pages. Anzia was able to do this because she didn't tell her story chronologically, but emotionally, as one would remember it — sharp scenes encrusted with memories of events before and later.

Obviously (although this was not perceived in 1950) it is *not* an autobiography, for Anzia selected only certain highlights of her life and invented many characters and incidents to fill them out. "One part of that

[book] that was purely made up by [my] guilty conscience," she remarked to some friends years after *Red Ribbon* was published, "was a man whose whole character I put into an imaginary letter to me while I was in Hollywood." The character she refers to bears a strong resemblance to Reb Yeziersky, Anzia's father. But in the book his letter, asking for money to help him return to his birthplace in Europe ("where a man is judged by what he is, and not by what he has"), is one of the begging letters she receives from strangers as a result of the movie studio publicity. Determined to answer this letter in person, she takes the train back to New York and finds that the man has just died, as had Anzia's father long before she wrote *Red Ribbon*.

Rather than autobiography, her real purpose in *Red Ribbon* was a summing up of what she had become because of her experiences, a view from the other side of success and failure of the truths she discovered afterward. In its brevity, yet fullness of insight, it seems as if her cluttering ambition, her false pride, and the terrible conflicts they inspired — the yearning for approval, success, love, money versus the need for the bottom layer of honesty — had been finally resolved. Writing about Dewey, for example, she saw their encounter more clearly than she had in earlier retellings of that love. She was now older than Dewey had been when she met him; she understood him better because anger and hurt over that relationship had been distilled out of her.

Red Ribbon's editor, John Wheelock, was partly responsible for the book's fine economy. He understood what Anzia had to say and with rare skill not only suggested where to eliminate the superfluous, but also where to insert a needed incident or memory to sharpen the point. But Anzia's growth as an artist in spite of the years of rejection, isolation, total obscurity, and while tormented by self-doubt, is the surprising, stunning force that created *Red Ribbon*.

Although she had begun and discarded other writing projects during her long exile from publishing, in accumulating the creative energy Anzia had been pregnant with this book *Red Ribbon* for eighteen years. Her joy in completing it transcended any worries about its sales. She finished the last pages — revisions — in response to John Wheelock's suggestions and admiring comments. She was back again among poets and editors who understood her and wanted only truth.

> Why had I no premonition in the wandering years when I was hungering and thirsting for recognition, that this quiet joy, this sanctuary, was waiting for me after I had sunk back to anonymity? I did not have to . . . sweat for glory, strain for the smile from important people. All that I could ever be . . . was in myself.

12

A R T

ANZIA THE WRITER WAS REBORN — the artist as an old woman — when *Red Ribbon* was published. The impressive critical applause pierced her silence — that is, the deafness surrounding her. It reassured her that she was not one of the ex-writers she had pitied on WPA, and so it released her, close to seventy, to write with youthful vigor again.

Although Scribner's was not advertising or promoting the book, and it could not be found in many bookstores, Anzia had been exhilarated by her working experience with Scribner editor John Wheelock.

Stories that had simmered in her mind or in scribbled notes now seemed worthier. Even in the years when she had not been published, she had never exhausted the emotions that impelled her to write. Now she had readers again.

Her first published writing after *Red Ribbon* began appearing within a few months (February 1951) in the *New York Times Book Review*. She reviewed more than fifty books for the *Times* over the next ten years. They amounted to warm-up exercises for the remarkable short stories she was starting to write. Limited in advance by the assignment editor, her reviews were usually brief mid-section pieces, the space given to books of third- or fourth-rate importance. Still, she worked over them. Never mind how small and obscure the space — to her a critic, especially for the *New York Times*, was godlike, and in contrast to some other critics from whom she had suffered, she aimed to be a kindly god.

She particularly enjoyed the feeling of power when she had the book of someone she knew. For instance, she grabbed the opportunity to review and praise *Judy's Surprising Day*, a children's book by Sally Scott, the daughter of Dorothy Canfield Fisher. Power over someone so powerful! (Fisher was a Book-of-the-Month Club judge): "Author Sally Scott, mother of four children, has inherited from her own mother . . . her storytelling gift, the art of revealing meaning within meanings in ordinary events." Or, as she had said in reviewing five children's books a few months earlier: "These last four books have gaiety, humor and originality, but they are of the moment. 'All Aboard,' with its meaning within meanings, is unforgettable." *All Aboard* was written by the poet-novelist Mary Britton Miller (Isabel Bolton), whom Anzia knew and admired.

But when the book turned out to be mediocre, knowing the author was an embarrassment; what could she say? "[This book] is different from anything that has been written about Jews in the past." Or: "The book is over-written in places. It also suffers from over-crowding of characters, and as a result there is occasional blurring. Yet these minor defects cannot mar its overall impact. [This book] is a pioneering work in American fiction." Sometimes, when she discovered a new writer whom she could wholeheartedly praise, she ignored the iron curtain supposed to protect the reviewer from the reviewed. She might telephone such a writer (once it was Elie Wiesel, just arrived in the United States) to talk to him, even perhaps to meet him and learn more about his purposes.

She was thus *not* a discriminating critic; although enthusiastic, her emotions, in fact her honesty, were not engaged. The books the *Times* chose for her were more often about immigrants — Russians, Poles, or Jews — but not otherwise related to her interests. In the course of ten years and fifty-odd books, there was only one that affected her deeply. This was *Teacher*, about Anne Sullivan Macy, the extraordinary teacher who had rescued blind, deaf, dumb seven-year-old Helen Keller from the stark isolation of darkness and silence. The story of a selfless, enduring love, *Teacher* was published twenty years after Macy's death, when author Helen Keller was in her mid-seventies, the same age as the reviewer. "For fifty years these two lived hand in hand, finger to finger, indissolubly bound to each other's fulfillment. Whatever Helen published represented the labor of Teacher as well." Anzia's review this time was equal to the book. Perhaps she was reminded by *Teacher* of the gift she had herself received from John Dewey.

Working on her own fiction at the same time, she might take two or three years, sometimes even more, to complete a short story. The writing never grew easier. However short, each story was almost like a novel because she was depicting a vast and to her unfamiliar spectrum of social circumstance — now it was the circumstance of being old and poor.

A new wave of immigrants had reached New York's Upper West Side, where she was living. Once-luxurious apartment houses and brownstones along Riverside Drive, West End Avenue, and Broadway, which had gradually changed into respectable but increasingly dingy rooming houses, were being filled, in fact overcrowded and worn down, by the poor from Puerto Rico. Single tenants who had occupied the rooms adjoining her own were replaced, one by one, by families with small children. Three times as many to share the apartment kitchen and bathroom and add their noise and garbage.

Because of a semantic change (the house was renamed a "hotel" and therefore decontrolled), her rent increased. The new tenants paid even more. The gross exploitation by landlords who seemed even greedier than those of her youth aroused in her the same fury. And yet: "All around us were people in comfortable houses unaware of what was going on in this jungle." So she moved to a room in a cleaner, less crowded apartment–rooming house with a lower rent and a magnificent view of the Hudson River because the landlady was impressed by her status as an author. This was an alternative not available to the large-familied Puerto Ricans. From that new room she wrote "The Lower Depths of Upper Broadway," published in the *Reporter* of January 19, 1954. Expressing her outrage as one of the oppressed, this story seems to be semidocumentary reportage; but it is larded with sentimental embroidery:

> Cleanliness, privacy, and a view of the sky are luxuries enough to make me humbly happy.
>
> But the cries of the children in that house from which I have escaped still haunt my dreams at night.

Anzia never gave up that sentimentality, the lush bathos in which many popular Yiddish plays and stories were steeped; they had been her literature growing up on the Lower East Side. Tschaikovsky's *Pathétique* or the Yiddish lament "Eli Eli" on the record player always stirred her emotions, and for years she followed certain radio soap operas ("Helen Trent," for instance) for companionship after work.

Even while she was making notes for a new fiction that became "A Chair in Heaven," a brilliant, tough-minded story about an old woman, Sara Rosalsky, holding tightly to her possessions against her meanly mercenary children, Anzia turned out a piece of sugared trivia, "The Day I Began to Live," for the Words to Live By page of *This Week* magazine, the Sunday newspaper supplement. It is about a night school teacher who taught an immigrant class:

> Yesterday is gone. Tomorrow may never be. *Now* is all we have. . . . Instead of looking back or worrying about tomorrow, let's stand up and look *now* in the face. It is all there is or ever can be.

Anzia, about seventy-two years old, in 1952. Photo by Charlotte Brooks.

and so on. "The Day I Began to Live" was for those who grope, as Anzia did. She wrote such admonitory nuggets into her notebook for self-help or for future stories, along with keener, more honest observations: "Growing old is like entering a new profession — forgiveness, acceptance of the worst that can happen. . . ." And years later, in her eighties, she copied into her notebook: "Self acceptance is the beginning of maturity." She also copied or clipped inspirational poems, including the lyrics to Bob Dylan's song "Blowing in the Wind," and kept them in a folder old and worn from frequent rereadings.

A cache of consolation — *Man's Quest for God, Stranger in the Earth, The Open Way: A Study in Acceptance, Dying We Live: Final Messages of Nazi Victims and Martyrs, The World's Great Religious Poetry, The Spirit of Zen* — these were some of the books she reread and underlined in her old age, revealing how alone and afraid she must have felt at times. And yet, although the corn syrup crept into all her writing, by the time she finished *Red Ribbon* she had learned, after writing it in, to cut most of it out.

Publishers Weekly, in a 1979 comment about the recently published Yezierska collection, *The Open Cage*, recognized the achievement of her last years: "In an irony as bitter as any in her stories, Yezierska's grasp of narrative improved after her fame subsided and she lost her audience. The later selections . . . [which begin with *Red Ribbon* and include short stories she wrote thereafter] are more skilled, the plot development more sure, the characters more complex, the insights more gripping."

Art was really all she had left. Her writing no longer had the shocking, explosive vitality and idiomatic style of her first books, but she had gained subtlety and a perspective from which she could see more. "A Chair in Heaven," for example, has a quiet certainty remarkable for Yezierska; the author-narrator is a professional, immediately understanding the demanding old woman:

> Sara Rosalsky's rapacious gray eye took swift inventory of the lines in my face, the shabbiness of my hat, the darned patches at the elbows of my sweater. "So you're a writer?"

The old woman is dying; her children are hostile or indifferent, awaiting their expected inheritance. There is nothing sentimental in "A Chair in Heaven"; but the narrator's observation at the deathbed is an affecting summation of Sara's life: ". . . the fierce obsession of a will to possess — the hunger for love which strives only to conquer." In Sara's aloneness, dying, the narrator sees her own isolation, "the shadows [of those] I had left behind me . . . father, mother, brothers and sisters — the relationships I had uprooted in my search for the life I had never found."

ANZIA WAS WRITING now for the sake of writing itself. It was only too evident in the first months after its publication that *Red Ribbon*, despite the glowing reviews, was not going to make money or win back her former place in the literary firmament. In fact, because the first edition was remaindered, Scribner's business department asked the author to pay back some of the advance. Book review fees she received from the *Times* were minimal; the honor of being invited to write them was considered payment in itself. But having long since lost her huckster's magic, Anzia still could not stop writing. It had become like breathing; and getting published again was all she needed as a stimulus.

Once, in that gloomy period before *Red Ribbon* was finished, while she was struggling with the unwieldy manuscript, then years in the making, she had declared that after she at last delivered herself of the burden, she would quit this painful, unrewarding occupation. She was drained physically and emotionally. "I rest a great deal," she had written to Fannie at the end of 1941.

> And because I have to rest so much the book is not even half done. I must get most of it done. Only then can I go to California and really retire from writing. But this book is on my chest.

And two years later, writing to Louise at an army post office address in Australia:

> I'm glad you do not listen to my greedy exhortations to write. Life is more important than literature — as you have found out for yourself. And if you can make your work out there full and rich enough, why worry about writing? Writing is only for such as me who have never found the right place in life as you have.

That and other gloomy notes to Louise (is writing pointless? has my life been wasted?) never mentioned that meanwhile her manuscript had been out and returned to her, rejected, and that she was of course sending it out again. Whatever she said to others, Anzia never intended to retire. She kept revising *Red Ribbon*.

Although sometimes humbled and remorseful, set back by the stomach disorders that came with constant emotional tension, as well as by the failure to sell her work, she remained the same vigorous egotist fiercely centered on herself and her own sufferings. Cataracts filming her eyes, headaches increasing in frequency, the shock of confronting an unrecognizable old face in the mirror — these facts of age were now inescapable. People of her vintage, and more resigned to it, shared with Anzia and the Puerto Ricans the rooming house ghetto on the Upper West Side; they spent much of their time sitting on the Broadway or Riverside Drive park benches, doing nothing. Seeing them as she walked past to do her grocery shopping was a constant reminder of her impending fate. The forced isolation, the waste!

Sometimes she came back to her room and discovered food and pot burnt on the hot plate. She had forgotten to turn off the switch. Close to eighty now, could she continue to live alone and take care of herself? Could she endure living in a "home"? She woke at night frightened, but in the morning she challenged these fears. ("Growing old is like entering a new profession.") She became a volunteer at an old age home within walking distance of her rooming house, despite the fact that to her it was a "house of doom" where "old men and old women stared into vacancy — joyless and griefless." She worked there as an unpaid receptionist and library clerk a couple of afternoons a week.

This was not really a response to others' need. She was trying to accept age in herself by examining it in others. One resident in his nineties was her constant companion in the library of the Home for Aged and Infirm Hebrews. He talked to her about the newsstand he formerly owned next to a subway entrance, and about the people he knew in the home. With Anzia's urging, he wrote her a letter in Yiddish about his impressions of the home as a "shtetl" (a Russian-Jewish ghetto village) of "have-beens," and about one "have-been," a former bread baker who in the home library discovered for the first time in ninety years the unusual pleasure of reading a book.

After Anzia telephoned an editor, this novice writer's letter was published in the *Forward*, New York's best-known Yiddish newspaper. Jacob Charniak, former newsstand owner, enjoyed the thrill of being a published author and a star among his elderly housemates. Anzia enjoyed the proof that she could still bring about small miracles.

THE SUCCESS of Anzia's efforts at the home inspired her. She elected herself a spokeswoman for the aged. She had conceived the idea of rehabilitation (as for the handicapped) to restore the elderly to jobs and social acceptance. Programs offering recreation for senior citizens were available at a local community center; adult education classes were advertised at the public library. But she wanted reeducation for intelligent, educated people like herself who were capable of work and not interested in bingo or finger painting.

She took this idea to Columbia University, where she was passed from one department to another by people trying to be polite, until at last she reached a psychology professor at Teachers College who was doing research on the learning abilities of the elderly. He said fine, if she could bring some other old women and herself to meet with him, they and the professor could create "a seminar on aging" and perhaps they could learn from each other.

He was probably honest with her, and with the seven, sometimes eight, others Anzia recruited for this seminar; and probably she didn't want to hear what he was saying. Whatever their hopes, he didn't promise them rejuvenation, only the opportunity to participate in a research project. He made some effort to be encouraging; he suggested they find volunteer work to do in the community, and that they adopt a "positive" attitude toward their present status as discards. But after the semester of sessions in which the women talked into a tape recorder about their past working lives, when they had had importance as human beings, how they felt about growing old and about death, the professor thanked them for their valuable contributions to his knowledge and dismissed them.

Cut off abruptly from their hope of absorbing the university's wisdom! Anzia had coaxed the other women into the class by convincing herself as well as them of the great possibilities. Now, although she had met this disillusionment in the same place before, she was freshly shocked (as she had been at twenty-two and fifty-two) at the rigidity of university scholarship. But out of that evaporation of hope she wrote a dramatized report, "One Thousand Pages of Research," in which the elderly students and their professor, talking about the same subject, were exposed as being on parallel, never-meeting courses, never able to understand each other.

It was published several years later as an "Observation" in the July 1963 issue of *Commentary*. Anzia must have been about eighty-two years old then. Because the writing, and therefore publication, came more slowly, she was cheered all over again; as if it were a new experience. "What a fool . . . at my age," she wrote to Louise, "to be still lifted up or cast down by the momentary see-saw."

Walking more slowly when she went out at noon, she was increasingly worried about the hazards of living alone. She told Louise that she was "disintegrating." Yet she had repeatedly turned her back on safer, alternative housing. By her excessive demands she had lost the help of most relatives and friends. One of the few she could telephone at any hour had always been Louise. Unfortunately Louise had just left the insecurity of free-lance magazine writing in New York and was now in Lafayette, Indiana, working as a science writer at Purdue University. Louise had consulted Anzia before accepting the job and Anzia had bravely urged her to take it. She had even agreed to let Louise hire a cook-cleaner a couple of hours a day to bring lunches and do errands for Anzia. Soon after her daughter left, however, Anzia dismissed this boring woman and used the money for more intellectual purposes.

Her sudden physical decline (and even stronger emotional need) was coinciding with the beginning of her daughter's new career and, soon afterward, her marriage to a professor at the university. Anzia, remembering how essential had been her own escape from parents, theoretically wanted Louise to be free. But whatever the daughter arranged for Anzia's benefit in advance or from a distance tended to unravel. Over the telephone Anzia could be buoyant as ever. She retained, on her good days (the optimistic lift of the seesaw), the adventurous willingness to test herself and trust in fate that sometimes produced new wonders in her life and sometimes black holes of despair.

"YOUR INVITATION that I come for a visit," Anzia wrote to Louise a few months after her daughter's departure for Indiana, "was such a shot in the arm to me that I suddenly thought — why not go flying?" She had never been on a plane, and the mere idea terrified her.

> If there should be a crash, why it'll be a quick end out of disintegrating old age. . . .
>
> . . . I must pour out my heart to you — in all my worstness — *Do you really want me to come?* Be honest with me as I am with you. . . . The only thing real left in me is *not to be a burden to you*. . . .
>
> Yesterday I was on the verge of exhaustion. . . . I managed to pull myself together to keep my appointment with the public relations woman on TWA. . . . The minute I walked in I liked her and she liked me and she caught instantly . . . my idea of a story for the airline.

For the free trip to Indianapolis and back (and an unasked for hundred dollars later on) she wrote "I'll Fly Again," a story of childlike wonder about soaring into the sky, which from the airline's viewpoint was evidently worth even more than this small payment. She reported to Louise:

> I may drop dead any moment — or maybe pass out in my sleep one of these nights. Nevertheless when the publicity woman of TWA

> asked me, would I care to take a flying trip to some of the capitals of Europe? I answered, "I'd love to." She looked at me and said, "You will have to have someone go with you." . . . But they want me to cut the story to 850 words. . . . I can't see how I can do it in less than a thousand.

Her age was like a mask she often forgot she was wearing. She felt the same emotions—fury, inspiration, excitement, despair, exaltation—she had known since adolescence, and then would be abruptly reminded by severe sciatic pain or a burnt pot forgotten on the stove that she was old and impotent. And yet she could still blaze again with some new purpose, and by her spontaneity and enthusiasm draw new people to her for whatever she proposed—as, for instance, the writers Marchette and Joy Chute.

She met the Chutes for the first time in January 1962, after reading a newspaper story about the sisters and their once active mother, who was now dependent on a wheelchair. The news story fascinated Anzia because the sisters were prominent writers and also because, unlike Anzia, who had left her parents as soon as possible, they were living with and caring for their mother. Their example was comforting. So she looked them up in the telephone book and must have sounded so urgent on the phone that the Chutes invited her to tea. The sisters and their mother listened as she told them a story she wanted to write.

On a hot summer morning four or five months earlier, when Anzia's wide window facing the Hudson was open to its limit, a small bird flew into her room and terrified her as it tried to get out again, fluttering frantically. Anzia ran to the next apartment, where there was a woman more involved with pet birds than with people. This neighbor rushed back with Anzia and cooed the chickadee into her hands, then put it into an empty cage. Now it was so docile that Anzia felt compassion for it. But after taking a sip of water the bird drooped; it could not survive in the cage. The next morning the neighbor carried the cage down to the park, opened its little door, and the bird flew free.

The incident gripped Anzia; she felt it was an overwhelming parable of her own situation. "But what did it mean?" she asked the Chutes.

They could see that, handicapped as she was by failing eyesight and other infirmities, she was choking with this story, trying to pull it out of herself. Instantly sympathetic, they gave her a magnanimous writer's gift: they hired a temporary secretary, who brought a tape recorder. He turned on the recorder as she talked the story over with the Chutes for more than an hour. A few days later the Chutes handed her the typed transcript of their conversation.

This transcript contains Anzia's jumbled recital of all the wrenching, discordant fears and sorrow of her life just then — the bleakness of the house in which she lived with 150 other, indifferent roomers; her helplessness when her hot plate burnt out and she misplaced her eyeglasses ("Inside me there were screams I couldn't vent"); the unfeeling landlady ("Just as truth is to the artist — her truth, the drive of her life, is money"); the tiny bird's powerful appearance; the neighbor "who was a chain smoker and a secret drinker . . . but . . . it was just as though a child of hers was in trouble when I told her about the bird." The bird's fatal decline in captivity, as she described it, might have been her own experience of age closing in on her.

"So you see it is a question I have brought you, not a story. Is it a story?" Throughout the recital, Anzia kept asking the Chutes for explication. She was still groping for meaning when Joy Chute told her helpfully that no wild bird ever flies into the hands of a human being; it is too perilous. Anzia's neighbor didn't know that; with her outstretched hands and cooing murmur, she expressed such love that the tiny bird lost its fear.

"I saw a miracle?" Anzia asks in awe. The Chutes confirm it.

"Well, was I wrong in coming to you?" she now demands as the tape reaches the end. "That was wonderful! Didn't you learn a lot?"

She wrote and rewrote this parable for two or three years, pouring into it her anger and impatience with herself for being slow-moving, forgetful; her wrinkled face, false teeth, and wretched gropings for help — "the outrage of being old!" — contrasted with the free flight of the bird. She called it "The Open Cage" — a harsh, poetic, deeply stirring glimpse of age that she couldn't sell to any magazine. Years after her death, after scholars had rediscovered Anzia Yezierska and wanted to read more of her work, her daughter resurrected it from Yezierska's files. It was published as the final story of the book *The Open Cage: An Anzia Yezierska Collection*.

The Chutes, after that first meeting, remained Anzia's friends and benefactors for the rest of her life. She made another instant friend a year later, when she was crossing the uptown Broadway traffic. She turned to a woman crossing at the same time to ask for help, because the sun's glare blinded her. This was Ardyth Ullman, with whom Anzia developed an extraordinary understanding. It was a final instance in her life of the intense relationship she yearned for but could not believe in and later purposefully destroyed.

Ullman was middle-aged, perceptive, a sensitive fellow writer who, from that first moment on the street, appreciated Anzia's rebellious, icon-smashing spirit. Volunteering help, which Anzia readily accepted, she was at once drawn into a crisis: Anzia had to undergo surgery promptly to remove a cataract in her right eye; the vision in her left had just been destroyed by a hemorrhage. She planned to enter the hospital without bothering Louise, and insisted that the medical insurance policy provided by her daughter and Social Security would cover the costs. But it didn't. Ullman, who took her to the hospital, wrote a check behind her back for the several hundred dollars the hospital asked before admitting Anzia and then wrote Louise.

Thus abruptly informed of Anzia's emergency, Louise arranged for her mother to convalesce at her fiancé's apartment on the campus of the Institute for Advanced Study in Princeton. During the convalescence, Ullman made the trip from New York City several times a week, bringing flowers and cake; she telephoned Anzia daily. Louise, who arrived on a weekend leave from her job, had paid for a housekeeper to help the rest of the time. But because Anzia disliked the housekeeper, an obliging but uneducated, ordinary person, Ullman was her chief comfort during the two-week period of rigid, enforced idleness. Anzia was tense with anxiety as she waited each day for Ullman's call, fearful that some bolt from heaven might end this unusual devotion.

When Anzia at last returned to normalcy in her room in New York, Ullman was still her friend. Ullman wrote to Anzia's niece, Cecelia:

> As you know, she's as independent as a hog on ice but . . . she can't live alone much longer, I don't believe.
>
> Her wish not to be a burden on or hamper Louise in any way is touching, but I assure you Louise is the only one she spares. Everybody else . . . she importunes and presses — or tries to press into service. . . . Having been, and in fact being still, a remarkable woman, she has been surprisingly successful at getting errands run, favors done, little purchases made, letters written, medical help, companionship (even the intellectual kind) etc., but it's a strain on her, she starts up out of naps — as I saw her do the other day — crying for help — and the patience of friends, neighbors and acquaintances, imposed upon without end, must grow shorter as her needs increase, as they cannot fail to do. . . . She's got about 14,000 people enlisted in her aid but nobody will really do anything when the chips are down. . . .
>
> She's as proud as Lucifer and more wildeyed than ever, now that the publication of that little story in the Reporter has restored her faith in herself and her gifts.

It was an appeal for some kind of planned, caretaker help for Anzia, which Anzia, if she had known of it, would have fiercely rejected even while she tried to get increasing personal attentions from people she liked. The "little story in the Reporter," "A Window Full of Sky," was in fact her impassioned rejection of the security in the imprisoning walls of a home for the aged.

Anzia had written it after a traumatic personal experience the year before. She had been beguiled by the apparent freedom and abundant conveniences the home seemed to offer to two elderly but still active acquaintances. Inside the home they were apparently leading lives a lot more comfortable than her own. Tossing aside further self-debate, she applied for a private room and asked Louise and Louise's fiancé to come to New York to impress the home's director. But she insisted on stage-managing the rest of the application process alone. And so, in the nick of time, she got overwhelming confirmation for her lifelong hatred of social workers and their institutions. She found out about the small, dark "coffin-like" room that would have been hers, the rigidity of the house rules, the prying into her personal finances, the imperviousness of the director to Anzia's onetime literary importance — and she halted the application, newly rewedded to the insecurity of her room with its window full of sky.

ARDYTH ULLMAN'S continuing help began to seem less valuable to Anzia after she recovered from the surgery. Telephoning more frequently, Anzia became dissatisfied when Ullman failed to respond as promptly as she once had. And if Ullman, answering one of Anzia's emergency-distress calls, for example, did take a pair of custom-made shoes back to the shoemaker and could not get Anzia's money back, that was a black mark against her in Anzia's mind; and she dispatched someone else on the same fruitless errand. "She's got everybody working and all kinds of things going for her, as you know," Ullman wrote to Louise, "bureaus, services, Social Security departments . . . private people, old and young. . . . One reason why she lowered the boom on me was [that] I had the temerity to . . . tease her . . . and say she was like Napoleon up there in that room of hers . . . deploying her troops."

Now cold and resentful, Anzia telephoned Ullman one day to say she was canceling their appointment, she didn't want to see Ullman again. "You're false — false," she told her over the phone. "I knew it was too good to be true, pretending to be Lady Bountiful!"

Without Ullman, her outlook was bleak — for a while. Having chopped off reliable lifelines, she managed her difficult existence miraculously. "I am fully competent to handle this business," she admonished in a letter asking Louise to stop trying to arrange for an apartment in a new "senior residence with sheltered walks." Although she often woke at night with the fear that she was helpless, dying, at other times Anzia's life was still magically touched with wonder. As if out of childhood fables, she still continued to receive *dei ex machina* every once in a while, dropping in to change her circumstances or at least her mood.

"One night last week I was roused from sound sleep by a long-distance call from . . . a group of freshmen at Michigan State University," she wrote in delight to Louise. In late January 1964, five young men in the same dormitory, students of a class in American Thought and

Language, had been talking about their required reading that night, Anzia's "How I Found America." They were astonished by her depiction of the sweatshop and the poverty in the ghetto tenement — here in America! — from which she had escaped. They wanted to find out what had happened to her.

Anzia tried to answer their innocent questions about a world they had never imagined; in turn, they told her of their remote world, Michigan State University, where young men were actually required to read one of her stories. She was enthralled.

Each of the five wrote her a letter that night, asking more questions, and she dictated to one of her volunteer helpers a brief but heartfelt letter in answer. She was about eighty-three years old then. To the Michigan State students she must have been a legend from the mythical past brought to life. Her letter, and their account of the phone conversation they had with her, so impressed the professors that she received another letter, asking whether she could come to the university to give a lecture.

She longed to do that, but it was physically too difficult. So she started writing the students a response that, over the next few years, grew into fifty-odd jumbled, nonconsecutive, partly handwritten pages of unfinished manuscript, "Letter to John Apple and Friends." It was an answer to their questions: how she had climbed out of the dark ghetto into the sunlight and then lost her way on the wonderful rags-to-riches American express.

Thriving on such stimulation, Anzia survived in her West 113th Street furnished room two years more. The appearance of "A Window Full of Sky" in the *Reporter* had brought her another boost of excitement, including even some admiring letters from social workers at old-age centers, requests by schools of social work to reprint the story free, and an invitation to speak to the students of Union Theological Seminary about being old in New York. Two students, a young man and his girl, who came to arrange for her talk had tea with her; and because she especially enjoyed their youth and grace, she tried to recruit them as friends. They got away gracefully, eluding her importunities. She was left with a gift package of tea and a deeper realization of how old she was.

The failure impelled her to write, over the next year and more, the sad, self-mocking "Taking Up Your Bed and Walk." But now it took a few years to find acceptance for this brief and subtle story about an old woman and the two young people who darted in and out of her grasp. After many rejections, Anzia managed to place it in the obscure, now-defunct quarterly *Chicago Jewish Forum*. Her last published story, it earned her twenty-five dollars, the same amount she had received for her first story, fifty years earlier.

Meantime there were other momentary lifts: an invitation to speak to an adult education class in New York; and at Purdue University, when she visited her daughter and son-in-law for two weeks, the flattering attention of English professors and their wives. She addressed an English composition class of freshmen who had no idea of who she was, and then a Hadassah meeting of older people, children and grandchildren of immigrants, who responded with excitement because their experiences matched her stories.

GOING BACK to her New York room this time was a letdown. Her dual existence then — daytime, when hope (her fairy tales) was possible; night, when she reencountered her bottomless despair — was barely mentioned in her letters to Louise. She was using the monthly check Louise sent for "a literary assistant and someone to walk with me and read to me as I'm getting blinder day by day."

"Even if I end up losing my sight," she added as a postscript to another letter the same month, "in my deepest moments I shall not regret what I have paid and must keep paying for having been a fool and a bungler in my egomania." But her tone changed abruptly with each letter:

> I discovered a letter you sent me . . . before you hooked a Prof of mathematics to keep you from being lonely. Now you worry over such trivial, earthly things as a cookstove, an ice-box and washing machine and you want to rescue me from my loneliness. The difference between you and me is that *I like loneliness*. I make an art of being lonely. You were afraid of it. Isn't that so?

June 4, 1966:

> How thankful I am that I had sufficient presence of mind in my lostness and rejected the security of The Old People's Home.

A few weeks later:

> I realize now it was my worst mistake not to have gone to the Home for the Aged. I no longer have what it takes to live alone in a rooming house.

When Louise phoned that summer from Berkeley, Anzia, remembering how cool Berkeley was, said in a quavering voice that New York's heat was cooking her alive. "Old age is hard. I made my bed, but it is hard. Don't give me sunshine fables." (She had discarded an air-conditioner because it made too much noise.)

By that fall, she was ready to move. Her many caprices may have delayed the move till then, but the primary obstacle had been that, though she yearned to live with her daughter, she couldn't get along with her son-in-law. For a brief period she had welcomed him as an addition to her life and Louise's. Then she found that she wasn't going to get his sustained help with her manuscripts, and she became aware that he was diverting Louise from similar obligations. She wrote to Louise some months after the wedding:

> I feel you are spending too much time cooking and doing chores. . . . You have a gift for writing for which you are responsible. In God's name realize you must find time to do your real work. . . . I don't know how to say what I have to say. Now — now is your time to write.

She never perceived that Louise had none of Anzia's compulsion.

After her marriage, Louise had to balance herself between the two opposing forces. When Anzia telephoned across the continent on a Sunday morning, waking her daughter and son-in-law at seven, if Mel answered she would demand abruptly, without greeting, "Where *is* she?" — blotting him out and innocently unaware that she was doing that. Her need was too great, too urgent for politeness. If he wasn't going to help her, then he amounted to an interference, for she had prior claim to her daughter.

Mel and Louise argued about it. She cannot go to a Home, Louise said; where can she live? Not in the same town with us, Mel said adamantly. But at last, during Anzia's visit to the Henriksens' home in Cleveland, where they were working at Case Western Reserve University, the three effected a compromise: an apartment for Anzia in a nearby hotel, which also had a restaurant dining room on the main floor.

Packing for Cleveland, closing out her fiercely independent life and leaving the city where she had lived for seventy-five years, was emotionally bruising. She confronted a roomful of files, fifty years of manuscripts, old letters, plans for more stories that now, she had to realize, she would never write. So she decided to be ruthless, to throw down the incinerator years of important, excruciating, fought-over work. Then she suffered aftershock: to recognize that death was so close and she so powerless!

During that feverish week, with Louise there to do the packing, Anzia also sometimes enjoyed the lift she always experienced when she changed course, a hope that her life might improve when she moved close to her daughter and her daughter's learned university friends. A devoted young volunteer, a solitary, lonely young man — one of Anzia's "14,000," in Ardyth Ullman's phrase — joined them. He turned himself into an abject burden bearer, lifting and roping boxes of books, carrying them on foot to the post office, intent on devoting these last days to Anzia, whom he did not expect to see again and who had been his confidante, a reminder of his dead mother.

But Cleveland was a slow step downward for Anzia. By making increasing demands she soon exhausted the people she met through her daughter; and instead of the motley tenants she used to meet each day in the elevator of her New York apartment–rooming house, the Cleveland hotel elevator usually carried one or two very well-dresed elderly ladies who might sit in the lounge downstairs through long afternoons and dine silently at night in the mournful dining room. It was starkly lonely — too Gentile, too hushed, too different from New York.

With the assistance of Case Western Reserve students employed a few hours a day, three days a week, she was revising "Take Up Your Bed and Walk," which had been rejected by several magazines. By mail or telephone she enlisted the Chute sisters, her niece Cecelia Ager and Cecelia's daughter, and a teacher of creative writing in a Cleveland high school, to edit and send out her manuscript. Declaring in these letters her physical exhaustion, the imminence of death, and her desperate loneliness, she still pushed and pulled with fierce energy for her manuscript.

Some of that energy she lost during two wintry years in Cleveland. When Mel and Louise moved to Berkeley in 1968 and she went along, she could no longer live alone. Now she had a room in a Berkeley "carehome"; her meals were served to her on a tray. But the University of California students hired to help her were more bohemian and more to her liking than those in Cleveland. Here she also had California relatives and other visitors aware of who Anzia Yezierska once was. A distinguished professor of American literature who knew of her work came to see her and decided to direct a doctoral thesis on long-forgotten Anzia Yezierska. The student he directed, an attractive female high school teacher, appeared regularly with a tape recorder to interview her. Since Anzia could no longer see well enough to read, she found it absorbing, at about eighty-seven, to look back again from this distance, without tears, and perhaps more succinctly revise her story once more.

"We lived on the taste of the food we couldn't get," she told this interviewer about her family's Hester Street poverty in 1895. Her failure to become an acceptable schoolteacher, she said, was partly because "my skirt and waist never came together." But about Dewey she said even more vehemently what she might have said fifty years earlier: "With him I was alive!" An unfinished, unkempt, half-aware savage, wild with doubt, always up or down — that was Anzia when she first opened his office door — and he had with a look, a few magical words, made her whole. "I never know what I know," she said she told him, and he gave her certainty. "You have in yourself the knowledge of what to write about your own people."

Summing up the long periods of lonely introspection she was now enduring, Anzia paused between sentences. "You think over what you did wrong," she said, "and what you failed to do — and with clarity comes grace — so you forgive yourself — and oblivion is welcome."

It wasn't yet true; it was a state of grace she hoped for. She was still writing, dictating to the students, but oblivion-death was often on her mind now. As she felt her strength going — harder now to walk on the sun-dazzled street or climb the carpeted stairs to her room — a wisp of a woman wrapped in shawls and dark glasses, she seemed to be preparing for it. All her files, as never before, were neatly organized and labeled by the students in large, dark, easy-to-read lettering.

Writing was an extraordinary feat of will — dictating, listening to how it sounded, redictating — but it was the only way she could keep on living. The last story, never finished, is a jumble of quotations and unresolved images:

> All at once, in the middle of the night, a door opened.
> "Who's there?" I cried. Silence was the only answer. . . .
> I knew that silence. I had fled from it all my life. . . .

In still other dictated notes, she swept up stray feelings that might belong to this story — that day's disappointments and those of years past, how she had tried to write about her daughter and could not, "the torment of the incommunicable." Accustomed to observing and describing her experiences, she was keeping to that habit as the last important event approached. On the manila envelope enclosing the notes, she had her young assistant hand-print:

HUNGER OF HUNGERS

FINAL VERSION

The hunger was for people — a lifetime's loneliness, yielded to at last.

> Now here is the beginning and end of my soul. Without regrets, without remorse.
>
> Now I surrender myself to Oblivion.

A small stroke, from which she recovered in a few weeks, took away another degree of power. Deprived of the private phone in her room because she had too often used it to summon the care-home's staff and doctors, she wrote to Louise by dictation only a week or so before she was to move near her in Southern California:

> I am not only blind but my heart aches, because I cannot say what I want to say to you. . . . I cannot phone and you cannot phone to me. . . .
>
> I have learned at last that no individual counts when his work is over.

But two days later, she sent a countermessage: "I feel sure that the *Village Voice* will take my article when you have a little time to edit it."

She lived another year, fighting to be recognized and important in a nursing home surrounded by blank faces, a desolate place. She was the only one in that place who had regular visitors, helpers from the world outside. No longer a writer, she would telephone her daughter when she woke during the night, lost. She telephoned the nurses, too, repeatedly, still alert and refusing the drugs with which other patients were tranquilized.

After the phone in her private room was removed, she doggedly lurched down the corridor, gripping an aluminum walker, her toes in slippers curling into the carpet with each step, to reach the nurses' station out front — humanity. She spent a half hour once teaching some of the nurses an old, joyful Hasidic song recalled from her childhood.

In the last weeks of her life, when she was about eighty-nine years old, she became sweet-tempered, grateful to the nurses' aides. Having hungered all her life, having been a devourer, she gradually stopped eating. Rail-thin, fragile, she gave up fighting, accepting annihilation. Death came gently, as she was being lifted from her chair to the bed.

A pocket notebook she left behind still had fragments of her thoughts, messages to herself, scrawled during the last two years. Amid the pages of scribble are these persistent shards:

> "Who am I? What am I? . . . Old age dissolving these sparks that are fading even as I try to catch them. . . .

> *The real mystery is oneself.*

Afterword

OUT OF LONELINESS and despair she made art. When I was a small child, I chose her against my father and never changed my allegiance. But whenever I was with her, close up, and fighting, she was always infuriating, demanding too much.

Only now, in her absence, can I come this close to her again.

Acknowledgments

I OWE THE INSPIRATION for and even some of the ingredients of this book to certain scholars who questioned me when they were studying Anzia Yezierska's work and life. When I started studying her life, too, without a scholar's training, and years after her death, I had gained from them a glimpse of how to do it.

Alice Kessler-Harris gave me more than that; she became a friend. A fine and discriminating writer and editor, she read parts of my manuscript at early stages and, with her perceptive advice, steered me in a productive direction.

Larzer Ziff, who at the University of California, Berkeley, rediscovered Anzia Yezierska when she was still alive and there directed the first contemporary doctoral thesis about her work, was a valuable critic. Carol Gartner, Carol Schoen, and Mary V. Dearborn, through research for their own studies, provided me with copies of Yezierska correspondence. I thank them for large pieces of the puzzle that, aided by memory, I could fit together into recognizable events in her life.

I owe a special debt to Joy and Marchette Chute, whose friendship with Yezierska and help to her at a crucial time, her old age, comforted me and, later, gave me insights about her thoughts on looking back over her life.

The relatives who shared some memories were Rose Goldberg, Louise Tamotzu, Viola Kates Stimpson, Ruth Shaffer, Victor Kates, Victor Rubenstein, Jennie Mayer, and Cecelia Ager.

And Jo Ann Boydston's assistance and encouragement, as director of the Center for Dewey Studies, providing me with copies of old documents that spurred and reinforced my own research, was so important that I have put her name on the title page.

To all these generous contributors, my thanks.

Sources and Notes

ABBREVIATIONS

The following abbreviations are used for Anzia Yezierska's books:

AB	*Arrogant Beggar.* New York: Doubleday, Page and Co., 1927.
AICNB	*All I Could Never Be.* New York: Brewer, Warren and Putnam, 1932.
BG	*Bread Givers.* New York: Doubleday, Page and Co., 1925. Reprinted, New York: Persea Books, George Braziller/Venture, 1975.
COL	*Children of Loneliness.* New York: Funk and Wagnalls, 1923.
HH	*Hungry Hearts.* Boston: Houghton Mifflin Co., 1920. Reprinted in *Hungry Hearts & Other Stories.* New York: Persea Books, 1985.
OC	*The Open Cage: An Anzia Yezierska Collection.* New York: Persea Books, 1979.
RR	*Red Ribbon on a White Horse.* New York: Charles Scribner's Sons, 1950. Reprinted, New York: Persea Books, 1981.
ST	*Salome of the Tenements.* New York: Boni and Liveright, 1922.

LETTERS

The letters excerpted in this book can be found in the following collections:

AY to Mary Austin	Mary Austin Papers, Huntington Library, San Marino, California
AY to Zona Gale	Zona Gale Papers, the State Historical Society of Wisconsin
AY to Louise Levitas Henriksen	Private files of Louise Levitas Henriksen, to be deposited in the Anzia Yezierska Papers, Boston University Libraries' Special Collections
AY to Arnold Levitas	Private files of Louise Levitas Henriksen, to be deposited in the Anzia Yezierska Papers, Boston University Libraries' Special Collections
AY to Amy Lowell	Houghton Library, Harvard University

AY (Hattie Mayer) to Rose Pastor Stokes April–October 1916	Rose Pastor Stokes Papers, Socialist Collection, Tamiment Library, New York University
15 September 1932	Rose Pastor Stokes Papers, Sterling Memorial Library Manuscripts and Archives, Yale University
AY's inscription to Marcet Haldeman-Julius in a numbered copy of *BG*	E. Haldeman-Julius Collection, Pittsburg (Kansas) State University
Between AY and Dorothy Canfield Fisher	Dorothy Canfield Fisher Papers, Special Collections, Bailey-Howe Library, University of Vermont
Between AY and Houghton Mifflin Co.	Houghton Library, Harvard University
Between AY and Charles Scribner's Sons	Charles Scribner's Sons Collection, Princeton University Libraries
Between John Dewey and A. C. Barnes; John Dewey to Alice Dewey	Joseph Ratner/John Dewey Collection, Special Collections, Morris Library, Southern Illinois University at Carbondale
Marcet Haldeman-Julius to her daughter Alice	E. Haldeman-Julius Collection, Pittsburg (Kansas) State University

NOTES

Preface

1 The phrases quoted are from newspaper stories of the 1920s.

3 *Publishers Weekly*, 24 September 1979.
The four reprinted books of Yezierska's writing are listed in "Abbreviations," above.

7 *The Poems of John Dewey*, ed. Jo Ann Boydston. Carbondale: Southern Illinois University Press, 1977.

8 "moral bankruptcy": from a letter of Anzia Yezierska in November 1917 to her second husband, after they were separated.

1. America

14 "looked out at . . . ": from "How I Found America," in *HH*.
"My mother . . . dried . . . ": from "Mostly about Myself," in *COL*.

16 "I was an unskilled . . . ": Yezierska quoted in interview by W. Adolphe Roberts, "My Ambitions at 21 and What Became of Them: III. Anzia Yezierska," *American Hebrew* 25 (August 1922).
"When all were asleep . . . ": from "America and I," in *COL*.
"Like a spark thrown . . . ": from "My Ambitions at 21 and What Became of Them."

18 "Every time I had to . . . ": from "Soap and Water," in *HH*.
"being out for a good time . . .," "I looked at these children of joy . . . ": from *BG*, pp. 212, 213.
"One day, the ache . . . ": ibid., pp. 218, 219.

23 "girl starving for beautiful clothes . . . ": from *ST*, p. 42.
"I can't bear to be . . . ": from *RR*, p. 103.

24 "Outside in the street . . . ": from *BG*, p. 186.
"couples . . . embraced . . . ": from *RR*, p. 110.

2. Love

46 "Anzia, I suppose . . . ": from Marcet Haldeman-Julius letter to her daughter Alice, Haldeman-Julius Collection, Pittsburg (Kansas) State University Library.

3. Hate

62 "Come! I'm waiting . . . ": from AY's letter to Fannie's son, Dr. Victor Rubenstein, 31 October 1961.

64 "the uptown ghetto . . . ": from "Wild Winter Love," *Century* 113 (February 1927).

67 "I Am a Spendthrift in Love" was later published in *Current Opinion* 73 (August 1922):240.

71 "Love Cheat," *Metropolitan* (July 1923).

76 "Where Lovers Dream," first collected in *HH*, is also reprinted in *OC*.

4. Real Love

85 On Dewey's speech, see "Democracy and Loyalty in the Schools," *New York Evening Post*, 19 December 1917.

On Feuer's comments about Dewey, see Lewis S. Feuer, "Dwelling on the Superficial," *New Leader* 57 (January 1974):20.

86 "Somehow they helped him . . . ": Feuer, "Dwelling," p. 18.

"He was a big man . . . ": *AICNB*, pp. 28, 29, 34, 35; *RR*, 105–106. This was how she remembered him, chiefly in her 1932 novel, *AICNB*. His character influenced and haunted her throughout her long life; she portrayed him repeatedly in her fiction. I first learned about their comparatively brief but deeply felt relationship through her recollections in conversations and in her writing. Then Dr. Jo Ann Boydston, director of the Center for Dewey Studies, added corroborating details with documents she accumulated in her research on Dewey's poems.

"big fences put up . . . ": from "Soap and Water," in *HH*.

88 "After graduation . . . ": ibid.

"The Free Vacation House," *Forum* 54 (December 1915):706–714; also in *HH* and *OC*.

"Where Lovers Dream," *Metropolitan* (March 1918):17–18; also in *HH* and *OC*.

"You've got none of that . . . ": from "To the Stars," in *COL*.

89 "transforming holiday spirit. . . . On her way back from work . . . ": from *AICNB*, p. 41.

90 "Generations of stifled worlds . . . ": *The Poems of John Dewey*, pp. 4–5. This poem was first published without credit and slightly altered by AY in *AICNB*. The first lines of her version are: "Generations of stifled words, reaching out *through you* / Aching for utterance, dying on lips . . ."

91 "Why do I need them . . . ": from *AICNB*, p. 74.

"If you want to understand . . . ": ibid., p. 77.

"damned Slavic seriousness": ibid., p. 76.

"You are translucent . . . ": ibid., pp. 58, 60, 61.

92 "At first I [was] embarrassed . . . ": from *RR*, p. 109.

"Why can't you write . . . ": from *AICNB*, p. 71.

"clear head and cold heart": from "The Miracle," in *HH*.

"Your book . . . was meant . . . ": from *AICNB*, pp. 70, 72.

"I wake from the . . . ": *The Poems of John Dewey*, pp. 5–6.

95 "the abnormalities . . . ": A. C. Barnes to John Dewey, 26 April 1918. Joseph Ratner/John Dewey Papers, Special Collections, Morris Library, Southern Illinois University.
"real work": from *AICNB*, p. 46.
"I have learned to . . . ": ibid., pp. 57–58.

96 "Dear Love of God . . . ": ibid., pp. 58, 59, 60.

98 "the three bastards who are opposing us": Barnes to Dewey, 26 May 1918.
"a small party . . . ": John Dewey to Alice Dewey, the John Dewey Papers.
On Barnes's report to Dewey on the research project, see his letter to Dewey, 12 June 1918.

99 "when she came to him . . . ": from *RR*, p. 105. (The letters quoted in *RR* and *AICNB* appear to be part of Yezierska-Dewey's actual correspondence.)
"recreating my every experience . . . ": ibid., pp. 110, 111.
"I know him as neither . . . ": from "Wild Winter Love," *Century* 113 (February 1927):490.
"evasion of life": from *RR*, pp. 111, 112.
"eloquent with the beauty of the world": from *AICNB*, p. 58.

100 "Across the white of . . . ": from *The Poems of John Dewey*, p. 18.

101 "He drew from his pocket . . . ": all the quoted text on this page and the next is from *AICNB*, pp. 64, 65.

102 "Riches, possessions hold me? Nay, . . . ": from *The Poems of John Dewey*, pp. 14–17. In addition to the internal evidence, Boydston adduced the physical evidence of typewriter face and watermark to establish that Dewey wrote this poem for AY (p. xxix).

104 John Dewey's "Confidential Report on Condition among the Poles in the United States" was privately printed in 1918; it is reprinted in vol. 2 of *The Middle Works of John Dewey*, ed. Jo Ann Boydston, pp. 259–330. Special Collections, Morris Library, Southern Illinois University at Carbondale, 1981.

105 "extensive": letter from John Dewey to Colonel Edward M. House, 23 August 1918.

106 "Interview with Mr. Alexander," 17 August 1918. Ratner/Dewey Papers.

5. Ambition

110 "There stirred within me . . . ": *The Poems of John Dewey*, pp. 11–12.

111 "Dear love of God": this letter appears on p. 112 of *RR*, which was published when AY was close to seventy.

"The feeling of familiarity . . . ": from *AICNB*, p. 35.

"We're drawn to each other . . . ": from "Wild Winter Love," *Century* 113 (February 1927).

112 "The light and shadows fell . . . ": from *AICNB*, pp. 99–101, and from *RR*, pp. 112–117 passim.

115 "the higher life": from "Hunger," in *HH*.

"Wherever I went . . . ": from *RR*, p. 117.

116 "He had given me . . . ": unpublished, handwritten notes in AY's papers, undated.

"I saw my own hump . . . ": from *RR*, p. 118.

117 "To my worthy wife . . . ": from "How I Found America," in *HH*.

"The writing became . . . ": from *RR*, p. 118.

118 "The Fat of the Land," in *HH*.

119 "Show him what's in you . . . ": from "Wings," in *HH*.

120 Columbia University records indicate that an Anzia Levitas took this course in the winter semester, 1918. The account of what happened in it is from "To the Stars," in *COL*.

"I was a hermit . . . ": from "My Ambitions at 21 and What Became of Them," *American Hebrew*, 25 August 1922.

"If the method I evolved . . . ": ibid.

121 "You want something good? . . . ": notes of Ralda Sullivan on her interview with AY, ca. 1968; and "An Immigrant among the Editors," in *COL*.

"The Miracle," in *HH*.

123 "In the intoxication . . . ": from *RR*, p. 119.

124 "There was in her now . . . ": from *AICNB*, p. 187.

"You make too much . . . ": from "To the Stars," in *COL*.

6. Fame

128 "a torture of chaos . . . ": "Mostly about Myself," in *COL*.

"The Immigrant Speaks": *Good Housekeeping* 70 (June 1920); reprinted as part of "Mostly about Myself," in *COL*.

131 Correspondence between AY and Houghton Mifflin Co. is in the Houghton Mifflin Collection, Houghton Library, Harvard University. "Hunger," *Harper's* (April 1920); reprinted in *HH*.

132 "My Own People," *Metropolitan* (February 1921); first published in *HH* (October 1920).

134 Letters from AY to Mary Austin are in the Austin Papers at the Huntington Library, San Marino, California.

135 "Soap and Water and the Immigrant," *New Republic* 18 (22 February 1919); reprinted as "Soap and Water," in *HH*.
Hungry Hearts was dedicated, dutifully, if perhaps reluctantly, to the lady bountiful "Mrs. Henry Ollesheimer," who had paid most of Anzia's Columbia University tuition. Anzia had wanted to include a literary benefactor, Ann Watkins, in her dedicatory thanks, but Mrs. Ollesheimer was evidently unwilling to share it.

137 "America Discovers the Immigrant," retitled "How I Found America," *Century* (November 1920); reprinted in *HH*.

138 "The Deported," *Nation* (24 July 1920).

140 Ferris Greenslet, *Under the Bridge: An Autobiography* (New York: Literary Classics, 1943; distributed by Houghton Mifflin).

144 "See! I've done . . . ": from *AICNB*, p. 187.

145 "Shivering with cold . . . ": "This Is What $10,000 Did to Me," *Cosmopolitan* (October 1925).

148 Dr. Frank Crane's column on AY, published by the Hearst chain of newspapers on different dates, appeared in the *New York Globe* in mid-December 1920.

150 "A man who had popularized . . . ": from AY's unpublished notes.

7. Fortune

151 "The high priestess of platitude": description of Ella Wheeler Wilcox in *American Authors*, ed. Stanley Kunitz and Howard Haycraft (New York: H. W. Wilson, 1938).

155 AY's review of John Dewey's *Democracy and Education* (New York: Macmillan, 1916) appears in her article "Prophets of Education," *Bookman* 52 (February 1921). In the same article she also reviewed the following 1920 books: John Erskine, *Democracy and Ideals* (New York: George H. Doran); Frank V. Thompson, *School of the Immigrant* (New York: Harper and Bros.); Ivor C. Brown, *The Meaning of Democracy*

(Chicago: A. C. McClurg); *Democracy and Education* was already, in 1920, a classic among professional educators. It was eventually translated into Arabic, Chinese, German, Italian, Japanese, Portuguese, Persian, Spanish, Swedish, and Turkish.

156 "To the Stars," *Century* (May 1921); reprinted in *COL*.

156 "Every man I saw . . . ": from *RR*, p. 34.

157 Howard Dietz, manager of studio publicity for the Goldwyn Co. in 1921, later became famous as a Broadway lyricist and musical comedy writer.

159 On Goldwyn Company negotiations with AY: the information comes from telegrams between New York and Hollywood in the MGM files. I am grateful to Dr. Carol Gartner for her research into the Goldwyn telegrams concerning the filming of *HH*, and to film historian Kevin Brownlow for further information on the film *Hungry Hearts*.

"I could treat myself . . . ": from "This Is What $10,000 Did to Me," *Cosmopolitan* (October 1925).

160 "For once in my life . . . ": from *RR*, p. 61.

"these lovely, important people": ibid., p. 59.

"Even if I turned . . . ": ibid., p. 62.

On Will Rogers, ibid., pp. 62, 63, 66–69.

161 "The familiar feel . . . ": ibid., p. 57.

162 The book reviews of *HH* appeared in the *Nation* (25 January 1921) and in *Grinnell Review* (December 1920).

163 "He looked at me . . . ": ibid., p. 73.

On William Fox and AY, see ibid., pp. 85, 86, 87.

166 "I hear your book . . . ": ibid., p. 81.

167 The interview with AY by Faith Service appeared in the British magazine *Motion Picture Classic* (November 1922).

8. Salome

169 "A sleek, smiling man . . . ": from *RR*, p. 81.

"betraying": ibid., p. 75.

"I no longer believed . . . ": ibid.

170 "outside of life . . . ": ibid., p. 74.

"The deeper, the finer . . . ": from *ST*, p. 151.

171 "I'm an American . . . ": ibid.

"I am a Russian Jewess . . . ": ibid., p. 65.

172 "she loved a high-souled saint . . . ": ibid., p. 155.
"The coward! . . . ": ibid., p. 153.
"any cry for justice . . . ": from AY's unpublished notes for a story, "Letter to John Apple and Friends."
175 "Sex is a universal fact . . . ": AY quoted in "My Ambitions at 21 and What Became of Them," interview in *American Hebrew* 25 (August 1922).
"Poverty is dirty . . . ": ibid.
"There is an unbridgeable chasm . . . ": from a news report of AY's speech in the *New York Evening Telegram*, 22 November 1921.
176 "My people": from "You Can't Be an Immigrant Twice," in *COL*, p. 263; and "Mostly about Myself," in *COL*, p. 9.
"generations sent to Siberian wastes": from *ST*, p. 65.
AY's letter to *New York Times Book Review* regarding Ludwig Lewisohn's *Up Stream* appeared on 23 April 1922.
177 "So at bottom . . . ": from *ST*, p. 289.
178 "My letters . . . ": from *AICNB*, p. 187.
179 "The advantage of your viewpoint . . . ": from the contract letter of 6 April 1922, signed by Bernarr Macfadden for Physical Culture Corp.
Carol B. Schoen, *Anzia Yezierska* (Boston: Twayne Publishers, 1983).
180 "An orgy of emotions . . . ": review of *ST* by W. Adolphe Roberts in the *New York Tribune*, 17 December 1922.
"Fighting Up from the Ghetto," by Gertrude Atherton, was a full-page Sunday magazine feature in the *New York Herald*, 7 January 1923.
181 James Harvey Robinson's review of *ST* appeared in the *Literary Digest International Book Review*, February 1923.
Scott Nearing's review of *ST*, "A Depraved Spirit," appeared in the *Nation*, 6 June 1923.
182 *New York Times* review of *ST*, by Louise Maunsell Field, is dated 24 December 1922.
"Those who welcomed 'Hungry Hearts'" . . . ": review of *ST* by Z.F.P., *American Hebrew*, 2 February 1923.
"People in the Ghetto . . . ": AY quoted by Burton Rascoe in "A Bookman's Day Book," *New York Tribune*, 31 December 1922.
183 "She is none of these things . . . ": AY quoted by interviewer Elizabeth Smith in *New York Evening Telegram*, 6 January 1923.
"And I suddenly thought of you . . . ": letter from AY to Mary Austin, in the Mary Austin Papers, Huntington Library, San Marino, California.

"I was afraid of literary people . . . ": AY quoted by Rascoe in "A Bookman's Day Book," 31 December 1922.
"Miss Yezierska is an . . . ": ibid.

185 "Love Hunger," *Metropolitan* (January 1924).

186 "Children of Loneliness," the short story first published in *Century* (March 1923), was reprinted in the book of the same name (New York: Funk and Wagnalls, 1923). Reprinted in *OC*.

186 "Brothers," *Harper's* (September 1921); reprinted in *COL*.
"The Husband They Picked for Rebecca," first published in *Metropolitan* (October 1923), was retitled "Dreams and Dollars" when reprinted in *COL*.

187 "There is an intensity . . . ": W. Adolphe Roberts, in interview with AY, "My Ambitions at 21 and What Became of Them," *American Hebrew* 25 (August 1922).

188 "society's puppy for the moment": from *AICNB*, p. 122.

189 "well-known . . . sculptor": "American Man Must Be Nearly Sixty Before He Really Loves, Says Novelist," news interview in *New York Evening Telegram*, 6 January 1923.

9. Loneliness

194 "tore the veil of ignorance . . . ": *London News Chronicle*, quoted in *New York Times* obituary, 11 July 1939.
"to end the turmoil . . . ": from "This Is What $10,000 Did to Me," *Cosmopolitan* (October 1925).

195 "In London . . . ": from AY's unfinished, unpublished manuscript, "Letter to John Apple and Friends," in her files.
The remarks on Joseph Conrad and Gertrude Stein are from AY's talk to an English class at Purdue University in October 1965, on "What Makes a Writer," in her files.

196 "Only by going back . . . ": from "This Is What $10,000 Did to Me."
"You Can't Be an Immigrant Twice," an interview with AY, was first published by the *New York Tribune* syndicate; reprinted in *COL*.
"I moved boldly into a hotel on Fifth Avenue": from "This Is What $10,000 Did to Me."

197 "For once I treated myself . . . ": from *RR*, p. 120.

201 Review of *COL* by William Lyon Phelps appeared in *International Book Review* (December 1923).

Edward J. O'Brien's criticism of *COL* appeared in his book *The Advance of the Short Story* (New York: Dodd, Mead, 1923).
"the club-leader of the settlement . . . ": from "Wild Winter Love," *Century* (February 1927).

202 "I envy the writers . . . ": from "Mostly about Myself," in *COL*, p. 10.
"Love Cheat," *Metropolitan* (July 1923); "Love Hunger," *Metropolitan* (January 1924). These short stories were never reprinted.
"dirt and disorder . . . ": from "Mostly About Myself," p. 17, *COL*.
"Writing is ordinarily . . . ": from "Mostly about Myself."

211 "Now I am cut off . . . ": from "This Is What $10,000 Did to Me."
"promoters, talent scouts . . . ": from *RR*, p. 126.

216 The numbered copy of *Bread Givers* that AY inscribed to Marcet Haldeman-Julius is in the Haldeman-Julius Papers, Pittsburg (Kansas) State University Library.

217 William Lyon Phelps's review of *BG* was published in the *International Book Review* (October 1925); the *New York Times'* review (unsigned), 13 September 1925; the *Springfield Republican*'s review, 27 September 1925; Samson Raphaelson's review in the *New York Herald Tribune*, 25 October 1925.

219 "I felt I had justified myself . . . ": from *RR*, p. 216.
"What is it I hear? . . . ": ibid.

10. Losing

231 "The whole object of her quest . . . ": from *AICNB*, p. 200.

233 "the restraint I lacked": this and other information about the Zona Gale–Anzia Yezierska friendship are from the chapter titled "Saint in Cellophane" (unpublished) in the Anzia Yezierska Papers, Boston University Libraries.

234 "Something unripe, unfinished . . . ": carbon copy of a letter from AY to Professor M. V. O'Shea, 31 May 1928, enclosed in letter of same date from AY to Zona Gale, Zona Gale Papers, State Historical Society of Wisconsin.

235 "Zona — dearest friend . . . ": ibid.
"You are Vision — Revelation": ibid.
"chasm between your world and mine . . . ": letter from AY to Zona Gale, 3 August 1928, Zona Gale Papers, State Historical Society of Wisconsin.

"I felt my criticism of education . . . ": letter to John Hall Wheelock, Scribner editor, Charles Scribner's Sons Papers, Princeton University Libraries.

"stale hash": from the chapter titled "The Death of Hamlet" in the Anzia Yezierska Papers, Boston University Libraries.

235 "not for an education . . . ": ibid.

"I thought at a University . . . ": this and her observations on Max Otto are from the chapter titled "The Bone in My Throat," ibid.

237 AY's experiences with the University of Wisconsin's Experimental College and Alexander Meiklejohn are from the unpublished chapter titled "We Can Change Our Moses but Not Our Noses," ibid.

238 "I was a prisoner of an experience . . . ": AY's letter to William Lyon Phelps, 20 October 1932, included in his book *Autobiography with Letters* (New York: Oxford University Press, 1939).

239 "She arrived, weeping . . . ": from the Dorothy Canfield Fisher Papers, Special Collections, Bailey/Howe Library, University of Vermont.

240 "a Russian Jewess of little education . . . ": ibid.

"You put the searchlight . . . ": ibid.

"Your chief character . . . ": ibid.

243 "Their becoming almost . . . ": ibid.

"That is the kind . . . ": ibid.

"A Russian Jewess could . . . ": ibid.

"The girl might have been . . . ": from the Dorothy Canfield Fisher Papers, Special Collections, Bailey/Howe Library, University of Vermont.

244 "Those sordid details . . . ": ibid.

"The full meaning . . . ": ibid.

"delicate intimation": ibid.

"This novel ends the cycle . . . ": from William Lyon Phelps Papers, Yale University Libraries.

"A hummingbird who flitted . . . ": from *RR*, p. 126.

245 "As a matter of fact the publishers lost heavily . . . ": from the Rose Pastor Stokes Papers, Sterling Memorial Library, Manuscripts and Archives, Yale University.

11. Silence

247 W. H. Auden's introduction to *Red Ribbon on a White Horse* (1950) also introduces the first edition issued by Persea Books in 1981.

248 "Without a country . . . ": from *RR*, p. 127.

249 "a society that feeds on the blood of . . . ": from AY's notes for an uncompleted, unpublished story, "Letter to John Apple."
"Bonds of Blood" is an unpublished story in the Anzia Yezierska Papers, Boston University Libraries.

258 On the farm strikes in Southern California in the 1930s, particularly the Imperial Valley lettuce strike of 1934, a brief history is included in Carey McWilliams, *Factories in the Field* (Boston: Little, Brown, 1939).

261 "I feel like a bit . . . ": from *RR*, p. 162.
"as lighthearted as if . . . ": ibid., p. 165.

262 "On the first payday . . . ": ibid., p. 161.
"To keep what we had . . . ": ibid., p. 170.

263 "he had the intelligence . . . ": ibid., p. 195.

264 "We . . . were forced . . . ": ibid., p. 193.
"Every day it became harder . . . ": ibid., p. 198.

265 Benjamin DeCasseres, *Spinoza: The Liberator of God and Man* (New York: E. Wickham Sweetland, 1932).

268 Letters to and from Charles Scribner's Sons regarding *RR* are in the Charles Scribner's Sons Collection, Princeton University Libraries.

270 AY to W. H. Auden letters (carbons) are also in the Charles Scribner's Sons Collection at Princeton.

273 "One part of that [book] . . . ": from a transcribed tape recording of AY's conversation with Joy and Marchette Chute in January 1962, private files of L. L. Henriksen.

274 "where a man is judged . . . ": ibid.

275 "Why had I no premonition . . . ": from *RR*, p. 220.

12. Art

278 Sally Scott, *Judy's Surprising Day* (New York: Harcourt Brace, 1958); AY's review appeared in the *New York Times*, 12 January 1958.
Mary Britton Miller, *All Aboard* (New York: Pantheon, 1958); AY's review appeared in the *New York Times*, 1 June 1958.
"[This book] is different . . . ": from AY's review of Hilde Abel's *The Guests of Summer* (Indianapolis: Bobbs-Merrill, 1951); AY's review appeared in the *New York Times*, 10 June 1951.
"This book is over-written . . . ": from AY's review of Charles Angoff,

Journey to the Dawn (New York: Beechhurst Press, 1951); AY's review appeared in the *New York Times*, February 1951.

279 Helen Keller, *Teacher: Anne Sullivan Macy, a Tribute by the Foster Child of Her Mind* (New York: Doubleday, 1955); AY's review appeared in the *New York Times*, 16 October 1955.

280 "All around us . . . ": from "The Lower Depths of Upper Broadway," *Reporter*, 19 January 1954.

"A Chair in Heaven," *Commentary* 22 (December 1956); reprinted in *OC*.

282 Abraham J. Heschel, *Man's Quest for God* (New York: Charles Scribner's Sons, 1954).

Thomas Sugrue, *Stranger in the Earth* (New York: Henry Holt & Co., 1948).

E. Graham Howe and I. LeMesurier, *The Open Way: A Study in Acceptance* (London: Methuen, 1939).

Helmut Gollwitzer, Reinhold Schneider, and Kathe Kuhn, eds., *Dying We Live: Final Messages and Records of the Victims and Martyrs, 1933–1945* (New York: Pantheon, 1956).

Caroline Miles Hill, ed., *The World's Great Religious Poetry* (New York: Macmillan, 1923).

Alan W. Watts, *The Spirit of Zen* (New York: Grove Press, 1958).

"In an irony . . . ": from "PW Forecasts," *Publishers Weekly* (24 September 1979):216.

284 "house of doom," "old men and old women . . . ": from "A Window Full of Sky," in *OC*, p. 230.

286 "One Thousand Pages of Research," *Commentary* (July 1963):60–63; reprinted in *Hungry Hearts & Other Stories* (New York: Persea Books, 1985).

287 "I'll Fly Again," *Modern Maturity* 6 (December–January 1963/64):25.

289 "the outrage of being old!": from "The Open Cage," short story in *OC*.

291 "A Window Full of Sky," *Reporter*, 2 July 1964; reprinted in *OC*.

294 "Take Up Your Bed and Walk," *Chicago Jewish Forum* 27 (Spring 1969):162–165; reprinted in *OC*.

Index